Value Guide to

BASEBALL COLLECTIBLES

M. Donald Raycraft
R. Craig Raycraft

COLLECTOR BOOKS
A Division of Schroeder Publishing Co., Inc.

Searching For A Publisher?

We are always looking for knowledgeable people considered to be experts within their fields. If you feel there is a real need for a book on your collectible subject and have a large comprehensive collection, contact us.

COLLECTOR BOOKS
P.O. BOX 3009
Paducah, Kentucky 42002-3009

Cover Design: Beth Summers
Layout Design: Jane White

Additional copies of this book may be ordered from:

Collector Books
P.O. Box 3009
Paducah, Kentucky 42002-3009

@ $16.95. Add $2.00 for postage and handling.

1 2 3 4 5 6 7 8 9 0

Printed by IMAGE GRAPHICS, INC., Paducah, Kentucky

ACKNOWLEDGMENTS

Alex Hood
Steve Quertermous
Grant Quertermous
Corwin Roop
Bill Striegel
Dean Bartges
Tyler Gee
Fred Wiedenhoefer
Andrew Stevens
Dick Kellogg
Michael Sheets
Steve Epperson
Jane White
Tim Siegworth
Dr. Duffy Bass
Steve Straub
E.L. Raycraft
Bob Christian
David Davis
E.M. Faulkner
J. Steven Sparks
Jim Moberly
Kevin Ellis
John Tedesco
Jeff Brumleve
Kelly Block
Jeff Wells
Dave DeBandi
Tim Pittman
Austin Wynn
Jim Phillips
John Flynn
Scott Raycraft
Don Marquart
Carol Raycraft
Craig Holly
Chuck Cain
Derek Schumm
Erik Bryant
Lisa Stroup

The authors would like to especially thank Lou Hagenbruch for his time, knowledge, and collection that he was kind enough to share with us.

PHOTOGRAPHY

R. Craig Raycaft
Carol Raycraft
Lou Hagenbruch
Cover: R. Craig Raycraft

FOREWORD

Over the years there have been countless times that we have found a baseball related piece of memorabilia at a card show, estate auction, or flea market and wondered about its value. In researching prices and attempting to secure information about a particular magazine, autographed item, or "game-used" bat, we collected a wealth of data and some knowledge. Recently, we decided to turn this accumulation into a book.

We sincerely hope you enjoy the final product as much as we did the process of putting it together.

M. Donald Raycraft
March 1992

My first piece of baseball memorabilia was an autographed Mickey Mantle ball my father purchased for me. The year was 1980 and the demand for autographs and memorabilia had not even begun to peak. Shows with guests signing autographs were almost non-existent in most regions of the United States and the attention of most collectors was focused on baseball cards.

I carried the Mantle ball around for five years to secure the signatures of other members of the Hall of Fame. On our yearly trips to Cooperstown, New York, for the annual Hall of Fame Induction Weekend, I had the oppurtunity to meet many baseball legends.

Although the baseball has slightly yellowed over the years, it sits on my desk in a prominent spot and is my most valuable baseball collectible. It symbolizes to me what memorabilia collecting should be about. It is not the monetary values of the pieces in a collection that are important, but the memories and experiences involved in finding them.

R. Craig Raycraft
March 1992

TABLE OF CONTENTS

INTRODUCTION

Collectors of baseball memorabilia are confronted with a much more difficult and complex task than baseball card collectors.

Card values are reported weekly by the *Sports Collectors Digest* and monthly by a multitude of publications. There are also several annual soft-cover books that index and evaluate baseball cards.

A card collector can make a telephone call and secure a price quote for a 1990 Leaf Frank Thomas rookie card or five hundred of the same card much like a stockbroker and his client communicate. Prices often rise and fall with the daily statistics of the individual player.

Collectors in New Mexico and New Jersey read the same publications and know the value of Will Clark's second Topps card as well as they know their telephone number.

Collectors of baseball memorabilia have interests as divergent as ticket stubs, game-used bats, Hartland statues, uniforms, patches, autographed baseballs, and copies of the *Sporting News* from 1938.

It is a physical and intellectual impossibility to have a firm grasp on the values of all the facets of baseball memorabilia because the field is so exceedingly broad.

We have attempted in this book to provide a cross-section of baseball related memorabilia and their current values. The values were secured from individual dealers' catalogs and price lists, auction results, advertisements in the numerous hobby publications, and surveying prices at baseball card shows and conventions throughout the United States.

The prices listed on the pages that follow are **not** estimates of value but actual retail and auction prices on the specific items described. They reflect current fair market retail values.

Future editions of this book will touch upon categories and values not included in this volume.

CHAPTER I
The Copeland Collection

The Copeland Collection of baseball cards and memorabilia was auctioned by Sotheby's in New York City on March 22-23, 1991.

The items below include the estimated price before the auction for the piece and the actual auction price in parentheses. The auction price **includes** a 10% buyer's premium.

The Copeland Collection auction featured the finest offering of baseball memorabilia ever offered for sale. The condition and rarity of the pieces auctioned by Sotheby's brought record-breaking prices and created new interest around the nation throught the extensive media coverage of the sale of the Honus Wagner card for $451,000.00.

1. 1951 Bowman#253 Mickey Mantle rookie Card – estimate: $4,000.00-6,000.00. ($7,425.00)
2. 1952 Bowman set (252 cards), near mint to mint – estimate: $7,000.00-10,000.00. ($9,350.00)
3. 1953 Bowman set (160 cards, color), near mint to mint – estimate: $12,000.00-15,000.00. ($20,900.00)
4. 1952 Topps #311 Mickey Mantle – estimate: $12,000.00-15,000.00. ($49,500.00)
5. 1952 Topps (407 cards), near mint to mint – estimate: $40,000.00-60,000.00. ($75,900.00)
6. 1953 Topps (280 cards), near mint to mint – estimate: $10,000.00-15,000.00. ($19,250.00)
7. 1954 Topps (250 cards), near mint to mint – estimate: $6,000.00-8,000.00. ($9,000.00)
8. R319 1933 Goudey #106 Napoleon Lajoie – estimate: $25,000.00-35,000.00. ($31,900.00)
9. R319 1933 Goudey set (240 cards), excellent to mint – estimate: $50,000.00-75,000.00. ($55,000.00)
10. George H. Ruth Candy Company candy wrapper, c. 1929, near mint – estimate: $3,500.00-4,500.00. ($3,300.00)
11. T 206 Honus Wagner, C. 1910 baseball card, Piedmont Cigarettes, mint, fewer than 40 Wagner cards known to exist, this is probably the finest example – estimate: $125,000.00-150,000.00. ($451,000.00)
12. T 206 Sweet Caporal Cigarettes Eddie Plank baseball card, c. 1910, near mint to mint – estimate: $15,000.00-20,000.00. ($16,500.00)
13. Complete set of 181 felt blankets, c. 1914, near mint to mint – estimate: $8,000.00-12,000.00. ($8,250.00)
14. Ty Cobb felt blanket, c. 1914, with rare red infield variation – estimate: $5,000.00-7,000.00. ($10,450.00)
15. *Who's Who in Baseball* (first edition), 1912, near excellent condition – estimate: $1,000.00-1,500.00. ($990.00)
16. Spalding Guides 1888-1941 (54 books), near mint condition – estimate: $9,000.00-12,000.00. ($9,900.00)
17. 1948 Honus Wagner exhibit card, autographed – estimate: $500.00-700.00. ($2,310.00)
18. Cy Young Day program from August 13, 1908 – estimate: $3,000.00-4,000.00. ($2,200.00)
19. 1909 Pittsburgh Pirates pocket mirror – estimate: $1,200.00-1,500.00. ($1,430.00)

20. Baseball yearbook collection, 700 different team yearbooks (1941-1987), excellent to mint condition, all important and rare yearbooks included - estimate: $25,000.00-35,000.00 ($19,800.00)
21. Roger Maris Hartland statue in original box - estimate: $900.00-1,200.00. ($550.00)
22. 1888 Cincinnati Reds scorecard collection, 8 different unscored programs, excellent to mint condition - estimate: $15,000.00-20,000.00. ($8,800.00)
23. 1891 Brooklyn vs. Chicago scorecard, unscored, excellent to mint condition - estimate: $1,500.00-2,000.00. ($880.00)
24. Dick Groat Hartland statue in original box - estimate: $1,500.00-2,000.00. ($1,650.00)
25. 1933 All Star Game program, scored, near mint, first all star game - estimate: $3,500.00-5,000.00. ($3,300.00)
26. 1933 All Star Game ticket stub, near mint - estimate: $1,200.00-1,500.00. ($2,750.00)
27. All Star Game ticket collection, 33 different ticket stubs 1935-1988 - estimate: $2,000.00-2,500.00. ($2,530.00)
28. 1905 World Series program at New York (N.L.) vs. Philadelphia, unscored, near mint - estimate: $15,000.00-20,000.00. ($24,200.00)
29. 1907 World Series program at Detroit vs Chicago Cubs, scored, near mint - estimate: $10,000.00-15,000.00 ($18,700.00)
30. 1912 World Series program at Boston (A.L.) vs. N.Y., scored, excellent condition - estimate: $2,000.00-3,000.00 ($2,200.00)
31. 1919 World Series program at Chicago (A.L.) vs. Cincinnati, scored, good condition - estimate: $4,000.00-6,000.00. ($2,750.00)
32. 1941 All Star Game program at Detroit - estimate: $800.00-1,200.00. ($660.00)
33. 1924 World Series program at Washington (A.L.) vs. N.Y., unscored, excellent condition - estimate: $1,500.00-2,000.00. ($1,650.00)
34. 1927 World Series program at Pittsburgh vs. N.Y. Yankees, scored, excellent to mint condition - estimate: $6,000.00 - 7,000.00. ($5,500.00)
35. World Series programs 1930-1973 (88 programs), all excellent or better - estimate: $20,000.00-30,000.00. ($13,200.00)
36. World Series ticket collection 1929-1988 (98 total tickets), very good to excellent condition - estimate: $3,000.00-4,000.00. ($3,300.00)
37. 1915 World Series program at Boston - estimate: $3,000.00-4,000.00. ($3,575.00)
38. Babe Ruth wrist watch, c. 1950, with original plastic baseball container, mint condition - estimate: $600.00-800.00. ($3,025.00)
39. 1931 Yankee autographed ball, excellent to mint condition, includes 9 Hall of Famers - estimate: $4,000.00-6,000.00 ($6,050.00)
40. Bobbing head doll, Roberto Clemente, dated 1962 - estimate: $ 800.00-1,200.00. ($880.00)
41. Bobbing head doll, Willie Mays, C. 1962 - estimate: $500.00-700.00. ($715.00)
42. Bobbing head doll, Roger Maris, C. 1962 - estimate: $500.00-700.00. ($715.00)
43. Red Man Tobacco collection (209 baseball cards), exceptional condition - estimate: $6,000.00-8,000.00. ($6,600.00)
44. 1946 All-Star Game press pin - estimate: $800.00-1,000.00. ($600.00)
45. 1982-89 Hall of Fame press pins - estimate: $3,500.00-5,000.00. ($5,775.00)
46. 1876 Chicago Baseball Club stock certificate signed by A.G. Spalding and William Hulbert - estimate: $10,000.00-15,000.00. ($11,000.00)
47. 1960 Topps baseball card set - estimate: $3,400.00-4,500.00. ($5,500.00)
48. 1902 sterling silver pass for Cincinnati ball park - estimate: $4,000.00-6,000.00 ($6,600.00)
49. Babe Ruth underwear box, c. 1930, includes one pair of underwear - estimate: $1,000.00-1,500.00. ($880.00)
50. Honus Wagner cigar band, c. 1910, very good condition, 3" long - estimate: $3,000.00-5,000.00. ($4,675.00)

The Copeland Collection consisted of 873 lots. The catalog was available by mail from Sotheby's for $35.00. It will become a very desirable collectible.

The ten items that appear below were also part of the Copeland Collection. We have included them because they were especially interesting to us.

In the future collectors will pay a premium for an item that was one of the 873 lots merely because it came out of this auction and is identified with the Copeland Collection.

1. 1954 Topps unopened pack, 6 cards in a five cent pack - near mint to mint condition ($1,870.00)
2. 1951 Bowman uncut sheet with Mantle rookie, 36 cards, near mint ($38,500.00)
3. Uncut sheet of 1954 Bowman cards, 4 card uncut sheet with rare Ted Williams and Mickey Mantle, near mint ($14,300.00)
4. Uncut sheet of 1934 Goudey cards, 25 cards including rare Lajoie, near mint ($79,750.00)
5. Frank Chance Booster Club pin, May 11, 1913, 1" diameter ($440.00)
6. "Honus Wagner for Sheriff" pin, mint condition, 1" diameter ($1,200.00)
7. 1946 All-Star Game press pin, mint condition ($660.00)
8. *Who's Who in Baseball*, 1912 (first edition), near excellent condition ($990.00)
9. Albert G. Spalding's *America's National Game*, c. 1911 ($495.00)
10. 1941 All-Star Game program, at Detroit, near mint, unscored ($660.00)

CHAPTER II
Autographs

Value Guide to Hall of Fame Autographs

The most valuable and desirable baseball autographs belong to members of the Hall of Fame. The possible exception to that statement would be the signature of "Shoeless" Joe Jackson. Jackson's career statistics would make him an automatic selection for Cooperstown but his alledged part in a plot to "fix" the 1919 World Series and his subsequent ban from baseball has destroyed that chance for immortality.

Many of Jackson's signatures owned by autograph collectors today were actually signed by his wife. Recently an authenticated "Shoeless" Joe signature sold for more than $30,000.00.

The autographs of players in the Hall of Fame who played before 1900 or shortly after are very difficult to locate and authenticate and expensive to purchase. Often the nineteenth century "autographs" that do make their way into the "hobby" have been "cut" from letters or legal documents. A "cut" contains only the signature with the rest of the letter or document thrown away.

The value guide that follows provides an autograph price for members of the Hall of Fame on single-signed baseballs, photographs, 3 x 5 cards, and "cuts." For many players (Radbourn, Cummings, Rusie, Etc.) finding a single-signed baseball, 3 x 5 card, or photograph is almost impossible. A "cut" is the best example that a collector could hope to locate of many nineteenth century and early twentieth century players.

	Single-signed baseball	Signed picture	"Cut"	3" x 5" card
Henry Aaron	35.00	23.00		8.00
Grover C. Alexander	3,500.00	600.00	225.00	300.00
Walter Alston	450.00	40.00		10.00
Cap Anson	20,000.00	3,000.00	1,500.00	
Luis Aparicio	28.00	16.00		12.00
Luke Appling	30.00	15.00		7.00
Earl Averill	175.00	35.00		9.00
Frank Baker	875.00	250.00	65.00	
Dave Bancroft	3,000.00	175.00		65.00
Ernie Banks	24.00	12.00		8.00
Al Barlick	20.00	12.00		6.00
Ed Barrow	2,500.00	325.00	65.00	125.00
Jake Beckley			1,500.000	
Cool Papa Bell	95.00	50.00		15.00
Johnny Bench	32.00	18.00		14.00
Chief Bender	3,500.00	500.00	225.00	275.00

	Single-signed baseball	Signed picture	"Cut"	3" x 5" card
Yogi Berra	30.00	18.00		8.00
Jim Bottomley	2,800.00	235.00	75.00	100.00
Lou Boudreau	13.00	10.00		3.00
Roger Breshahan	4,000.00	1,200.00	400.00	
Lou Brock	20.00	15.00		8.00
Dan Brouthers	9,000.00		1,300.00	
Mordecai Brown	5,000.00	500.00	300.00	
Morgan Bulkeley			1,500.00	
Jesse Burkett	5,000.00	600.00	300.00	
Roy Campanella*	2,500.00	250.00		200.00
Rod Carew	25.00	18.00		8.00
Max Carey	350.00	100.00		15.00
Alexander Cartwright			700.00	
Henry Chadwick			1,800.00	
Frank Chance	5,000.00	2,000.00	750.00	
Happy Chandler	50.00	35.00		10.00
Oscar Charleston	4,500.00	1,200.00	650.00	
Jack Chesbro	5,000.00	1,800.00	1,000.00	
Fred Clarke	2,500.00	400.00	125.00	150.00
John Clarkson		2,500.00	1,000.00	
Roberto Clemente	2,500.00	350.00		125.00
Ty Cobb	3,500.00	900.00	250.00	350.00
Mickey Cochrane	1,500.00	250.00	75.00	100.00
Eddie Collins	4,500.00	500.00	150.00	200.00
Jimmy Collins	5,000.00	1,300.00	500.00	
Earle Combs	1,500.00	175.00		35.00
Charles Comiskey	3,000.00	650.00	300.00	
Jocko Conlan	80.00	35.00		10.00
Tom Connolly	3,000.00	700.00	200.00	
Roger Connor		2,500.00	1,000.00	
Stan Coveleski	350.00	55.00		10.00
Sam Crawford	2,000.00	175.00		75.00
Joe Cronin	350.00	35.00		15.00
Candy Cummings			1,100.00	
Kiki Cuyler	1,500.00	400.00	150.00	
Ray Dandridge	25.00	15.00		7.00
Dizzy Dean	1,000.00	300.00		65.00
Ed Delahanty			1,500.00	
Bill Dickey	100.00	45.00		20.00
Martin Dihigo	4,000.00		650.00	
Joe DiMaggio	225.00	65.00		25.00
Bobby Doerr	16.00	12.00		3.00
Don Drysdale	20.00	12.00		6.00
Hugh Duffy	2,000.00	400.00	350.00	
Billy Evans	3,500.00	500.00		200.00
Johnny Evers	3,000.00	800.00	300.00	
Buck Ewing			1,000.00	
Red Faber	1,000.00	55.00		20.00
Bob Feller	13.00	8.00		2.00
Rick Ferrell	20.00	12.00		5.00

* Items signed prior to Mr. Campanella's auto accident

	Single-signed baseball	Signed picture	"Cut"	3" x 5" card
Elmer Flick	1,500.00	165.00		35.00
Whitey Ford	22.00	13.00		8.00
Rube Foster			2,000.00	
Jimmy Foxx	3,000.00	300.00	100.00	175.00
Ford Frick	750.00	75.00		30.00
Frank Frisch	1,200.00	115.00		35.00
Pud Galvin			1,000.00	
Lou Gehrig	5,000.00	1,600.00	650.00	750.00
Charles Gehringer	50.00	20.00		12.00
Josh Gibson	3,500.00	1,200.00	700.00	
Bob Gibson	20.00	13.00		10.00
Warren Giles	600.00	65.00		25.00
Lefty Gomez	75.00	35.00		12.00
Goose Goslin	2,000.00	175.00		100.00
Hank Greenberg	300.00	50.00		14.00
Clark Griffith	1,500.00	350.00	130.00	185.00
Burleigh Grimes	200.00	35.00		16.00
Lefty Grove	800.00	100.00	35.00	50.00
Chick Hafey	900.00	125.00		50.00
Jesse Haines	800.00	85.00		25.00
Billy Hamilton	4,000.00		500.00	
Will Harridge	1,000.00	150.00		90.00
Bucky Harris	750.00	100.00	20.00	30.00
Gabby Hartnett	900.00	125.00	35.00	
Harry Heilmann	2,000.00	400.00	175.00	
Billy Herman	14.00	10.00		3.00
Harry Hooper	700.00	75.00	35.00	
Rogers Hornsby	3,000.00	325.00	175.00	225.00
Waite Hoyt	150.00	65.00		15.00
Cal Hubbard	700.00	150.00		35.00
Carl Hubbell	70.00	30.00		10.00
Miller Huggins	5,000.00	1,500.00	200.00	
Jim Hunter	20.00	12.00		5.00
Monte Irvin	20.00	10.00		5.00
Travis Jackson	175.00	50.00		15.00
Ferg. Jenkins	18.00	15.00		4.00
Hugh Jennings	6,000.00	1,000.00	650.00	
Ban Johnson	3,500.00	550.00	150.00	
Judy Johnson	85.00	25.00		12.00
Walter Johnson	3,500.00	1,000.00	400.00	475.00
Addie Joss			1,500.00	
Al Kaline	20.00	16.00		6.00
Tim Keefe	4,500.00	2,000.00	750.00	
Willie Keeler		2,000.00	1,000.00	
George Kell	17.00	12.00		3.00
Joseph Kelley	5,000.00	1,500.00	650.00	
George Kelly	500.00	55.00		12.00
Mike Kelly			1,500.00	
Harmon Killebrew	20.00	16.00		5.00
Ralph Kiner	20.00	15.00		4.00

	Single-signed baseball	Signed picture	"Cut"	3" x 5" card
Chuck Klein	2,800.00	350.00	125.00	
Bill Klem	3,000.00	1,500.00	300.00	
Sandy Koufax	25.00	22.00		8.00
Nap Lajoie	3,200.00	650.00	185.00	300.00
Kenesaw Landis	2,800.00	425.00	200.00	
Tony Lazzeri	1,700.00	700.00	325.00	375.00
Bob Lemon	18.00	12.00		3.00
Buck Leonard	50.00	24.00		7.00
Freddy Lindstrom	650.00	125.00		18.00
John Lloyd	5,000.00		650.00	
Ernie Lombardi	1,000.00	150.00	35.00	50.00
Al Lopez	55.00	28.00		12.00
Ted Lyons	150.00	50.00		11.00
Connie Mack	1,500.00	400.00	75.00	175.00
Larry MacPhail	1,300.00	350.00	65.00	175.00
Mickey Mantle	65.00	35.00		25.00
Heinie Manush	1,500.00	250.00	35.00	75.00
Rabbit Maranville	2,000.00	350.00	150.00	
Juan Marichal	22.00	17.00		8.00
Rube Marquard	750.00	90.00	8.00	15.00
Eddie Mathews	22.00	15.00		6.00
Christy Mathewson	10,000.00	2,500.00	1,000.00	
Willie Mays	28.00	20.00		10.00
Joe McCarthy	950.00	100.00		25.00
Tom McCarthy			2,000.00	
Willie McCovey	22.00	18.00		8.00
Joe McGinnity			850.00	
John McGraw	6,000.00	1,500.00	700.00	
Bill McKechnie	1,300.00	275.00		100.00
Joe Medwick	1,300.00	100.00	25.00	50.00
Johnny Mize	17.00	8.00		5.00
Joe Morgan	20.00	14.00		6.00
Stan Musial	40.00	25.00		7.00
Kid Nichols	3,500.00	750.00	150.00	
Jim O'Rourke			1,200.00	
Mel Ott	3,000.00	350.00	150.00	
Satchel Paige	750.00	200.00	50.00	65.00
Jim Palmer	22.00	18.00		6.00
Herb Pennock	1,500.00	500.00	150.00	
Gaylord Perry	24.00	16.00		5.00
Eddie Plank			1,500.00	
Charles Radbourn			2,500.00	
Pee Wee Reese	25.00	20.00		8.00
Sam Rice	1,500.00	150.00	35.00	45.00
Branch Rickey	1,500.00	850.00	125.00	225.00
Eppa Rixey	1,500.00	200.00	75.00	125.00
Robin Roberts	20.00	17.00		6.00
Brooks Robinson	20.00	17.00		4.00
Frank Robinson	25.00	20.00		9.00
Jackie Robinson	2,200.00	700.00	150.00	200.00

	Single-signed baseball	Signed picture	"Cut"	3" x 5" card
Wilbert Robinson	5,000.00	1,500.00	750.00	
Edd Roush	125.00	40.00		15.00
Red Ruffing	300.00	50.00	50.00	12.00
Amos Rusie	5,000.00	1,500.00	750.00	
Babe Ruth	2,500.00	1,750.00	500.00	850.00
Ray Schalk	1,000.00	250.00	55.00	100.00
Al "Red" Schoendienst	28.00	20.00		7.00
Joe Sewell	50.00	25.00		8.00
Al Simmons	2,500.00	350.00	100.00	125.00
George Sisler	1,200.00	150.00	35.00	75.00
Enos Slaughter	16.00	10.00		3.00
Duke Snider	20.00	16.00		5.00
Warren Spahn	17.00	12.00		4.00
Al Spalding		1,800.00	1,000.00	
Tris Speaker	3,000.00	500.00	200.00	
Willie Stargell	20.00	17.00		4.00
Casey Stengel	700.00	125.00		35.00
Bill Terry	100.00	55.00		12.00
Sam Thompson			1,800.00	
Joe Tinker	5,500.00	1,000.00	850.00	
Pie Traynor	1,000.00	300.00	90.00	
Dazzy Vance	3,200.00	750.00	150.00	185.00
Arky Vaughn	3,500.00	650.00	250.00	
Bill Veeck	250.00	100.00		35.00
Rube Waddell	13,000.00		1,400.00	
Honus Wagner	3,500.00	750.00	250.00	350.00
Bobby Wallace	3,500.00	750.00	300.00	
Ed Walsh	3,500.00	550.00	200.00	
Lloyd Waner	250.00	75.00		15.00
Paul Waner	2,200.00	300.00	100.00	135.00
Monte Ward			1,000.00	
George Weiss	1,000.00	250.00		65.00
Mickey Welch			1,500.00	
Zack Wheat	750.00	225.00		80.00
Hoyt Wilhelm	20.00	13.00		4.00
Billy Williams	20.00	16.00		6.00
Ted Williams	65.00	35.00		12.00
Hack Wilson	4,500.00	1,000.00	400.00	
George Wright			850.00	
Harry Wright			1,500.00	
Early Wynn	25.00	15.00		7.00
Tom Yawkey	1,200.00	350.00	135.00	175.00
Carl Yastrzemski	28.00	22.00		10.00
Cy Young	4,500.00	650.00	300.00	400.00
Ross Youngs	5,000.00	1,500.00	750.00	

Examples of Baseball Autographs and Prices

Hall of Fame pitcher Grover Cleveland Alexander
Died: 1950

Single-signed baseball: $3,500.00
Signed picture: $600.0
"Cut": $225.00
3" x 5" Card: $300.00

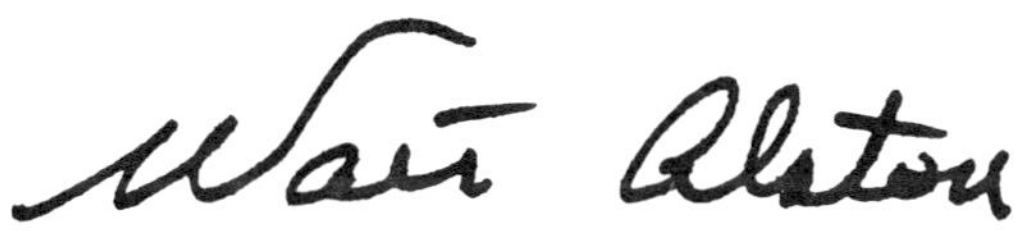

Hall of Fame manager Walter Alston
Died: 1984

Single-signed baseball: $450.00
Signed picture: $40.00
3" x 5" Card: $10.00

Hall of Fame short-stop "Luke" Appling
Died: 1991

Single-signed baseball: $30.00
Signed picture: $s15.00
3" x 5" Card: $7.00

Hall of Fame Baseball executive Ed Barrow
Died: 1953

Single-signed baseball: $2,500.00
Signed picture: $325.00
"Cut": $65.00
3" x 5" Card: $125.00

Hall of Fame Negro League outfielder James "Cool Papa" Bell
Died: 1991

Single-signed baseball: $95.00
Signed picture: $50.00
3" x 5" Card: $15.00

Hall of Fame catcher "Yogi" Berra

Single-signed baseball: $30.00
Signed picture: $18.00
3" x 5" card: $8.00

Hall of Fame first baseman Jim Bottomley
Died: 1959

Single-signed baseball: $2,800.00
Signed picture: $235.00
"Cut": $75.00
3" x 5" card: $100.00

Hall of Fame short-stop Lou Boudreau

Single-signed baseball: $13.00
Signed picture: $10.00
3" x 5" card: $3.00

Hall of Fame outfielder Lou Brock

Single-signed baseball: $20.00
Signed picture: $15.00
3" x 5" card: $8.00

Hall of Fame catcher Roy Campanella

Single-signed baseball: $2,500.00 (signed prior to automobile accident)
Signed picture: $250.00
3" x 5" card: $200.00

Hall of Fame outfielder Max Carey
Died: 1976

Single-signed baseball: $350.00
Signed picture: $100.00
3" x 5" card: $15.00

Hall of Fame outfielder Ty Cobb
Died: 1961

Single-signed baseball: $3,500.00
Signed picture: $900.00
"Cut": $250.00
3" x 5" card: $350.00

Hall of Fame outfielder Earle Combs
Died: 1976

Single-signed baseball: $1,500.00
Signed picture: $175.00
3" x 5" card: $35.00

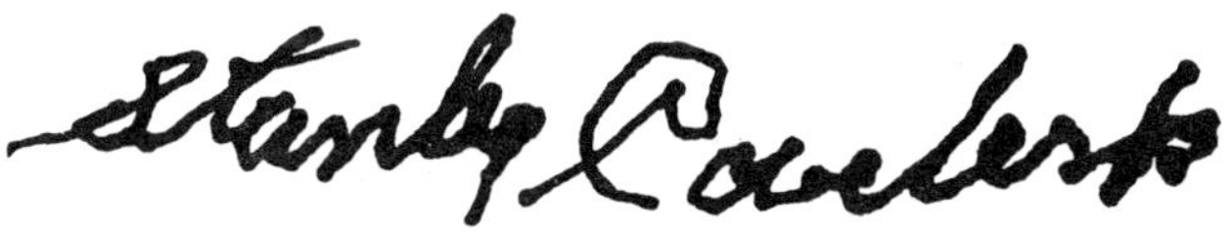

Hall of Fame pitcher Stanley Coveleski
Died: 1984

Single-signed baseball: $350.00
Signed picture: $55.00
3" x 5" card: $10.00

Hall of Fame short-stop Joe Cronin
Died: 1984

Single-signed baseball: $350.00
Single picture: $35.00
3" x 5" card: $15.00

Hall of Fame outfielder "KiKi" Cuyler
Died: 1950

Single-signed baseball: $1,500.00
Single picture: $400.00
"Cut": $150.00

Hall of Fame pitcher "Dizzy" Dean
Died: 1974

Single-signed baseball: $1,000.00
Single picture: $300.00
3" x 5" card: $65.00

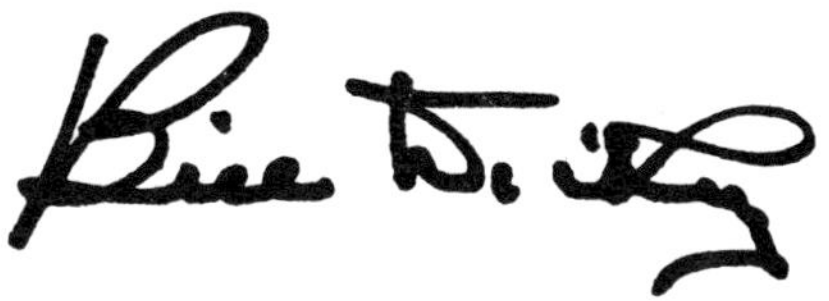

Hall of Fame catcher Bill Dickey

Single-signed baseball: $100.00
Single picture: $65.00
3" x 5" card: $20.00

Hall of Fame center fielder Joe DiMaggio

Single-signed baseball: $225.00
Single picture: $50.00
3" x 5" card: $25.00

Hall of Fame catcher Rick Ferrell

Single-signed baseball: $20.00
Single picture: $12.00
3" x 5" card: $5.00

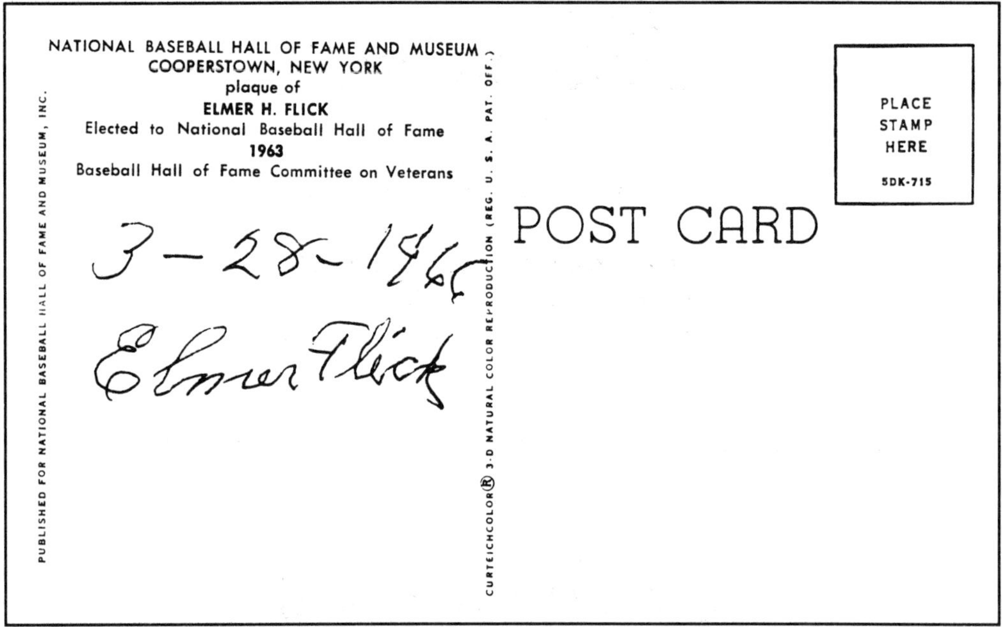

NATIONAL BASEBALL HALL OF FAME AND MUSEUM
COOPERSTOWN, NEW YORK
plaque of
ELMER H. FLICK
Elected to National Baseball Hall of Fame
1963
Baseball Hall of Fame Committee on Veterans
PUBLISHED FOR NATIONAL BASEBALL HALL OF FAME AND MUSEUM, INC.
CURTEICHCOLOR® 3-D NATURAL COLOR REPRODUCTION (REG. U. S. A. PAT. OFF.)
POST CARD
PLACE
STAMP
HERE
5DK-715

Hall of Fame outfielder Elmer Flick
Died: 1971

Single-signed baseball: $1,500.00
Single picture: $165.00
3" x 5" card: $35.00

Future member of the Hall of Fame catcher Carlton Fisk

Single-signed baseball: $24.00
Single picture: $18.00
3" x 5" card: $5.00

Hall of Fame first baseman Jimmie Foxx
Died: 1967

Single-signed baseball: $3,000.00
Single picture: $300.00
3" x 5" card: $175.00

Hall of Fame baseball executive Ford Frick
Died: 1978

Single-signed baseball: $750.00
Single picture: $75.00
3" x 5" card: $30.00

Hall of Fame second baseman Frank Frisch
Died: 1973

Single-signed baseball: $1,200.00
Single picture: $115.00
3" x 5" card: $35.00

Hall of Fame second baseman Charles Gehringer

Single-signed baseball: $50.00
Single picture: $20.00
3" x 5" card: $12.00

Hall of Fame pitcher Vernon "Lefty" Gomez
Died: 1989

Single-signed baseball: $75.00
Single picture: $35.00
3" x 5" card: $12.00

"Goose" Goslin

Hall of Fame outfielder "Goose" Goslin
Died: 1971

Single-signed baseball: $2,000.00
Single picture: $175.00
3" x 5" card: $100.00

Hall of Fame first baseman Hank Greenberg
Died: 1986

Single-signed baseball: $300.00
Single picture: $50.00
3" x 5" card: $14.00

Hall of Fame first baseman Lou Gehrig
Died: 1941

Single-signed baseball: $5,000.00
Single picture: $1,600.00
"Cut": $650.00
3" x 5" card: $750.00

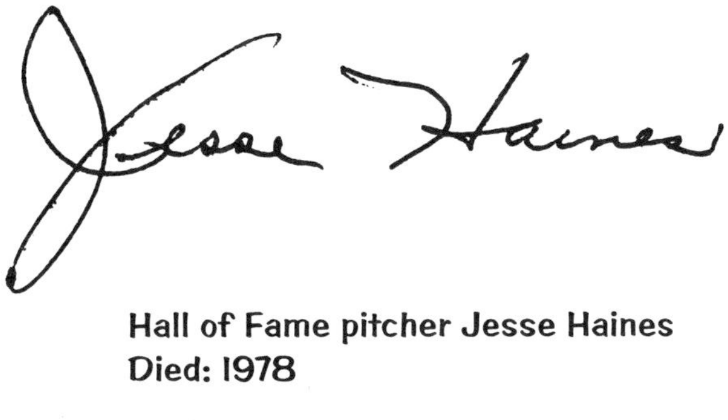

Hall of Fame pitcher Jesse Haines
Died: 1978

Single-signed baseball: $800.00
Single picture: $85.00
3" x 5" card: $25.00

Hall of Fame second baseman Rogers Hornsby
Died: 1963

Single-signed baseball: $3,000.00
Single picture: $325.00
"Cut": $175.00
3" x 5" card: $225.00

Hall of Fame pitcher Jim "Catfish" Hunter

Single-signed baseball: $20.00
Single picture: $12.00
3" x 5" card: $5.00

Future Hall of Fame outfielder Reggie Jackson

Single-signed baseball: $30.00
Single picture: $24.00
3" x 5" card: $9.00

Hall of Fame short-stop Travis Jackson
Died: 1987

Single-signed baseball: $175.00
Single picture: $50.00
3" x 5" card: $15.00

Hall of Fame Negro League third baseman Judy Johnson
Died: 1989

Single-signed baseball: $85.00
Single picture: $25.00
3" x 5" card: $12.00

Hall of Fame first baseman George Kelly
Died: 1984

Single-signed baseball: $500.00
Single picture: $55.00
3" x 5" card: $12.00

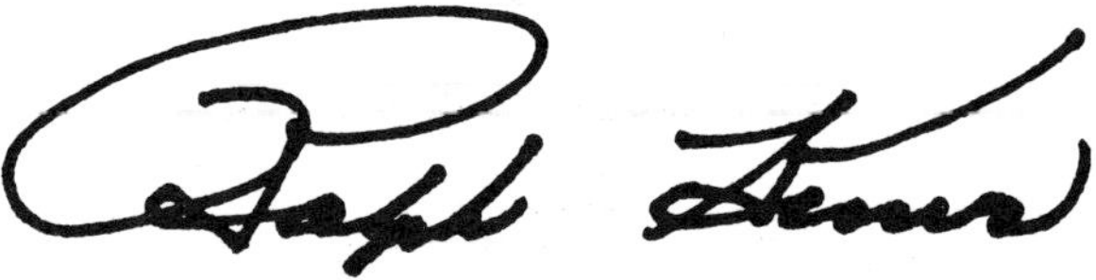

Hall of Fame outfielder Ralph Kiner

Single-signed baseball: $20.00
Single picture: $15.00
3" x 5" card: $4.00

Hall of Fame second baseman Larry Lajoie
Died: 1959

Single-signed baseball: $3,200.00
Single picture: $650.00
"Cut": $185.00
3" x 5" card: $300.00

Hall of Fame third baseman Fred Lindstrom
Died: 1981

Single-signed baseball: $650.00
Single picture: $125.00
3" x 5" card: $18.00

Hall of Fame manager Al Lopez

Single-signed baseball: $55.00
Single picture: $28.00
3" x 5" card: $12.00

Hall of Fame center fielder Mickey Mantle

Single-signed baseball: $65.00
Single picture: $35.00
3" x 5" card: $25.00

Hall of Fame left fielder Heinie Manush
Died: 1971

Single-signed baseball: $1,500.00
Single picture: $250.00
"Cut": $35/00
3" x 5" card: $75.00

Former Yankee rightfielder Roger Maris
Died: 1985

Single-signed baseball: $300.00
Single picture: $175.00
3" x 5" card: $125.00

Hall of Fame outfielder Stan Musial

Single-signed baseball: $40.00
Single picture: $25.00
3" x 5" card: $7.00

Hall of Fame pitcher Satchel Paige
Died: 1982

Single-signed baseball: $750.00
Single picture: $200.00
"Cut": $50.00
3" x 5" card: $65.00

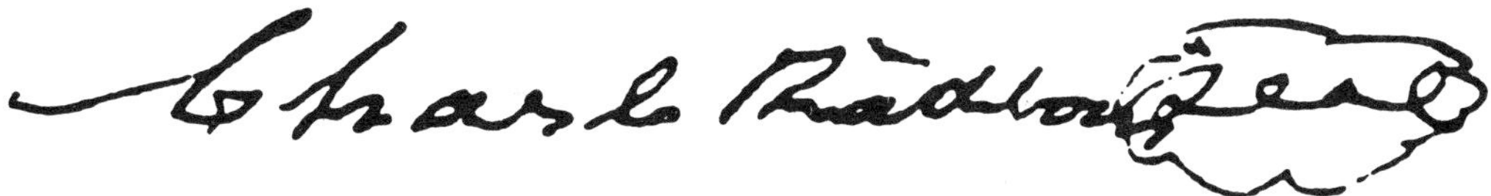

Hall of Fame pitcher Charles "Old Hoss" Radbourn
Died: 1897

"Cut": $2,500.00

Hall of Fame baseball executive Branch Rickey
Died: 1965

Single-signed baseball: $1,500.00
Single picture: $850.00
"Cut": $125.00
3" x 5" card: $225.00

Hall of Fame pitcher Robin Roberts

Single-signed baseball: $20.00
Single picture: $17.00
3" x 5" card: $6.00

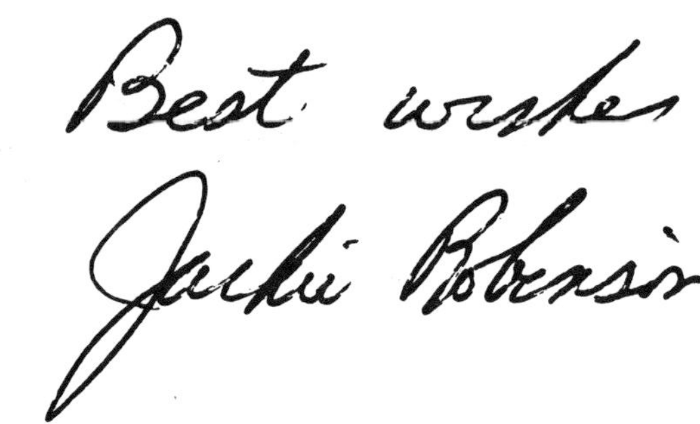

Hall of Fame second baseman Jackie Robinson
Died: 1972

Single-signed baseball: $2,200.00
Single picture: $700.00
3" x 5" card: $200.00

Hall of Fame outfielder Babe Ruth
Died: 1948

Single-signed baseball: $2,500.00
Single picture: $1,750.00
3" x 5" card: $850.00

Future Hall of Fame third baseman Mike Schmidt

Single-signed baseball: $40.00
Single picture: $25.00
3" x 5" card: $12.00

Hall of Fame second baseman "Red" Schoendienst

Single-signed baseball: $28.00
Single picture: $20.00
3" x 5" card: $7.00

NATIONAL BASEBALL HALL OF FAME AND MUSEUM
COOPERSTOWN, NEW YORK

Hall of Fame first baseman George Sisler
Died: 1973

Single-signed baseball: $1,200.00
Single picture: $150.00
"Cut": $35.00
3" x 5" card: $100.00

Hall of Fame pitcher Warren Spahn

Single-signed baseball: $17.00
Single picture: $12.00
3" x 5" card: $4.00

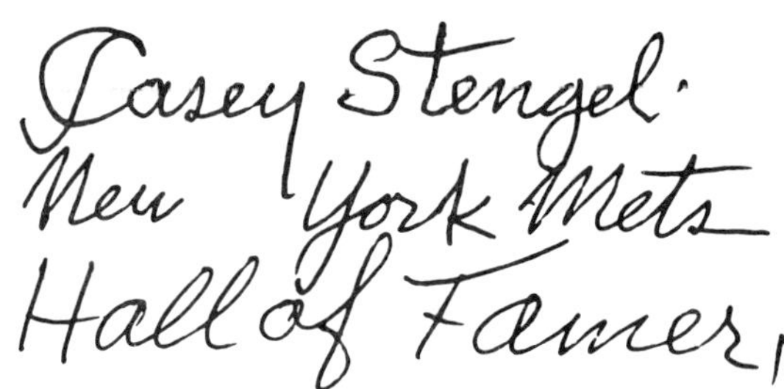

Hall of Fame manager Casey Stengel
Died: 1975

Single-signed baseball: $700.00
Single picture: $125.00
3" x 5" card: $45.00

Wm H (Bill) Terry

Hall of Fame first baseman Bill Terry
Died: 1989

Single-signed baseball: $100.00
Single picture: $55.00
3" x 5" card: $12.00

Honus Wagner

Hall of Fame short-stop Honus Wagner
Died: 1955

Single-signed baseball: $3,500.00
Single picture: $750.00
"Cut": $250.00
3" x 5" card: $350.00

Hall of Fame outfielder Paul Waner
Died: 1965

Single-signed baseball: $2,200.00
Single picture: $300.00
3" x 5" card: $135.00

Hall of Fame pitcher Hoyt Wilhelm

Single-signed baseball: $20.00
Single picture: $15.00
3" x 5" card: $5.00

Hall of Fame pitcher Cy Young
Died: 1955

Single-signed baseball: $4,500.00
Single picture: $650.00
"Cut": $300.00
3" x 5" card: $400.00

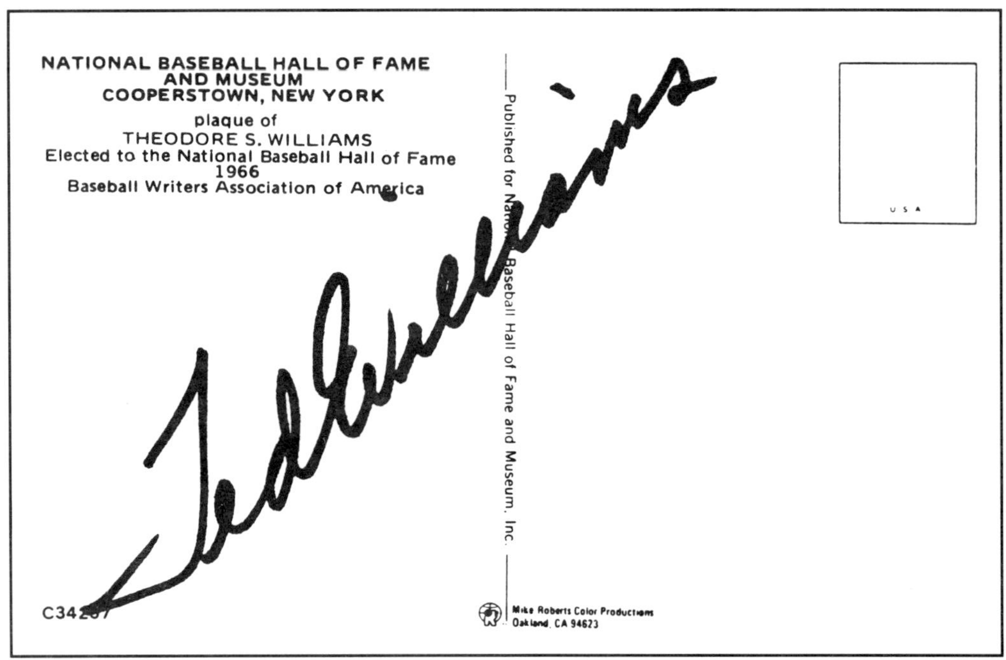

Hall of Fame outfielder Ted Williams

Single-signed baseball: $50.00
Single picture: $25.00
3" x 5" card: $12.00

"Picture" ball sold in the gift shop in Cooperstown and signed by Cardinal pitcher Bob Gibson in 1984. $20.00-25.00.

Baseball autographed by former Commisioner of Baseball, Peter Ueberroth. $30.00-35.00.

Signed Baseball from Hall of Fame umpire Al Barlick. $20.00-25.00.

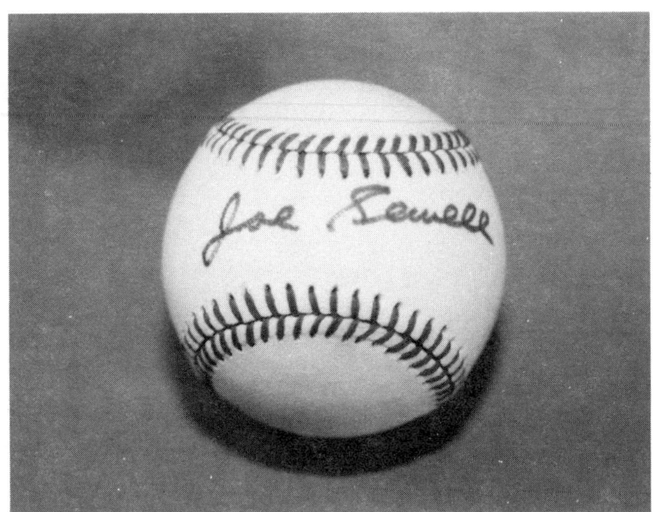

Autographed baseball from New York Yankee and Cleveland Hall of Fame short-stop Joe Sewell. $50.00.

Ball autographed and dated October 8, 1956 by Yankee pitcher Don Larsen. $18.00-20.00

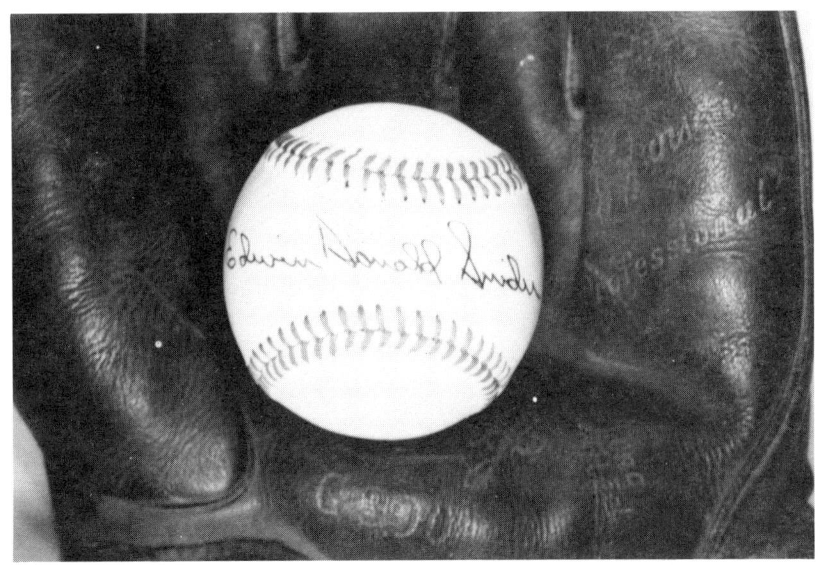

Ball autographed "Edwin Donald Snider" by Hall of Fame Dodger center fielder "Duke" Snider. $20.00-25.00.

Baseball autographed by the Yankee Clipper, Joe DiMaggio. $225.00-275.00.

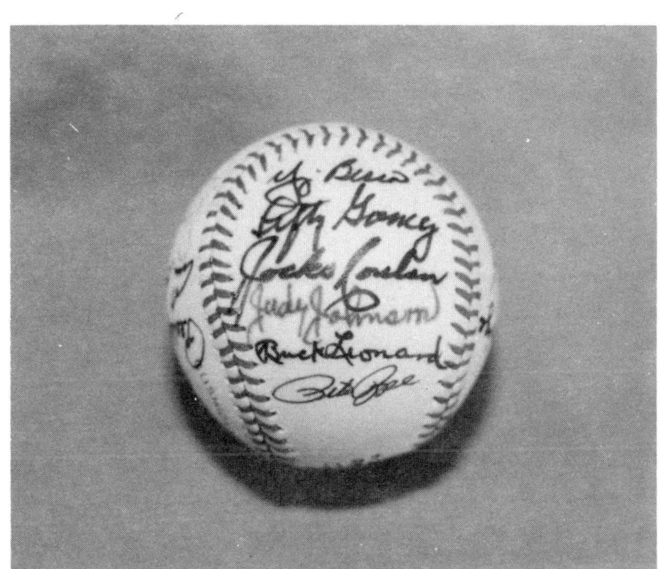

Ball signed by 25 members of the Hall of Fame and Pete Rose. Signatures include Berra, Gomez, Conlon, Judy Johnson and Leonard. $250.00-275.00.

Baseball signed in 1946 in fountain pen by Babe Ruth. $2,000.00-2,500.00.

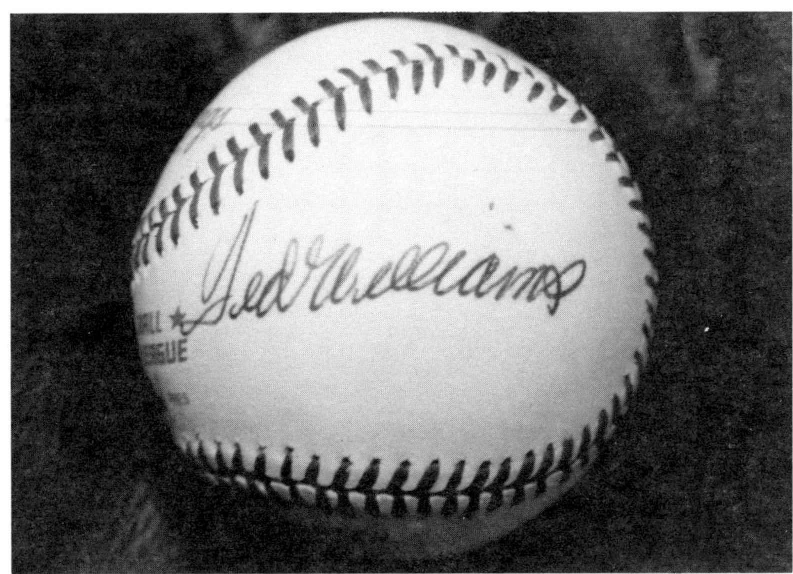

Ted Williams autographed American League baseball. $55.00-70.00.

Edd Roush autograped baseball. Mr. Roush is a Hall of Fame outfielder who played with the Reds in the 1919 World Series. $100.00-125.00.

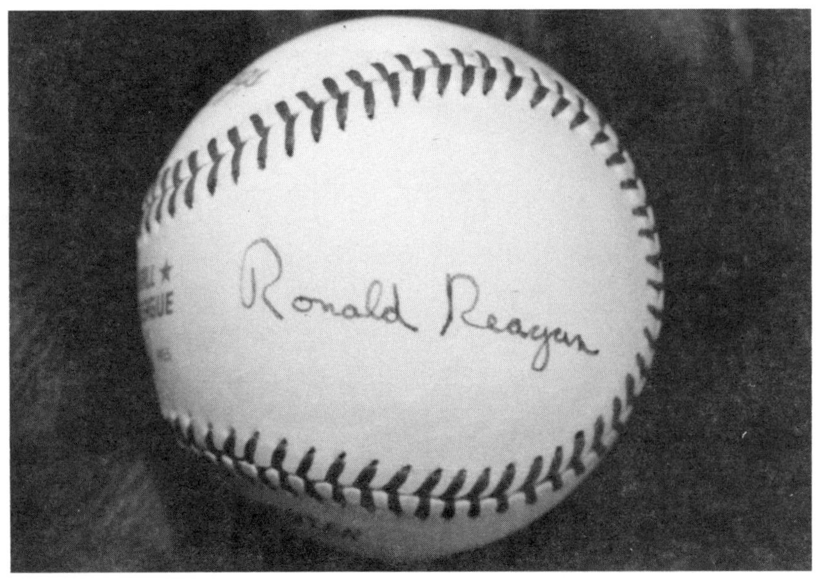

Baseball signed by U.S. President Ronald Reagan. $300.00-400.00.

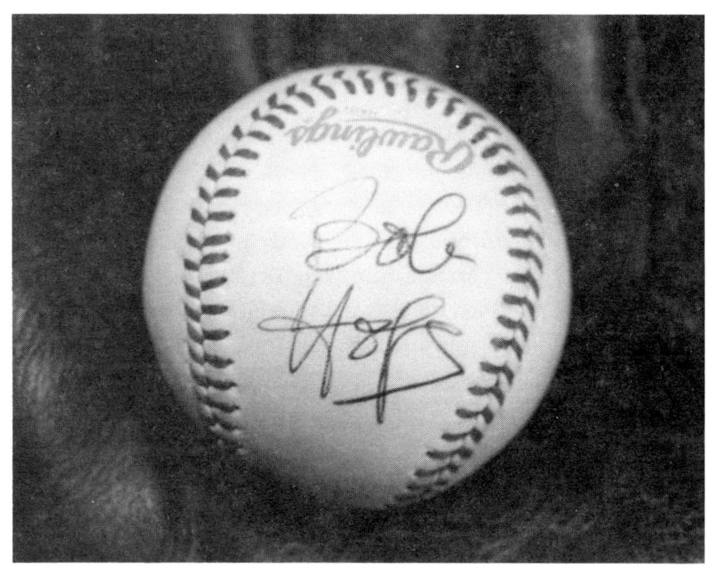

Baseball signed by comedian Bob Hope, a former owner of the Cleveland Indians. $50.00-75.00.

Baseball autographed by boxer Sugar Ray Leonard. $75.00-100.00.

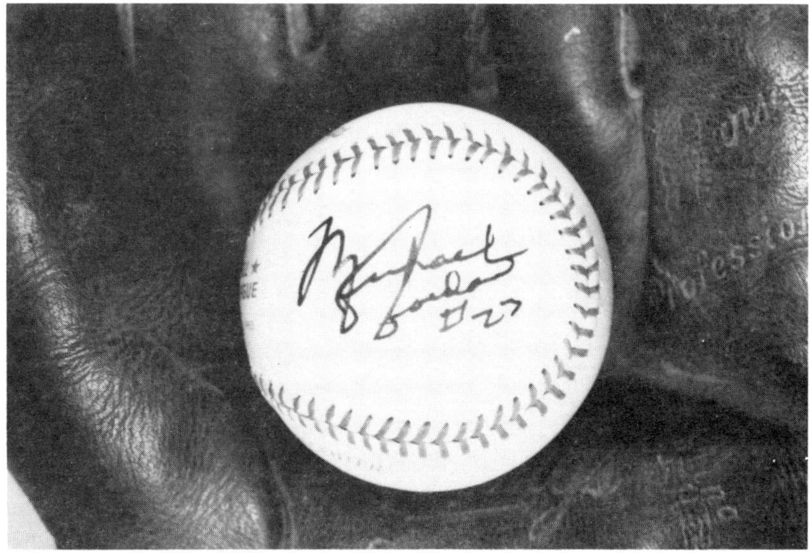

Michael Jordan's signature on an American League baseball. $100.00-150.00.

Autographed 8" x 10" Photographs

Collectors of autographed pictures of current and former major league players have hundreds from which to select. It is essential that the collector make every effort to ascertain that the signature is legitimate before the purchase is made unless the buyer is physically present when the picture is signed.

In the January 25, 1991 issue of *Sports Collectors Digest,* former Philadelphia third baseman Mike Schmidt wrote a letter to the editor warning collectors to be wary of buying his autographed picture from several dealers. Schmidt enclosed two signed pictures that were forgeries and an authentic example of his signature.

The pictures that tend to be faked most often carry the signatures of players like Schmidt, Nolan Ryan, Reggie Jackson, Mickey Mantle, Ted Williams, and Joe DiMaggio. These players do not do shows constantly and their autograph fees are high. The demand for their autographed items by collectors is equally strong.

The profit margin in a $45.00 "Mickey Mantle" forged picture is much greater than a $6.00 "Billy Herman" or a $5.00 "Sam Mele" photograph.

It is not difficult to understand that a collector can be more certain the $7.00 "Matt Nokes" picture is legitimate than a $75.00 "Ted Williams" when he encounters both in a stack at a flea market or swap meet in San Jose, California.

Each Sunday baseball card shows are held in hundreds of locations throughout the United States. Many of the shows contract with current and former major league players to be in attendance to sign autographs for a fee. Most of the promoters offer autographed baseballs and pictures gathered at the show to customers who order by mail. Collectors who purchase these items through the mail can normally do so with confidence. Dealers do not wish to jeopardize their ability to advertise in hobby publications by selling fraudulent items through the mail that will bring reader complaints.

The United States Postal Department also frowns on using the mails to defraud.

* denotes membership in the National Baseball Hall of Fame
b/w denotes a black and white photo rather than color

Hank Aaron* 25.00
Tommy Agee 9.00
Sparky Anderson 8.00
Johnny Antonelli 10.00
Louis Aparicio* 15.00
Richie Ashburn 10.00
Marty Barrett 8.00
Hank Bauer 7.00
Ernie Banks* 20.00
George Bell 8.00
Johnny Bench* 20.00
Todd Benziger 8.00
Yogi Berra* 20.00
Joe Black (b/w) 10.00
Ewell Blackwell 7.00
Vida Blue 10.00
Mike Boddicker 7.00
Wade Boggs 20.00
Bobby Bonilla 8.00
Lou Boudreau* 6.00
Jim Bouton 8.00
Harry Brecheen (b/w) 8.00
George Brett 20.00
Greg Brock 7.00
Tom Browning 8.00
Lou Burdette 8.00
Jose Canseco 20.00
Rod Carew* 20.00
Andy Carey (b/w) 8.00
Steve Carlton 18.00
Orlando Cepeda 10.00
Ron Cey 7.00
Happy Chandler* (b/w) 15.00
Jack Clark 6.00
Will Clark 15.00
Vince Coleman 12.00
Roger Clemons 20.00
David Cone 10.00
Del Crandell (b/w) 10.00
Frank Crosetti 12.00
Ray Dandridge* 10.00
Ron Darling 8.00
Kal Daniels 10.00
Al Dark 10.00
Eric Davis 20.00
Tommy Davis 8.00
Willie Davis 8.00
Andre Dawson 15.00

Bill Dickey* (b/w) 50.00
Dom DiMaggio (b/w) 12.00
Joe DiMaggio (b/w) 75.00
(color) 100.00
Bobby Doerr* (b/w) 8.00
Don Drysdale* 10.00
Mariano Duncan 8.00
Mike Dunne 6.00
Leo Durocher 35.00
Lenny Dykstra......................8.00
Carl Erskine..........................8.00
Nick Esasky 6.00
Elroy Face 8.00
Tony Fernandez 8.00
Rick Ferrell* 15.00
Carlton Fisk........................20.00
Whitey Ford* 20.00
Bob Friend 7.00
Carl Furillo 100.00
Gary Gaetti 8.00
Andres Galarraga.................8.00
Joe Garagiola 10.00
Steve Garvey 8.00
Bob Gibson* 9.00
Dwight Gooden 12.00
Mark Grace 10.00
Pete Gray (b/w) 15.00
Ken Griffey Jr. 15.00
Dick Groat 10.00
Ron Guidry 12.00
Tony Gwynn 10.00
Harvey Haddix 8.00
Billy Hatcher 7.00
Rickey Henderson 25.00
Keith Hernandez 10.00
Orel Hershiser 15.00
Billy Herman* (b/w) 10.00
Teddy Higuera 7.00
Bob Hoerner 8.00
Frank Howard 9.00
Catfish Hunter* 10.00
Reggie Jackson 20.00
Fergie Jenkins* 12.00
Tommy John 8.00
Wally Joyner 8.00
Jim Kaat 9.00
George Kell*..........................8.00
Al Kaline* 12.00
Harmon Killebrew* 12.00
Ralph Kiner*..........................9.00
Sandy Koufax* 25.00
Tony Kubec (b/w)..................8.00

Clem Labine 10.00
Barry Larkin 10.00
Vern Law 8.00
Al Leiter 7.00
Bob Lemon* 10.00
Buck Leonard* (b/w) 12.00
Eddie Lopat (b/w) 10.00
Al Lopez* (b/w) 75.00
Sparky Lyle 8.00
Jim Maloney (b/w) 8.00
Mickey Mantle* 45.00
Juan Marichal* 12.00
Ed Mathews* 12.00
Don Mattingly 35.00
Willie Mays* 25.00
Jon Matlock 7.00
Willie McCovey* 12.00
Lindy McDanial 7.00
Sam McDowell 8.00
Fred McGriff 10.00
Mark McGwire 20.00
Denny McLain 9.00
Ken McMullen 7.00
Sam Mele (b/w) 10.00
Lloyd Mosby 8.00
Jack Morris 9.00
Minnie Minoso (b/w) 12.00
Bip Roberts 7.00
Robin Roberts*....................12.00
Brooks Robinson* 10.00
Frank Robinson*..................12.00
Rick Rhoden 8.00
Bobby Richardson...............10.00
Dave Righetti.........................8.00
Cal Ripken Jr. 12.00
Pete Rose 15.00
Al Rosen (b/w) 12.00
Ryne Sandberg 15.00
Juan Samuel 12.00
Ron Santo............................10.00
Hank Sauer 8.00
Mike Schmidt.....................40.00
Red Schoendienst* 10.00
Mike Shannon 8.00
Bobby Shantz 7.00
Larry Sheets 5.00
Roy Sievers (b/w) 8.00
Moose Skowron (b/w) 10.00
Dwight Smith 8.00
Duke Snider* 10.00
Willie Stargell* 12.00
Dave Stewart.......................15.00

Dave Steib 10.00
Kevin Mitchel 12.00
Johnny Mize* (b/w) 10.00
Paul Molitor 12.00
Joe Morgan (Red Sox) (b/w) ..8.00
Eddie Murray 10.00
Stan Musial* 35.00
Don Newcombe...................10.00
Hal Newhouser....................10.00
Jim Northrup 6.00
Tony Oliva 8.00
Joe Oller (b/w) 6.00
Gregg Olson 10.00
Andy Pafko..........................10.00
Mike Pagliarulo 8.00
Jim Palmer* 18.00
Milt Pappas 7.00
Dave Parker 10.00
Dan Pasqua 7.00
Jim Piersall 10.00
Johnny Podres 8.00
Gaylord Perry* 12.00
Boog Powell 8.00
Kirby Puckett.........................8.00
Dick Radatz 8.00
Tim Raines 10.00
Jeff Reardon 9.00
Pee Wee Reese* 30.00
Allie Reynolds 8.00
Danny Tartabull 8.00
Birdie Tebbetts (b/w) 10.0
Walt Terrell 6.00
Bill Terry* 45.00
Mickey Tettleton 8.00
Joe Torre.............................10.00
Gus Triandos 7.00
Tom Tresh 9.00
Allan Trammel.......................9.00
Jeff Treadway 6.00
Mickey Vernon 7.00
Bill White (b/w) 6.00
Devon White 7.00
Hoyt Wilhelm* (b/w)..............10.00
Billy Williams* 8.00
Mitch Williams 8.00
Ted Williams* 40.00
Maury Wills.........................10.00
Gene Woodling 6.00
Early Wynn* 10.00
Carl Yastrzemski* 15.00
Ed Yost (b/w) 8.00
Todd Zeil 9.00

Values of black and white photographs autographed by retired major league baseball players

* denotes member of the Hall of Fame

Cal Abrams 8.00
Joe Adcock 8.00
Tom Alston 8.00
Luke Appling* 15.00
Ernie Banks* 15.00
Hank Bauer 8.00
Gus Bell 10.00
Yogi Berra* 15.00
Lou Boudreau* 10.00
Justin Boyd 5.00
Ralph Branca 10.00
Harry Brecheen 8.00
Nellie Briles 8.00
Lou Brissie 8.00
Lou Brock* 12.00
Bob Buhl 8.00
Jim Bunning 10.00
Lou Burdette 10.00
Smokey Burgess 10.00
Jim Busby 8.00
Steve Carlton 15.00
Phil Caveretta 8.00
Orlando Cepeda 10.00
Bubba Church 8.00
Ellis Clary 8.00
Joe Coleman 8.00
Ray Coleman 8.00
Walker Cooper 8.00
Del Crandell 10.00
Frank Crosetti 12.00
Joe Cunningham 8.00
Al Dark 10.00
Jim Delsing 8.00
Joe DeMastri 8.00
Dom DiMaggio 15.00
Bob Doerr* 10.00
Walt Dropo 8.00
Don Drysdale* 12.00
Leo Durocher 20.00
Del Ennis 8.00
Carl Erskine 10.00
Hoot Evers 15.00
Elroy Face 10.00
Bob Feller* 10.00
Rick Ferrell* 12.00
Tom Ferrick 8.00
Whitey Ford* 15.00
Bob Friend 8.00
Joe Garagiola* 12.00
Ned Garver 8.00
Bob Gibson* 12.00
Al Gionfriddo 10.00
Dick Groat 8.00
Harvey Haddix 8.00
Grady Hamner 8.00
Clint Hartung 8.00
Solly Hemus 10.00
Tom Henrich 10.00
Billy Herman* 10.00
Tommy Holmes 8.00
Johnny Hopp 8.00
Ralph Houk 10.00
Al Hrbrosky 8.00
Billy Hunter 8.00
Larry Jansen 8.00
Julian Javier 12.00
Eddie Joost 8.00
Al Kaline* 12.00
George Kell* 10.00
Ken Keltner 10.00
Martin Kennedy 8.00
Ralph Kiner* 12.00
Jack Kramer 8.00
Dick Kryhoski 8.00
Whitey Kurowski 8.00
Bob Kuzana 8.00
Clem Labine 10.00
Max Lanier 10.00
Don Larsen 10.00
Vernon Law 10.00
Bob Lemon* 10.00
Don Lenhardt 8.00
Whitey Lockman 10.00
Ed Lopat 10.00
Stan Lopata 8.00
Mickey Mantle* 30.00
Marty Marion 10.00
Willard Marshall 8.00
Phil Masi 8.00
Walter Masterson 8.00
Eddie Mathews* 12.00
Gene Mauch 10.00
Willie Mays* 22.00
Bill Mazeroski 10.00
Lindy McDaniel 10.00
Von McDaniel 10.00
Gil McDougald 10.00
Cal McLish 10.00
Sam Mele 10.00
Minnie Minoso 12.00
Johnny Mize* 10.00
Vinegar Bend Mizell 8.00
Terry Moore 10.00
Walt Moryn 8.00
Les Moss 8.00
Don Mueller 8.00
Bob Muncrief 8.00
Stan Musial* 22.00
Charlie Neal 10.00
Don Newcombe 12.00
Hal Newhouser 10.00
Mickey Owen 10.00
Andy Pafko 8.00
Mel Parnell 8.00
Johnny Pesky 8.00
Billy Pierce 10.00
Jimmy Piersall 10.00
Johnny Podres 8.00
Ken Raffensburger 8.00
Pee Wee Reese* 20.00
Allie Reynolds 10.00
Bobby Richardson 10.00
Bill Rigney 10.00
Phil Rizzuto 10.00
Robin Roberts* 10.00
Frank Robinson* 15.00
"Preacher" Roe 10.00
Al Rosen 12.00
Pete Runnels 10.00
Bob Rush 8.00
Johnny Sain 10.00
Hank Sauer 8.00
Eddie Sawyer 8.00
Johnny Schmitz 8.00
Red Schoendienst* 12.00

Name	Value
Dick Schofield	8.00
Herb Score	10.00
Andy Seminick	8.00
Joe Sewell*	25.00
Mike Shannon	10.00
Bobby Shantz	8.00
Spec Shea	10.00
Roy Sievers	8.00
Dick Sisler	8.00
Moose Skowron	10.00
Enos Slaughter*	10.00
Duke Snider*	12.00
Warren Spahn*	10.00
Eddie Stanky	10.00
Dick Starr	8.00
Wayne Terwilliger	8.00
Frank Thomas	8.00
Bobby Thomson	10.00
Joe Torre	10.00
Virgil Trucks	8.00
Bob Turley	10.00
Elmer Valo	8.00
Johnny Vander Meer	12.00
Mickey Vernon	8.00
Bill Virdon	10.00
Bill Voiselle	8.00
Harry Walker	8.00
Alan Weintraub	4.00
Wally Westlake	8.00
Wes Westrum	8.00
Dick Whiteman	8.00
Hoyt Wilhelm*	10.00
Early Wynn*	10.00
Ed Yost	8.00
Al Zarilla	8.00
Gus Zernial	8.00

Autographed Commemorative Envelopes

The Gateway Stamp company of Florissant, Missouri has been marketing commemorative baseball envelopes since 1977. The envelopes, many of which are autographed by the player being honored, are typically hand cancelled at a post office in the major league city on the day a record-breaking, historic, or memorable baseball event takes place.

The initial Gateway series was offered following Lou Brock's breaking the career stolen base record of Ty Cobb on August 29, 1977 in San Diego, California.

Steve Ciniglio, one of the nation's leading dealers in autographed commemorative envelopes, issues a periodic catalog of Gateway offerings that he has for sale. Mr. Ciniglio can be contacted at P.O. Box 1126, Malibu, California 90265.

The following example will illustrate how the descriptions and prices of the Gateway envelopes can be interpreted:

Joe Cowley No hitter 9-19-86 (299) $200.00

White Sox pitcher Joe Cowley pitched a no-hitter on September 19, 1986. His Gateway commemorative envelope was issued in a series of 299, postmarked on the date of the no-hitter, and is currently valued at $200.00.

Name	Description	Price
Hank Aaron	HOF ind. 5/1/82 (4000)	21.95
Walt Alston	HOF Ind. 7/31/83 (1520)	34.95
Sparky Anderson	100 victories in both leagues 9/23/84 (1500)	11.95
L. Aparicio	HOF Ind. 8/12/84 (2000)	19.95
Ernie Banks	50th anniversary of A/S game 7/6/83 (1200)	49.95
Len Barker	Perfect game 5/15/81 (1000)	69.95
Al Barlick	HOF Ind. 7/23/89 (1500)	14.95
Yogi Berra	50th anniversary/Coop. 6/12/89 (2000)	16.95
Bert Blyleven	3000 Ks, 2 env. set 8/1/86 (3000) w/1 autograph	12.95
Bob Boone	All time catching record 9/16/87 (1000)	12.95
Lou Brock	3000 hits, 2 end. set 8/14/79 (6000) w/1 autograph	12.95
Lou Brock	HOF Ind. 7/28/85 (2000)	12.95
Tom Browning	Perfect game 9/16/88 (1200)	14.95
Roy Campanella	50th anniversary HOF (personally autographed 6/10/89) (257)	650.00

Canadian FDI	150th anniversary of baseball in Canada unautographed 9/14/88	4.50
Joe Canseco	40/40 9/23/88 (1400)	85.00
Rod Carew	3000 hits, env. set 8/4/84 (2000) w/2 autographs	24.95
Steve Carlton	Left hand strikeout rec. 7/6/80 (1000)	95.00
Steve Carlton	3000 Ks, 2 env. set 4/29/81 (3500) w/1 autograph	21.95
Steve Carlton	All time strikeout rec. 6/7/83 (2000)	21.95
Happy Chandler	HOF Ind. 8/1/82 (1000)	59.95
Roger Clemens	20 Ks, single game 4/29/86 (750)	250.00
Roberto Clemente	1st day cover, unautographed 8/17/84 (6000)	3.95
Vince Coleman	Rookie stolen base record 8/15/85 (3500)	11.95
Jocko Conlon	50th HOF 6/12/89 (1000) Unautographed	3.95
Cooperstown	1st day cover, 50th anniversary, unautographed 6/12/89 (1700)	4.50
Joe Cowley	No hitter 9/19/86 (299)	200.00
R. Dandridge	HOF Ind. 7/26/87 (1200)	11.95
Eric Davis	3 grand slams in one month 5/30/87 (1250)	49.95
Jim Deshaies	Strikeout record 9/23/86 (1000)	11.95
Bill Dickey	50th anniversary A/S game 7/6/83 (1000)	75.00
Joe DiMaggio	40th anniversary of 56 hit streak 7/16/81 (2000)	125.00
Don Drysdale	HOF Ind. 8/12/84 (2000)	11.95
Bobby Doerr	HOF Ind. 8/3/86 (1200)	11.95
Darrell Evans	40 HR Club, oldest member 10/2/85 (600)	74.95
Darrell Evans	400 HRs 9/20/88 (1000)	14.95
Bob Feller	50th anniversary of 1st game 8/23/86 (1700)	11.95
Fenway Park	75th anniversary 4/20/87 (unautographed)	35.00
Rick Ferrell	HOF Ind. 8/12/84 (1500)	11.95
Rollie Fingers	All time saves rec. 4/13/85 (1500)	11.95
Carlton Fisk	1807 games caught 8/19/88 (1000)	16.95
500 HR Club	12 autographs 1/14/89 (1000)	495.00
Whitey Ford	HOF Ind. 6/12/79 (1000)	79.95
Bob Forsch	2nd No-hitter 9/26/83 (950)	49.95
Steve Garvey	1000 consecutive games 6/7/82 (2000)	16.95
Steve Garvey	1118 consecutive games 4/16/83 (2000)	16.95
Steve Garvey	Padres retire uniform number 4/16/88 (1000)	14.95
Lou Gehrig	FDI 6/10/89 (3000) unautographed	4.00
C. Gehringer	50th anniversary of A/S game 4/16/83 (500)	175.00
Bob Gibson	HOF Ind. 8/21/81 (3000)	11.95
Kirk Gibson	1988 dramatic WS home run (1400)	19.95
Lefty Gomez	50th anniversary of A/S game 4/16/83 (1000)	49.95
Dwight Gooden	K record 9/24/84 (1500)	74.95
Dwight Gooden	Youngest 20 game winner 8/25/85 (1500)	74.95
Goose Gossage	300 saves 8/6/88 (1000)	11.95
Ken Griffey Sr.	4/3/89 (1000)	14.95
Rickey Henderson	Stolen base record, 2 env. set 8/27/82 (2000) w/1 autograph	24.95
Orel Hershiser	59 scoreless innings 9/28/83 (1300)	75.00
Bob Horner	4 HRs in one game 7/6/86 (1200)	12.95
Carl Hubbell	50th anniversary of A/S feat 7/10/84 (1000)	74.95
Catfish Hunter	HOF Ind. 7/26/87 (2000)	11.95
Monte Irvin	50th anniversary Cooperstown 6/12/89 (2000)	11.95
Travis Jackson	HOF Ind. 8/1/82 (1000)	59.95
Reggie Jackson	400 HRs 8/11/80 (1200)	49.95
Reggie Jackson	500 HRs 9/17/84 (500)	124.95
Reggie Jackson	500 HRs, numbered version (500)	225.00
Bo Jackson	1989 All Star MVP 7/11/89 (800)	75.00

Ferguson Jenkins	3000 Ks, 2 env. set 5/25/83	11.95
Ferguson Jenkins	Canadian HOF INd. 11/19/87 (1000)	11.95
Jim Kaat	25 years 4/5/83 (2000)	11.95
George Kell	HOF Ind. 7/31/83 (1500)	11.95
Harmon Killebrew	HOF Ind. 8/12/84 (2000)	11.95
Sandy Koufax	50th anniversary of Cooperstown 6/12/89 (2000)	24.95
Rick Langford	21 complete games 9/6/80 (500)	250.00
Rick Langford	22 complete games 9/12/80 (1000)	49.95
Don Larsen	30th anniversary of perfect game 10/8/86 (1000)	11.95
E. Lombardie	HOF Ind., unautographed 8/3/86 (1000)	3.95
Willie Magee	N.L. switch hitting record 10/6/85 (2000)	11.95
Mickey Mantle	40th Anniversary of HOF 6/`12/79 (1000)	149.95
Juan Marichal	HOF Ind. 7/31/83 (2000)	11.95
Billy Martin	Tragedy in Baseball 12/29/89 (1000) unautographed	4.00
Don Mattingly	Hits record 10/5/86 (1500)	49.95
Don Mattingly	Consecutive HRs 7/18/87 (1000)	69.95
Willie Mays	HOF Ind. 8/2/79 (2000)	149.95
Willie McCovey	500 HRs 6/30/78 (2000)	124.95
Willie McCovey	HOF Ind. 8/3/86 (3000)	14.95
Mark McGwire	Rookie HR record 8/14/87 (2000)	29.95
Mark McGwire	5 Hrs in 2 games 6/28/87 (1000)	49.95
Minnie Minoso	5 decades in baseball 10/4/80 (500)	550.00
Johnny Mize	HOF Ind. 8/2/81 (2000)	14.95
Paul Molitor	39 game hit streak 8/25/87 (1500)	12.95
Jack Morris	No-hitter 4/7/84 (1500)	16.95
Phil Niekro	300 wins 6/10/85 (1500)	14.95
Phil Niekro	3000 Ks, 2 env. set 7/4/84 (2000)	14.95
Niekro/Sutton	1st time two 300 game winners opposed each other 6/28/86 (800)	74.95
Niekro Bros.	Winningest combo 6/1/87 (1000)	24.95
Juan Nieves	No-hitter 4/15/87 (850)	69.95
Olympic Team	1984 U.S. Olympic Baseball Team Reunion, 21 autographs, #10 env. (500)	225.00
Satchell Paige	40th anniversary of HOF 6/12/79 (1000)	400.00
David Palmer	5 inning perfect game 4/22/84 (1500)	11.95
Gaylord Perry	300 wins, 2 env. set 5/6/82 (3000)	14.95
Perry Bros.	Winningest brother combo 6/1/87 (1000) autograhped by Jim and Gaylor Perry	24.95
Kirby Puckett	10 consecutive hits 8/30/87 (1500)	14.95
Jeff Reardon	40 saves both leagues 9/30/88 (1200)	11.95
Dave Righetti	No-hitter 7/4/83 (1650)	19.95
Cal Ripken Jr.	Consecutive innings played 9/14/87 (2000)	14.95
	Autographed by Cal Jr. and Cal Sr.	24.95
Jackie Robinson	1st day issue 8/2/82 (8000) unautographed	3.95
Brooks Robinson	HOF Ind. 7/31/83 (3000)	14.95
Frank Robinson	HOF INd. 8/1/82 (2250)	14.95
Edd Roush	70th anniversary of batting title 9/30/87 (1000) unautographed	3.95
Pete Rose	N.L. hit record Nos. 3630 & 3631, 2 env. set 6/10/81 (5000) 1 autograph	24.95
Pete Rose	3000 hits, 2 env. set 5/5/78 (5000) w/1 autograph	69.95
Pete Rose	3,309 games played 6/29/84 (1000)	69.95
Pete Rose	4,000 hits 4/13/84 (1000)	95.00
	With Ottawa postmark	124.95
Pete Rose	All time hit record 4192, 4 env. set 9/1/84 (2500) w/1 autograph	29.95

	w/2 autographs	49.95
Pete Rose	Managerial debut, large env. 8/17/84 (only 104 exist)	1650.00
Pete Rose	Banishment 8/24/89 (1500)	24.95
Babe Ruth	1st day issue, unautographed 7/6/83 (5000)	4.50
	Autographed by Ben Chapman, Mel Allen, Jimmie Reese	74.95
Nolan Ryan	3000 Ks, 2 env. set 7/4/80 (5000)	29.95
Nolan Ryan	3509 Ks, all time strikeouts 4/27/83 (2000)	29.95
Nolan Ryan	5th No-hitter 9/26/81 (1000)	225.00
Nolan Ryan	4000 Ks 7/11/85 (2000)	29.95
Nolan Ryan	5000 Ks 8/22/89 (2000)	125.00
Brett Saberhagen	2nd youngest 20-game winner 9/30/85 (200)	375.00
S.D. Padres	3 HRs to start game 4/13/87 (500)	195.00
S.D. Padres	20th anniversary, autographed by Randy Jones 4/12/88 (2000)	16.95
B. Santiago	Rookie hitting streak 10/2/87 (1000)	19.95
Mike Schmidt	400 HRs 5/15/85 (1500)	19.95
Mike Schmidt	500 HRs 4/18/87 (3000)	24.95
Red Schoendienst	HOF 7/23/89 (1500)	14.95
Mike Scott	No-hitter 9/25/86 (1500)	11.95
Tom Seaver	Uniform retirement 7/24/88 (1500)	21.95
Tom Seaver	Opeining Day rec. 4/9/85 (1500)	21.95
Tom Seaver	300 wins 8/4/85 (1800)	21.95
Tom Seaver	3000 Ks, 2 env. set 4/18/81 1 autograph	21.95
Tom Seaver	No-hitter 6/16/78 100 #10 six env.; 42 reg size (142 exist)	1650.00
Joe Sewell	50th anniversary Cooperstown 6/12/89 (200)	79.95
Shea Stadium	25th anniversary, unautographed 4/17/89 (200)	3.95
Enos Slaughter	HOF Ind. 7/28/85 (2000)	11.95
Warren Spahn	300 Club 5/6/82 (1000)	59.95
Rusty Staub	100 pinch hits 9/21/83 (800)	69.95
Rusty Staub	Last game, 2 env. set w/2 autographs 7/13/86 (2000)	21.95
Willie Stargell	HOF Ind. 7/31/88 (2000)	16.95
Don Sutton	3000 Ks, 2 env. set 6/24/83 (2000) w/1 autograph	11.95
Don Sutton	300 wins 6/18/86 (1500)	11.95
Bill Terry	50th anniversary A/S/ game 7/6/83 (750)	100.00
Jim Thorpe	1st day issue 5/24/84 (3500) unautographed	3.95
Triple Crown	4 autographs 1/14/89 (650) Mantle, Yaz, Williams, F. Robinson	250.00
Fernando Valenzuela	ERA rec. 4/28/85 (1000)	49.95
J. VanderMeer	Anniversary of back-to-back no-hitters, 2 env. set 6/11, 6/15/88 (2000) w/1 autograph	19.95
Arky Vaughn	HOF Ind. unautographed 7/8/85 (1000)	3.95
Hoyt Wilhelm	HOF INd. 7/2/85 (2000)	11.95
Ted Williams	40th anniversary of .400 season 9/29/81 (2000)	49.95
Billy Williams	HOF Ind. 7/26/87 (2000)	11.95
Willie, Mick & Duke	Snider, Mays, Mantle - 3 autographs 1/14/89 (650)	200.00
Maury Wills	25th anniversary 104 steals 10/3/87 (1000)	11.95
Mike Witt	Perfect game 9/30/84 (1500)	11.95
Todd Worrell	Rookie saves record 8/10/86 (1200)	11.95
Wrigley Field	1st night game 8/8 & 8/9/88, 2 env. set (4000) unautographed	7.95
	w/1 autograph	14.95
	w/2 autographs	21.95
Wrigley Field	75th anniversary 4/25/89 (2000) unautogrpahed	3.95
Early Wynn	300 Club 5/6/82 (1000)	59.95
Carl Yastrzemski	3000 hits 9/12/79 (3000)	79.95
Carl Yastrzemski	HOF Ind. 7/23/89 (2000)	24.95

Unautographed Gateway envelope from the 1980 Philadelphia-Kansas City World Series. $3.00-4.00.

Team Autographed Baseballs

Autographed baseballs signed by a team or a portion of a team roster can present a serious problem for collectors. Many team balls may have key autographs missing or contain the signatures of a clubhouse attendant or bat boy rather than the player who didn't take the time to sign the ball.

To verify the date attributed to a team ball, use the *Baseball Encyclopedia* (Macmillan) to make sure the players on the baseball were actually members of the team during that season.

A 1951 Yankee ball signed by the team and Joe DiMaggio is much more desirable than a 1952 ball because DiMaggio had retired after the 1951 World Series.

The values that follow on team signed baseballs assume minimal fading and the legible signatures of the major stars. The baseballs are "official" National or American League balls.

Notes on Collecting "Team" Autographed Baseballs

1. It is important that the ball be an official American League or National League baseball to have maximum value. If it is a minor league team, the ball should be an "official" ball from the specific league in which the team played (Midwest League, American Association, Pacific Coast League, etc..)
2. Faded or illegible signatures severely diminish the value of a baseball. If the ball was signed by the 1927 New York Yankees, it can take more damage than a ball signed by the 1973 Detroit Tigers and still hold its relative value.
3. Baseballs exposed to light or periodic games of catch tend to darken or scuff over time and signatures that were once bold become difficult to read.
4. Shellac tends to darken or "yellow" a baseball and will eventually crack and negatively affect the signatures and the value.
5. The primary players or "stars" must be on the baseball with legible signatures. A 1927 Yankee team ball without Ruth and Gehrig would be worth only a fraction of a ball with the legible signatures of the two immortals.
6. Many times a ball signed by a single player is worth much more than a team ball signed by the same player and 23 teammates. A 1938 Chicago Cub ball autographed by Gabby Hartnett and 19 fellow Cubs is worth less than a ball in similar condition signed only by Hartnett.
7. If a Hall of Fame member serving as a coach signs a team ball, the value of the ball can be significantly enhanced. Yogi Berra on a Houston Astros team baseball will not add significant dollars to its value but Honus Wagner on a 1947 Pirates ball can at least double or triple its worth.
8. Mechanically stamped "autographed" baseballs have been sold at concession stands in ball parks since the early 1950's. These balls have minimal value today but often confuse collectors who have difficulty in differentiating between machine and "hand signed" baseballs.

Year	Team	# of signatures (prominent players)	Condition	Value
1928	New York Yankees	20	near mint	2,400.00
1928	Philadelphia Athletics	19	excellent	800.00
1930	New York Yankees	20 (Ruth and Gehrig)	excellent	3,995.00
1931	Philadelphia Athletics	24	excellent	2,350.00
1931	Philadelphia Athletics	13	mint	925.00
1933	All-Star National League	22	excellent	1,000.00
1933	Pittsburgh Crawfords	17 (Bell and Gibson)	excellent	3,550.00
1934	New York Yankees	21 (Ruth and Ruffing)	good	2,200.00
1935	Boston Red Sox	23	very good	350.00
1936	New York Yankees	26	excellent	1,695.00
1937	NL All-Stars	33	near mint	900.00
1937	Pittsburgh Pirates	23 (Wagner and Vaughan)	near mint	700.00
1938	A's	22	excellent	295.00
1938	Boston Braves	24 (Stengel and Lopez)	near mint	240.00
1938	Philadelphia Athletics	22 (Mack)	excellent	320.00
1939	New York Yankees	28 (DiMaggio and Dickey)	near mint	2,500.00
1940	New York Yankees	29	very good	300.00
1940	AL Champ Tigers	25 (Averill and Greenberg)	near mint	950.00
1940	Brooklyn Dodgers	23 (Reese and Walker)	excellent	400.00
1941	Brooklyn Dodgers	19 (Reese and Herman)	excellent	400.00
1941	Cleveland Indians	20	excellent	200.00
1941	New York Yankees	25 (DiMaggio)	very good	900.00
1941	Chicago White Sox	16 (Lyons)	near mint	250.00
1943	Washington Senators	27 (Wynn and Vernon)	near mint	225.00
1943	Cleveland Indians	23 (Boudreau)	very good	100.00
1945	Boston Red sox	26 (Cronin)	near mint	125.00
1946	Boston Red Sox	28	excellent	325.00
1946	Brooklyn Dodgers	20 (Reese, Durocher)	near mint	1,000.00
1947	New York Yankees	27	excellent	700.00
1947	Brooklyn Dodgers	28	excellent	650.00
1948	New York Yankees	21 (DiMaggio)	mint	850.00
1948	Cleveland Indians	23	near mint	500.00
1948	Detroit Tigers	37	excellent	250.00
1948	Brooklyn Dodgers	26 (Hodges and Furillo)	excellent	700.00
1948	Senators	27 (Ferrell)	mint	290.00
1949	Browns	24	excellent	375.00
1949	Tigers	27 (Kell and Lyons)	excellent	350.00
1949	New York Yankees	23 (DiMaggio and Dickey)	near mint	650.00
1949	New York Giants	24	mint	295.00
1949	Cleveland Indians	32 (Feller, Garcia)	excellent	525.00
1950	New York Giants	26	near mint	295.00
1950	Phillies	23 (Ashburn and Roberts)	excellent	400.00
1950	Yankees	24 (Berra and DiMaggio)	excellent	1,200.00
1950	Indians	16	near mint	375.00
1950	St. Louis Cardinals	22 (Musial and Marion)	mint	395.00
1951	New York Giants	21 (Dark and Irvin)	excellent	350.00
1951	Dodgers	21 (Robinson and Hodges)	near mint	700.00
1951	Yankees	25 (Mantle and DiMaggio)	mint	1,695.00
1951	Giants	30 (Thomson and Durocher)	near mint	795.00
1951	Boston Braves	22	excellent	375.00

Date	Team	# of signatures (prominent players)	Condition	Value
1952	Brooklyn Dodgers	25 (Campanella)	excellent	550.00
1952	Browns	24 (Paige)	excellent	425.00
1953	St. Louis Browns	26 (Paige and Marion)	near mint	325.00
1953	Announcers Ball	12 (Red Barber and Allen)	excellent	250.00
1953	Yankees	29 (Mantle and Ford)	near mint	1,100.00
1953	Yankees	25 (Martin and Mantle)	mint	925.00
1954	Indians	26 (Rosen and Doby)	excellent	400.00
1954	Braves	25 (Mathews and Spahn)	excellent	325.00
1954	Boston Red Sox	24 (Williams and Piersall)	mint	250.00
1955	NL All Stars	30 (Hodges and Mays)	excellent	300.00
1955	Dodgers	23 (Campanella and Hodges)	near mint	750.00
1955	NL All Stars	13 (Mantle, Williams, Fox)	excellent	225.00
1956	New York Yankees	28 (Mantle and Howard)	near mint	895.00
1956	Phillies	24	mint	200.00
1956	Yankees	25 (Mantle and Dickey)	mint	995.00
1957	Braves	18 (Spahn and Aaron)	near mint	525.00
1957	NL All Stars	21 (Campanella)	mint	795.00
1957	Dodgers	29 (Alston and Koufax)	excellent	995.00
1957	Braves	13 (Aaron and Covington)	near mint	600.00
1957	Yankees	27 (Shantz and Mantle)	near mint	875.00
1957	Braves	31	fair	225.00
1958	NL All Stars	26 (Mays, Moon, Banks)	near mint	300.00
1958	Reds	26 (Kluzewski)	near mint	225.00
1958	Pirates	30 (Clemente and Groat)	very good	300.00
1958	KC Athletics	26 (Maris and Lemon)	excellent	500.00
1958	Yankees	21 (Berra and Ford)	near mint	950.00
1958	Braves	19 (Aaron and Mathews)	near mint	450.00
1959	L.A. Dodgers	23 (Drysdale and Snider)	near mint	400.00
1959	White Sox	27 (Aparicio and Fox)	near mint	800.00
1959	AL All Stars	27 (Lopez and Alston)	excellent	375.00
1960	NL All Stars	30 (Musial, Aaron, Mays)	mint	700.00
1960	Yankees	22 (Mantle and Berra)	near mint	900.00
1960	Pirates	27 (Clemente)	near mint	875.00
1960	L.A. Dodgers	27 (Snider and Drysdale)	excellent	275.00
1961	S.F. Giants	28 (Mays and Kuenn)	excellent	245.00
1961	Yankees	28 (Mantle and Howard)	excellent	500.00
1961	Indians	23	excellent	125.00
1962	Yankees	23 (Maris and Mantle)	mint	325.00
1962	S.F. Giants	24 (Dark and Mays)	near mint	325.00
1962	Yankees	27 (Maris andHoward)	mint	1,100.00
1962	Colt 45s	22 (Ferrell and Craft)	near mint	650.00
1962	S.F. Giants	23 (Mays and Marichal)	near mint	350.00
1962	Cubs	25 (Hubbs and Brock)	excellent	375.00
1963	Yankees	28 (Berra and Maris)	excellent	600.00
1963	Indians	24 (Adcock and HInton)	mint	350.00
1963	Mets	27 (Hodges and Snider)	mint	400.00
1964	Chicago Cubs	22 (Williams and Banks)	excellent	275.00
1964	Cubs	25 (Santo and Williams)	excellent	300.00
1964	Cardinals	27 (Gibons and Boyer)	mint	540.00
1964	Dodgers	28 (Koufax and Wills)	excellent	350.00

Date	Team	# of signatures (prominent signatures)	Condition	Value
1965	Twins	29 (Killebrew and Oliva)	excellent	425.00
1965	L.A. Dodgers	24 (Alston and Wills)	mint	385.00
1965	AL All Stars	20 (Howard and Kaline)	mint	275.00
1965	L.A. Dodgers	24 (Sutton and Alston)	excellent	300.00
1965	Yankees	26 (Mantle and Howard)	mint	325.00
1966	L.A. Dodgers	24 (Koufax and Alston)	excellent	385.00
1966	Orioles	30 (B. and F. Robinson)	mint	425.00
1966	Orioles	19 (Aparicio and Palmer)	excellent	375.00
1966	L.A. Dodgers	21	mint	400.00
1967	Phillies	21 (Bunning and White)	mint	200.00
1967	Cardinals	30 (Brock and Maris)	excellent	550.00
1967	Red Sox	21 (Yastrzemski and Tiant)	mint	575.00
1968	Tigers	19 (Cash and Kaline)	excellent	400.00
1968	Dodgers	22 (Boyer and Sutton)	mint	225.00
1969	Mets	27 (Ryan and Seaver)	excellent	900.00
1969	Orioles	17 (Palmer and F. Robinson)	near mint	475.00
1970	Cubs	25 (Banks and Williams)	excellent	140.00
1970	Phillies	20 (Luzinski and Ozark)	near mint	95.00
1970	Mets	18 (Seaver and Ryan)	mint	285.00
1971	Cardinals	23	excellent	160.00
1971	Phillies	25	near mint	85.00
1971	KC Royals	20	very good	75.00
1972	Padres	23	excellent	65.00
1972	Angels	19	near mint	60.00
1972	Padres	24	good	45.00
1972	Red Sox	29	mint	125.00
1972	Angels	19	mint	70.00
1973	Philles	17	mint	80.00
1974	Dodgers	15	near mint	115.00
1975	Padres	25	excellent	85.00
1975	New York Yankees	24	excellent	325.00
1975	Pirates	21	mint	150.00
1975	Phillies	30	excellent	95.00
1975	Dodges	20	excellent	60.00
1976	Dodgers	15	excellent	65.00
1976	Padres	28	mint	90.00
1977	Yankees	21 (Munson)	mint	500.00
1978	NL All Stars	22	mint	125.00
1979	Tigers	15	mint	115.00
1979	Royals	21	mint	120.00
1979	Rangers	25	mint	115.00
1979	Orioles	24	excellent	235.00
1979	Expos	18	mint	90.00
1979	Tigers	15	mint	115.00
1979	Royals	21	near mint	120.00
1979	Rangers	30	excellent	70.00
1979	Orioles	18	excellent	150.00
1981	AL All Stars	25	mint	325.00
1982	Expos	19	mint	65.00
1982	A's	32	near mint	225.00

Date	Team	# of signatures (prominent signatures)	Condition	Value
1982	Giants	21	excellent	50.00
1982	Brewers	21	near mint	65.00
1982	Expos	19	mint	60.00
1983	Pirates	13	near mint	55.00
1983	Orioles	25	excellent	195.00
1983	New York Yankees	23	very good	155.00
1983	Orioles	32	near mint	290.00
1983	Angels	24	excellent	145.00
1983	Pirates	13	near mint	65.00
1984	Blue Jays	21	near mint	95.00
1984	Orioles	26	excellent	75.00
1984	Mets	29	excellent	75.00
1984	Braves	16	excellent	35.00
1984	New York Yankees	11	excellent	100.00
1984	Phillies	28	near mint	85.00
1984	Padres	24	mint	295.00
1984	Tigers World Champs	23	mint	350.00
1985	Orioles	22	near mint	65.00
1985	Cardinals	18	mint	150.00
1985	Phillies	22	near mint	100.00
1985	White Sox	28	excellent	95.00
1985	Rangers	29	mint	50.00
1985	Astros	27	near mint	75.00
1985	Twins	25	excellent	100.00
1985	Expos	29	excellent	75.00
1986	Orioles	27	near mint	90.00
1986	Padres	32	excellent	75.00
1986	Braves	23	excellent	60.00
1986	Expos	21	mint	50.00
1986	Red Sox	33	mint	210.00
1987	White Sox	22	mint	95.00
1987	Orioles	28	excellent	75.00
1987	New York Yankees	26	excellent	125.00
1987	Expos	25	excellent	50.00
1987	Astros	27	excellent	100.00
1988	Giants	15	near mint	65.00
1988	A's	28	mint	195.00
1988	Braves	22	near mint	75.00
1988	Padres	22	near mint	50.00
1988	Orioles	30	mint	65.00
1988	Giants	15	mint	95.00
1988	A's	24	mint	250.00
1988	Detroit Tigers	25	excellent	75.00
1988	Padres	22	near mint	70.00
1989	Red Sox	21	mint	80.00
1989	Brewers	22	mint	65.00
1989	Expos	23	near mint	60.00
1989	Twins	27	mint	50.00
1989	White Sox	21	mint	55.00
1989	Astros	24	mint	50.00

Date	Team	# of signatures (prominent signatures)	Condition	Value
1989	Brewers	22	mint	75.00
1989	Blue Jays	10	mint	25.00
1989	Royals	21	near mint	55.00
1989	Angels	20	mint	75.00
1990	Mets	31	mint	110.00
1990	Cubs	25	near mint	95.00
1990	Yankees	28	near mint	110.00
1990	Detroit Tigers	29 (Fielder)	mint	85.00

The baseballs described below were recently advertised in a national "hobby" publication. The dealer commented in the ad that "These balls are in pretty bad shape. They are tarnished. It appears to be some type of polyurethane on them. Many of the signatures are not legible." The signatures that <u>are</u> listed with the balls <u>are legible</u>. A "plain" baseball is an unofficial ball.

1950 Yankees plus a few celebrities (24 signatures on a plain ball), Bob Hope, Jack Benny, Crosetti, Rizzuto, Berra, Reynolds, Lopat, Collins, McDougald ... 125.00

1950 Cleveland Indians (29 signatures on a plain ball). Lobe, Easter, Wynn, Boone, Gordon, Feller, Boudreau, Rosen, Vernon, Doby, Garcia, Rozek, Hagen, Kennedy, Mitchell ... 150.00

1952 All Stars (16 signatures on a plain ball). Avila, Wertz, Mantle, Raschi, Reynolds, Dom DiMaggio, Satchell Paige, Rosen, Kell, Berra, Rizzuto, Yost ... 195.00

1950 Chicago White Sox (26 signatures on a plain ball). Corriden, Scarbrough, Rickert, Holdcombe, Judson, Robinson, Wight, Pierce, Fox, Maasi, Kozar, Aloma, Erautt, Goldsberry, Baker, Zernial, Judson, Cain, Appling ... 150.00

1949 St. Louis Browns (26 signatures on a plain ball). Coleman, Taylor, Dresling, Winegarner, Sommers, Pillette, Demars, Starr, Arft, Upton, Stirnweiss, Dorish, Wood, Overmire, Lenhardt ... 95.00

1950 Boston Braves (26 signatures on a National League ball). Southworth, Spahn, Johnson, Elliot, Almo, Reiser, Chipman, Bickford, Torgensen ... 75.00

1950 Boxton Red Sox (22 signatures on a plain ball). Stephens, Schantz, Zarilla, Wright, Ted Williams, Pesky, Stobbs, Goodman, Dropo, Vollmer ... 150.00

1950 Washington Senators (23 signatures on a plain ball). Vernon, Hudson, Grasso ... 50.00

1950 Cincinnati Reds (28 signatures on a National League ball). Adcock, Scheffing, Kluszewski, Stallcup, Hatton, Landrith, Ryne, Raffensburger, Ford, Ransdell, Lowery ... 150.00

Mini ball with Connie Mack, Hank Greenberg and 11 other non-legible signatures ... 75.00

1950 Pittsburgh Pirates (24 signatures on a National League ball). Dickson, Castiglione, Beard, Lombardi, Pierce, Dillinger, Mueller, Rojek, Westlake, Law, Werle, O'Connell, Phillips, Chambers, Bell, Queen, McDonald, McCullough, Riddle ... 75.00

1950 Philadelphia A's (16 signatures on a Reach ball). Fain, Kellner, Hitchcock, Meyers, Suder, Shantz, McCosky, Miller, Brisse, Joost, Tipton, Connie Mack ... 125.00

1950 Chicago Cubs (24 signatures on a National League ball). Frisch, Leonard, Sauer, Klippstein, Ward, Jackson, Terwilliger, Walker, Jeffcoat, Lade, Schmitz, Pafko, Owen, Cavarretta ... 95.00

1950 St. Louis Cardinals (26 signatures on a National League ball). Miller, Brazlie, Bucha, Staley, Kozak, Howerton, Slaughter, Walker, Musial, Brechen, Pollet, Wares, Moore, Munger ... 150.00

1949 New York Giants (24 signatures on National League ball). Hoffman, Jansen, Mueller, Park, Stanky, Westrum, Irvin, Hansen, Maglie, Hartung ... 95.00

1962 Detroit (28 signatures of a National League ball). Wertz, Trucks, Evers, Groth, Bartell, Berry, Rolfe, White, Robinson, Kolloway, Lake ... 75.00

1950 Dodgers (24 signatures on a National League ball). Campanella, Furillo, Reese, Newcombe, Hodges Branca, Snider, Cox, Abrams, Barney, Edwards .. 195.00

1950 Yankees (30 signatures on a plain ball). Berra Raschi, Brown, Houk, Ostrowski, Ferrick, Hopp Reynolds, Jensen, Crosetti ... 150.00

Autographed "Government" Postcards

Autograph collectors have been purchasing postcards at United States Post Offices ("government post cards") for more than 70 years to send to their baseball heroes for an autograph. The prices for the cards have escalated over the years from 1¢ to almost 20¢ and relatively few autograph collectors use them today. The preference now is for unlined index cards, baseball cards, or limited edition cards.

Collectors addressed one side of the postcard to themselves and then enclosed it in a letter to the player. The signature came back on the blank side of the postcard with a postmark from the city in which it was mailed and the date.

It is important that the government postcards be postmarked and that the autograph has not been distorted by ink from the postmark that has worked its way through the card to the blank side.

The "government" post cards below date from the 1930's to the 1950's. They can be accurately dated by the postmark from the day they were returned.

Values of Autographed Government Postcard of Members of the Hall of Fame

Grover Cleveland Alexander 350.00
Dave Bancroft 100.00
Al Barlick 10.00
Max Carey 55.00
Fred Clarke 200.00
Mickey Cochrane 200.00
Earle Combs 55.00
Joe Cronin 55.00
Dizzy Dean 125.00
Bill Dickey 15.00
Bob Doerr 10.00
Red Faber 80.00
Rick Ferrell 15.00
Whitey Ford 15.00
Jimmy Foxx 200.00
Fork Frick 90.00
Frank Frisch 80.00
Charlie Gehringer 10.00
Lefty Gomez 55.00
Hank Greenberg 40.00
Chick Hafey 45.00
Jessie Haines 65.00
Harry Hooper 65.00
Rodgers Hornsby 325.00
Waite Hoyt 15.00
Carl Hubbell 12.00
Travis Jackson 15.00
Ralph Kiner 10.00
Freddie Lindstrom 55.00
Ernie Lombardi 65.00
Al Lopez 25.00
Ted Lyons 35.00
Connie Mack 150.00
Joe McCarthy 55.00
Joe Medwick 80.00
Stan Musial 35.00
Mel Ott 250.00
Sam Rice 80.00
Robin Roberts 10.00
Jackie Robinson 250.00
Edd Roush 15.00
Red Ruffing 40.00
Ray Schalk 100.00
George Sisler 50.00
Enos Slaughter 10.00
Tris Speaker 275.00
Bill Terry 20.00
Pie Traynor 150.00
Honus Wagner 350.00
Lloyd Waner 35.00
Zack Wheat 55.00

Values of Autographed Government Postcards of Major League Players

Bobby Avila 20.00
Dick Bartell 10.00
Max Bishop 35.00
Joe Black 15.00
Ossie Bluege 15.00
George Case 20.00
Spud Chandler 20.00
"Rip" Collins 25.00
Billy Cox 35.00
Frank Crosetti 15.00
George Cutshaw 35.00
Dom DiMaggio 25.00
Larry Doby 20.00
Chuck Dressen 35.00
Leo Durocher 30.00
Bob Elliott 25.00
Fred Fitzsimmons 25.00
Carl Furrillo 20.00
Jim Gilliam 20.00
Billy Goodman 30.00
Joe Gordon 25.00
Charlie Grimm 35.00
Stan Hack and Bill Lee 30.00
Bill Hallahan 25.00
Babe Herman 40.00
Mike Higgins 25.00
Shoeless Joe Jackson (signed by his wife) 250.00
Ellis Kinder 30.00
Jim Konstanty 20.00
John Kotarba 6.00
Duffy Lewis 30.00
Pepper Martin 125.00
Terry Moore 20.00
Lou Novikoff 35.00
Lefty O'Doul 30.00
Steve O'Neil 30.00
Mel Parnell 10.00
Babe Pinelli 20.00
Vic Raschi 15.00
Phil Rizzuto 10.00
Red Rolfe 25.00
Charlie Root 25.00
Al Schacht 30.00
Vern Stephens 30.00
Bill Stewart 30.00
Stuffy Stirnweiss 20.00
Johnny VanderMeer 7.00
Bucky Walters 30.00
Ted Wilks 30.00
Smokey Joe Wood 20.00
Whitlow Wyatt 25.00

The procedure in sending out postcards was relatively simple. A self-addressed card was included with a letter addressed to the team or player. The player read the letter, signed the postcard, and returned it to the collector. The postmark on the autographed card provides today's collectors with an approximate date of the signature.

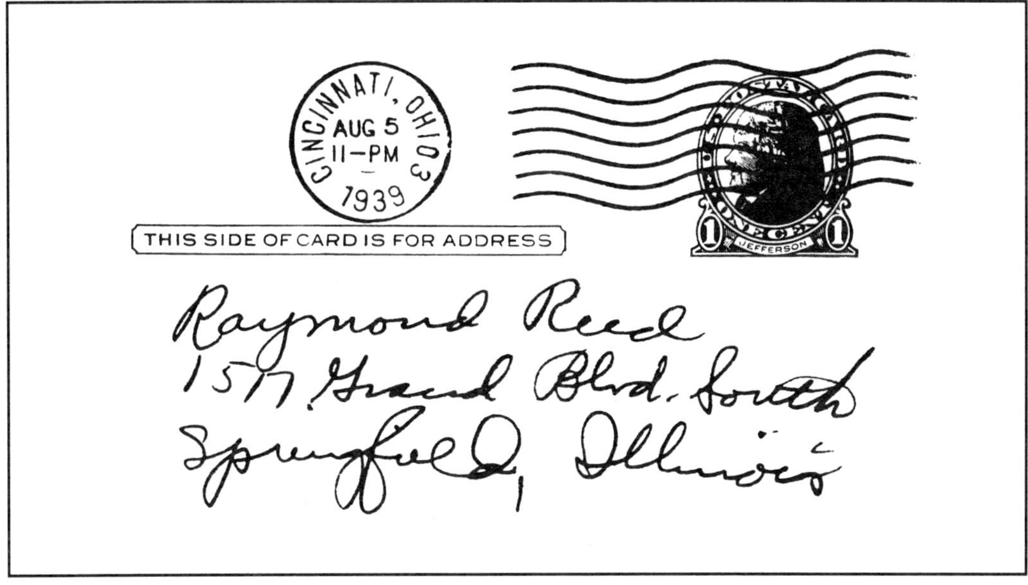

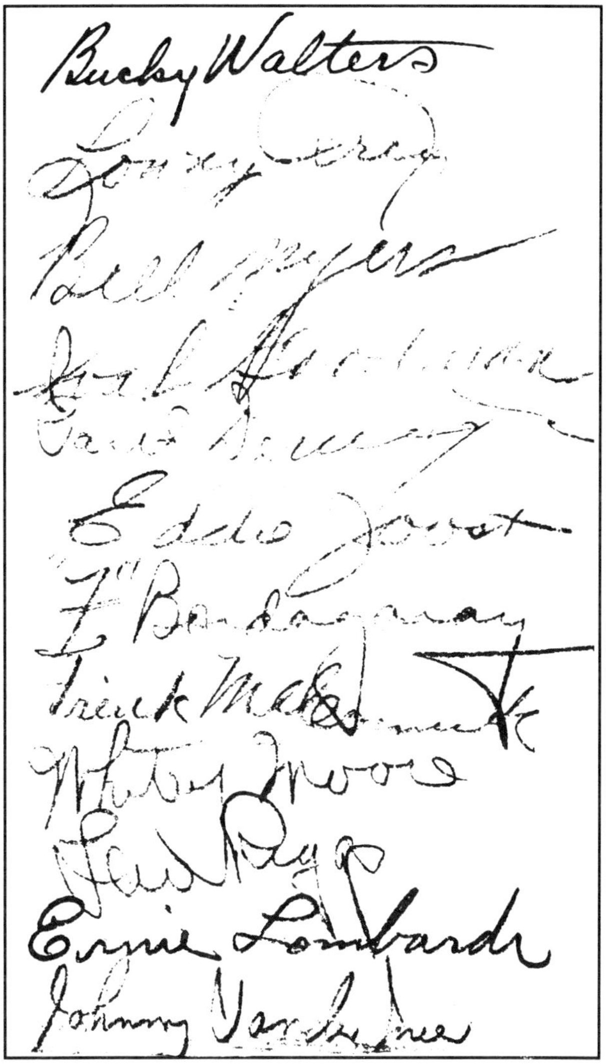

This government postcard was signed by the pennant-winning Cincinnati Reds and returned to Raymond Reed in Springfield, Illinois on August 5, 1939.

To Raymond: your friends are right, I have not pitched a no-hit-no run game during my career—
Sincerely
"Dizzy" Dean

This government postcard was returned by "Dizzy" Dean. The ink from the postmark permeated the card but did not disturb Dean's autograph. $125.00.

Nine members of the St. Louis Cardinals' "Gas House Gang" autographed this government postcard. Four of the players-Dean, Medwick, Haines, and Frisch-went on to be elected to the Hall of Fame. $150.00-225.00.

Hall of Famers Bill Terry and Travis Jackson and seven New York Giants teammates signed this government postcard. $100.00-115.00.

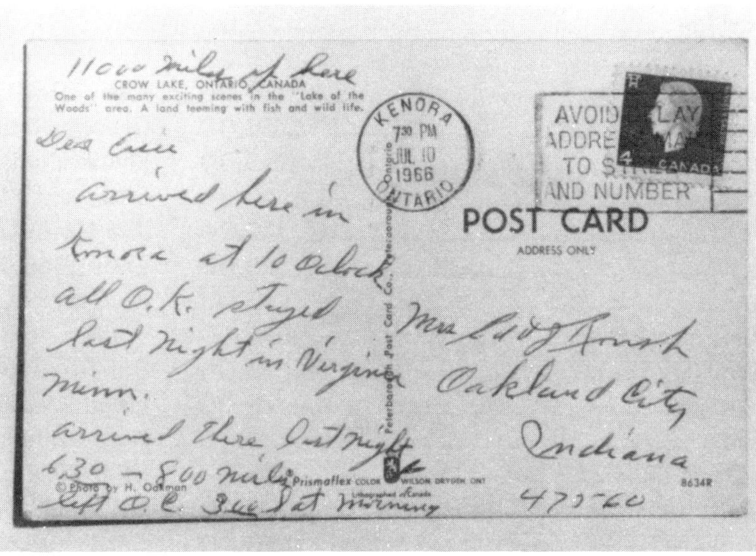

Postcard sent by Edd Roush to his wife in 1966. $15.00-20.00.

Perez-Steele Cards

To date the Perez-Steele Gallery of Ft. Washington, Pennsylvania has produced four distinct sets of limited edition cards that have been eagerly collected.

1. Perez-Steele postcards. 10,000 numbered postcard sets depicting members of the Hall of Fame with the first series issued in 1980. The sets are updated every two years with the cards of new inductees during that period.
2. Great Moments cards were offered in 1985 with 5,000 numbered sets. Periodically a new series of Hall of Fame members is released.
3. The Celebration set of 44 boxed cards was offered in 1989 in celebration of the 50th anniversary of the Hall of Fame. There were 10,000 sets made available to collectors. Unlike the other sets from Perez-Steele, the Celebration cards will not be periodically updated. The set is complete with the 44 cards.
4. The Masterworks set was introduced in 1990. Series I contained five different card styles of five players - Mantle, Mays, Snider, Gehringer, and Spahn-for a total of 25 cards. There were 10,000 sets made available. Additional five card sets of players will be updated.

Values of Autographed Perez-Steele Postcards

(D) denotes deceased

Hank Aaron 40.00
Walter Alston (D) 1,100.00
Luis Aparicio 25.00
Earl Averill 950.00
Al Barlick 25.00
Lou Brock 25.00
Happy Chandler (D) 65.00
Jocko Conlan (D) 100.00
Stan Coveleski 750.00
Ray Dandridge 25.00
Bill Dickey 125.00
Bob Doerr 20.00
Don Drysdale 25.00
Bob Feller 35.00
Rick Ferrell 30.00
Whitey Ford 40.00
Bob Gibson 30.00
Lefty Gomez (D) 125.00
Charley Gehringer 100.00
Carl Hubbell (D) 125.00
Catfish Hunter 25.00
Monte Irvin 25.00
Travis Jackson (D) 175.00
George Kell 20.00
George Kelly (D) 750.00
Harmon Killebrew 30.00
Ralph Kiner 25.00
Bob Lemon 30.00
Buck Leonard 50.00
Al Lopez 125.00
Juan Marichal 25.00
Willie Mays 95.00
Willie McCovey 25.00
Stan Musial 95.00
Satchel Paige (D) 3,500.00
Pee Wee Reese 40.00
Robin Roberts 20.00
Brooks Robinson 25.00
Frank Robinson 30.00
Edd Roush (D) 125.00
Joe Sewell (D) 95.00
Enos Slaughter 25.00
Ed Stack 15.00
Willie Stargell 25.00
Bill Terry (D) 125.00
Lloyd Waner (D) 3,500.00
Hoyt Wilhelm 25.00
Billy Williams 25.00
Ted Williams 225.00
Carl Yastrzemski 35.00

Values of Autographed Great Moments Cards

(D) denotes deceased

Hank Aaron	35.00
Luis Aparicio	25.00
Ernie Banks	40.00
Cool Papa Bell (D)	110.00
Johnny Bench	35.00
Yogi Berra	35.00
Lou Boudreau	20.00
Lou Brock	25.00
Roy Campanella	425.00
Ray Dandridge	25.00
Bill Dickey	125.00
Bobby Doerr	20.00
Rick Ferrell	20.00
Whitey Ford	30.00
Lefty Gomez (D)	125.00
Billy Herman	25.00
Carl Hubbell (D)	100.00
Monte Irvin	25.00
Al Kaline	30.00
George Kell	25.00
Harmon Killebrew	25.00
Sandy Koufax	45.00
Buck Leonard	32.00
Al Lopez	175.00
Mickey Mantle	125.00
Juan Marichal	25.00
Eddie Mathews	25.00
Willie Mays	55.00
Willie McCovey	25.00
Johnny Mize	25.00
Stan Musial	65.00
Pee Wee Reese	55.00
Robin Roberts	25.00
Brooks Robinson	35.00
Red Schoendienst	20.00
Enos Slaughter	25.00
Warren Spahn	25.00
Willie Stargell	25.00
Billy Williams	20.00
Ted Williams	100.00
Carl Yastrzemski	35.00

Miscellaneous Autographed Baseball Memorabilia

The autographed items that follow include bats, balls, pictures, index cards, and Hall of Fame plaques. All were advertised for sale recently in national hobby publications. The bats that are listed below are not game bats.

* denotes member of the Hall of Fame

Aaron, Hank*	ball	30.00
	bat	125.00
	picture	25.00
Abbott, JIm	ball	18.00
	picture	12.00
Abrams, Cal	ball	14.00
	picture	8.00
Adcock, Joe	picture	8.00
Agee, Tommy	picture	8.00
Aker, Jack	ball	14.00
	picture	8.00
Allen, Dick	ball	15.00
	picture	8.00
Alomar, Sandy Jr.	ball	18.00
Alston, Walter*	ball	250.00
	index card	25.00
Amoros, Sandy	ball	14.00
	picture	8.00
Anderson, Sparky	ball	25.00
Anthony, Eric	ball	17.00
	picture	9.00
Aparicio, Luis*	ball	25.00
	picture	15.00
Appling, Luke*	ball	35.00
	bat	85.00
	index card	6.00
	picture	15.00
Ashburn, Richie	ball	15.00
	picture	10.00
Averill, Earl*	HOF plaque	35.00
	index card	8.00
Bancroft, Dave*	index card	60.00
Banks, Ernie*	ball	30.00
	picture	20.00
Baines, Harold	picture	6.00
Barber, Red	ball	25.00
Bauer, Hank	picture	6.00
Bell, James "Cool Papa" *	ball	60.00
Barlick, Al*	ball	20.00
	picture	15.00
Bench, Johnny•	ball	35.00
	Celebration card	35.00
	picture	25.00
Berra, Yogi*	ball	25.00
	index card	6.00
	picture	20.00
Black, Joe	picture	8.00
Blackwell, Ewell	picture	8.00
Blanchard, John	picture	8.00
Blefary, Curt	ball	14.00
	picture	8.00
Blomberg, Ron	ball	14.00
	picture	8.00
Blue, Vida	picture	8.00
Boggs, Wade	ball	25.00
	picture	20.00
Bonds, Barry	ball	20.00
Bordagaray, Frenchy	ball	14.00
	picture	8.00
Boston, Darryl	picture	8.00
Boudreau, Lou*	ball	18.00
	HOF plaque	5.00
	index card	4.00
	picture	12.00
Bouton, Jim	picture	8.00
Bragan, Bob	ball	14.00
	picture	8.00
Branca, Ralph	picture	8.00
Brett, George	ball	28.00
	picture	15.00
Brock, Lou*	ball	20.00
	picture	10.00
Buckner, Bill	ball	18.00
Campanella, Roy*	bat	595.00
Canseco, Jose	ball	40.00
	bat	165.00
	picture	25.00
Carew, Rod*	ball	25.00
	picture	15.00
Carey, Max*	index card	20.00
	HOF plaque (b/w)	50.00
Carlton, Steve	ball	25.00
	picture	14.00
Carter, Gary	picture	20.00
Carter, Joe	ball	19.00
	picture	10.00
Cepeda, Orlando	ball	15.00

	picture	8.00
Chambliss, Chris	ball	14.00
	picture	8.00
Chandler, Happy*	ball	50.00
	bat	85.00
	picture (b/w)	35.00
Chapman, Ben	ball	50.00
Charles, Eddie	picture	8.00
Clark, Jack	picture	8.00
Clark, Will	ball	25.00
	bat	125.00
	picture	16.00
Clemens, Roger	ball	30.00
	picture	18.00
Clemente, Roberto*	signed check	550.00
Clendenon, Don	picture	8.00
Clift, Harlond	ball	15.00
	picture (b/w)	10.00
Cochrane, Mickey*	ball	1500.00
Coleman, Vince	ball	25.00
Combs, Earle*	index card	35.00
Combs, Pat	ball	15.00
	picture	8.00
Cone, David	picture	8.00
Conlan, Jocko*	ball	80.00
	index card	10.00
	HOF plaque	25.00
Coveleski, Stanley*	index card	10.00
Cronin, Joe*	index card	15.00
Crosetti, Frank	picture (b/w)	10.00
Dandridge, Ray*	ball	25.00
	bat	75.00
	picture	15.00
Daniels, Kal	ball	17.00
Dark, Al	ball	13.00
	picture	5.00
Daulton, Darren	ball	15.00
	picture	8.00
Davis, Glen	picture	15.00
Davis, Tommy	picture	8.00
Dawson, Andre	ball	22.00
Day, Leon	picture	8.00
Dean, Dizzy*	index card	65.00
De Shields, Delino	picture	8.00
Dickey, Bill*	ball	100.00
	bat	275.00
	picture (b/w)	45.00
DiMaggio, Dom	ball	30.00
	picture (b/w)	12.00
DiMaggio, Joe*	ball	225.00
	picture	65.00
DiMaggio, Vince	index card	15.00
Doby, Larry	ball	14.00
	picture	8.00
Doerr, Bobby*	ball	15.00
	index card	4.00
	picture	5.00
Donatelli, Augie	ball	35.00
Drysdale, Don*	ball	20.00
	index card	5.00
	picture	13.00
Dunston, Shawon	picture	6.00
Durocher, Leo	ball	65.00
	picture	30.00
Dykstra, Len	ball	24.00
	picture	15.00
Ennis, Del	picture	8.00
Erskine, Carl	ball	14.00
	picture	8.00
Faber, Urban*	index card	20.00
Feller, Bob*	ball	13.00
	bat	40.00
	index card	2.00
	picture	8.00
Fernandez, Sid	picture	8.00
Ferrell, Rick*	ball	20.00
	bat	50.00
	index card	5.00
	picture	12.00
Fielder, Cecil	ball	30.00
Fingers, Rollie	ball	18.00
	picture	5.00
Finley, Charlie O.	ball	40.00
Fisk, Carlton	ball	30.00
	picture	16.00
Ford, Whitey*	ball	22.00
	index card	8.00
	picture	13.00
Foster, George	ball	14.00
	picture	8.00
Fox, Nellie	index card	90.00
Friend, Bob	picture	5.00
Frisch, Frankie*	index card	35.00
Garrett, Wayne	picture	8.00
Garvey, Steve	ball	20.00
	picture	12.00
Gehringer, Charlie*	ball	50.00
	HOF plaque	15.00
	index card	12.00
Gentry, Gary	ball	14.00
	picture	8.00
Gibson, Bob*	ball	20.00
	picture	13.00
Gibson, Kirk	ball	28.00
	picture	15.00
Gomez, Lefty*	ball	75.00

	index card	15.00
	picture	25.00
	picture (b/w)	35.00
Gonzalez, Juan	ball	18.00
	picture	8.00
Gooden, Dwight	ball	24.00
	picture	15.00
Grace, Mark	ball	18.00
Gray, Pete	picture (b/w)	15.00
Greenberg, Hank*	ball	300.00
	index card	18.00
Greenwell, Mike	ball	20.00
Griffey, Ken Jr.	ball	25.00
	bat	115.00
	picture	15.00
Grimes, Burleigh*	index card	25.00
Grimsley, Jason	picture	5.00
Grove, Lefty*	index card	35.00
Guererro, Pedro	ball	15.00
Guidry, Ron	ball	20.00
Gywnn, Tony	ball	15.00
	picture	10.00
Hafey, Chick*	index card	50.00
Haines, Jesse*	index card	25.00
Hall, Dick	ball	14.00
	picture	8.00
Harkey, Mike	ball	15.00
	picture	5.00
Harrelson, Bud	ball	14.00
Harris, Bucky*	index card	30.00
Hartnett, Gabby*	index card	60.00
Hassett, Buddy	picture (b/w)	7.00
Hayes, Charlie	ball	12.00
	picture	6.00
Henderson, Rickey	ball	30.00
	picture	18.00
Henrich, Tom	ball	14.00
	picture (b/w)	12.00
Herman, Billy*	ball	14.00
	HOF plaque	8.00
	index card	3.00
	picture	10.00
Hernandez, Keith	picture	14.00
Hershiser, Orel	ball	18.00
Herzog, Whitey	ball	25.00
Hrabosky, Al	ball	16.00
Holmes, Tommy	picture	8.00
Hooper, Harry*	index card	30.00
Horton, Willie	picture	8.00
Howard, Elston	index card	15.00
Howell, Dixie	picture	8.00
Hoyt, Waite	index card	15.00
Hubbell, Carl*	ball	70.00

	HOF plaque	25.00
	index card	10.00
	picture	30.00
Hunter, Jim "Catfish" *	ball	20.00
	picture	12.00
Incaviglia, Pete	ball	14.00
	picture	8.00
Irvin, Monte*	ball	20.00
	index card	5.00
	picture	12.00
Jackson, Al	ball	14.00
	picture	8.00
Jackson, Bo	ball	30.00
	bat	175.00
	picture	20.00
Jackson, Ransom	ball	14.00
	picture	8.00
Jackson, Reggie	ball	40.00
	bat	150.00
	picture	20.00
Jackson, Travis*	index card	15.00
Jefferies, Greg	ball	22.00
	picture	15.00
Jenkins, Ferguson*	picture	12.00
John, Tommy	picture	9.00
Johnson, Alex	picture	8.00
Johnson, Howard	ball	19.00
	picture	10.00
Johnson, Judy*	HOF plaque	25.00
	picture	30.00
Johnstone, Jay	picture	8.00
Jones, Cleon	picture	8.00
Jones, Tracy	picture	8.00
Jordan, Rickey	ball	16.00
Jorgenson, Spider	ball	14.00
	picture	8.00
Justice, Dave	ball	22.00
	picture	15.00
Kaline, Al*	ball	20.00
	index card	5.00
	picture	16.00
Kanehl, Rod	picture	8.00
Kell, George*	ball	17.00
	index card	3.00
	picture	12.00
Kelly, George*	index card	12.00
Killebrew, Harmon*	ball	20.00
	index card	5.00
	picture	16.00
Kiner, Ralph*	ball	20.00
	bat	40.00
	HOF plaque	12.00
	index card	4.00

Name	Item	Value
	picture	12.00
Koonce, Cal	ball	14.00
	picture	8.00
Koufax, Sandy*	ball	35.00
	index card	15.00
	picture	22.00
Kranepool, Ed	ball	14.00
	picture	8.00
Kubek, Tony	ball	30.00
Labine, Clem	ball	14.00
	picture	8.00
Larsen, Don	ball	16.00
LaSorda, Tommy	ball	25.00
Lavagetto, Cookie	picture	8.00
Leiter, Al	ball	12.00
	picture	8.00
Lemon, Bob*	ball	15.00
	HOF plaque	5.00
	index card	6.00
	picture	10.00
Leonard, Buck*	ball	30.00
	bat	75.00
	HOF plaque (pre-stroke)	15.00
	picture	22.00
Lindstrom, Fred*	index card	10.00
Linz, Phil	picture	8.00
Loes, Billy	ball	14.00
	picture	8.00
Lolich, Mickey	ball	14.00
	picture	8.00
Lombardi, Ernie*	index card	30.00
Lonborg, Jim	picture	8.00
Lopat, Ed	picture	8.00
Lopez, Al	index card	15.00
Lyle, Sparky	picture	8.00
Lyons, Ted*	index card	13.00
Maas, Kevin	ball	17.00
Maddox, Elliott	picture	8.00
Magadan, Dave	picture	8.00
Mantilla, Felix	picture	8.00
Mantle, Mickey*	ball	55.00
	bat	650.00
	index card	35.00
	picture	35.00
Manush, Heinie*	index card	45.00
Marichal, Juan*	ball	20.00
	picture	9.00
Maris, Roger	ball	300.00
	index card	75.00
Martin, Billy	ball	125.00
Martin, J.C.	picture	8.00
Marquard, Rube*	index card	45.00
Marzano, John	picture	8.00
Matchick, Tom	picture	5.00
Mathews, Eddie*	ball	20.00
	index card	5.00
	picture	10.00
Matlock, Jon	ball	14.00
	picture	8.00
Mattingly, Don	ball	35.00
	picture	25.00
Mays, Willie*	ball	25.00
	bat	145.00
	picture	18.00
Mazeroski, Bill	ball	15.00
	picture	11.00
McAndrew, Jim	ball	14.00
	picture	8.00
McCaskill, Kurt	ball	10.00
McCarthy, Joe*	index card	20.00
McClain, Denny	picture	8.00
McCovey, Willie*	ball	30.00
	picture	16.00
McGwire, Mark	ball	25.00
	picture	16.00
McLish, Cal	picture	8.00
McMillan, Roy	picture	8.00
McReynolds, Kevin	ball	16.00
	picture	8.00
Medwick, Joe*	index card	20.00
Melton, Bill	picture	5.00
Meusel, Bob	index card	12.00
Micheal, Gene	ball	14.00
	picture	8.00
Miksis, Ed	ball	20.00
	picture	8.00
Millan, Felix	ball	14.00
	picture	8.00
Miller, Keith	picture	6.00
Mize, Johnny*	ball	18.00
	bat	55.00
	HOF plaque	10.00
	index card	5.00
	picture	12.00
Morgan, Bobby	ball	14.00
	picture	8.00
Morgan, Joe*	ball	25.00
	picture	17.00
Moryn, Moose	ball	14.00
	picture	8.00
Mueller, Don	ball	14.00
	picture	8.00
Mullholland, Terry	ball	13.00
	picture	8.00
Murphy, Rob	picture	7.00

Name	Item	Value
Murray, Eddie	ball	20.00
Musial, Stan*	ball	35.00
	picture	26.00
Neal, Charlie	picture	8.00
Nettles, Craig	picture	8.00
Newcombe, Don	ball	14.00
	picture	8.00
Newhouser, Hal	ball	14.00
	picture	7.00
Niekro, Joe	ball	14.00
	picture	8.00
Niekro, Phil	ball	18.00
	picture	10.00
Northrup, Jim	picture	6.00
Nuxhall, Joe	ball	25.00
Oleurd, John	ball	18.00
Oliva, Tony	picture	8.00
Olson, Greg	ball	17.00
	picture	15.00
Owen, Mickey	ball	14.00
	picture	8.00
Pafko, Andy	ball	14.00
	picture	8.00
Paige, Satchel*	index card	35.00
Palmer, Jim*	ball	25.00
	bat	50.00
	picture	18.00
Pasqua, Dan	picture	8.00
Pepitone, Joe	ball	14.00
	picture	8.00
Perez, Tony	ball	24.00
	picture	13.00
Perry, Gaylord*	ball	18.00
Petrocelli, Rico	picture	8.00
Piersall, Jim	ball	15.00
	picture	8.00
Pignatano, Joe	ball	14.00
	picture	8.00
Pinella, Lou	ball	14.00
	picture	8.00
Podres, John	ball	14.00
	picture	8.00
Puckett, Kirby	ball	28.00
	picture	15.00
Radatz, Dick	picture	8.00
Raines, Tim	ball	15.00
Reed, Jody	ball	14.00
	picture	8.00
Reese, Pee Wee*	ball	35.00
	index card	5.00
	picture	25.00
Rice, Jim	picture	9.00
Rice, Sam*	index card	40.00
Righetti, Dave	picture	9.00
Ripken, Cal Jr.	ball	24.00
	picture	16.00
Rizzuto, Phil	ball	16.00
	index card	6.00
	picture	12.00
Roberts, Bip	picture	5.00
Roberts, Robin*	ball	20.00
	picture	10.00
Robinson, Brooks*	ball	22.00
	bat	50.00
	index card	5.00
	picture	13.00
Robinson, Frank*	ball	30.00
	picture	18.00
Robinson, Jackie*	index card	250.00
Rose, Pete	ball	30.00
	picture	20.00
Rosen, Goody	picture	8.00
Roush, Edd	HOF plaque	20.00
	index card	10.00
Ruffing, Red*	ball	300.00
	index card	25.00
Ryan, Nolan	ball	45.00
	index card	10.00
	picture	20.00
Saberhagen, Bret	ball	15.00
Sabo, Chris	ball	18.00
	picture	10.00
Sain, Johnny	ball	18.00
Sandberg, Ryne	ball	35.00
	picture	18.00
Santo, Ron	ball	18.00
Sasser, Mackey	picture	8.00
Sax, Steve	ball	13.00
	picture	10.00
Schoendienst, Red*	ball	20.00
	index card	8.00
Schmidt, Mike	ball	45.00
	bat	215.00
	picture	25.00
Scott, George	picture	8.00
Seaver, Tom	ball	30.00
	picture	20.00
Sewell, Joe*	ball	45.00
	index card	6.00
Shamsky, Art	ball	14.00
	picture	8.00
Sheffield, Gary	ball	15.00
Shuba, George	ball	14.00
	picture	8.00
Sierra, Ruben	ball	19.00
	picture	10.00

Sievers, Roy	ball	15.00
Sisler, George	index card	45.00
Skowron, Moose	picture	8.00
Slaughter, Enos*	ball	18.00
	bat	45.00
	index card	8.00
	picture	10.00
Smith, Dwight	ball	20.00
	picture	12.00
Snider, Duke*	ball	25.00
	Great Moments card	25.00
	index card	10.00
	picture	16.00
Spahn, Warren*	ball	25.00
	bat	45.00
	index card	5.00
	picture	10.00
Stanky, Eddie	ball	15.00
Stargell, Willie*	ball	20.00
	index card	5.00
	picture	12.00
Staub, Rusty	ball	20.00
Strawberry, Darryl	ball	25.00
	picture	18.00
Stengl, Casey*	index card	50.00
Sutton, Don	picture	10.00
Swoboda, Ron	ball	14.00
	picture	8.00
Tartabull, Danny	picture	8.00
Terry, Bill*	ball	75.00
	index card	20.00
	picture (b/w)	25.00
Teuful, Tim	picture	8.00
Thomas, Frank	picture	18.00
Thomson, Bobby	picture	8.00
Tiant, Louis	ball	14.00
	picture	9.00
Torrez, Mike	picture	8.00
Trammell, Alan	ball	18.00
	picture	8.00
Uecker, Bob	ball	40.00
Valo, Elmer	ball	14.00
	picture	8.00
VanderMeer, Johnny	ball	16.00
	index card	10.00
	picture	12.00
Viola, Frank	ball	23.00
	picture	15.00
Walter, Bucky	ball	25.00
Walton, Jerome	ball	18.00
	picture	9.00
Waner, Lloyd*	index card	12.00
Weiss, Al	ball	14.00
	picture	8.00
Weiss, Walt	ball	10.00
Wheat, Zack*	index card	50.00
White, Roy	picture	8.00
Wilhelm, Hoyt*	ball	20.00
	index card	5.00
	picture	12.00
Williams, Billy*	ball	19.00
	index card	6.00
	picture	10.00
Williams, Dick	picture	10.00
Williams, Matt	ball	20.00
	picture	8.00
Williams, Mitch	picture	5.00
Williams, Ted*	ball	55.00
	bat	500.00
	Celebration card	45.00
	picture	35.00
Wills, Maury	ball	25.00
Wilson, Mookie	picture	6.00
Winfield, Dave	ball	20.00
	picture	12.00
Witt, Bobby	ball	10.00
Womack, Dooley	ball	14.00
	picture	8.00
Worthington, Craig	picture	5.00
Wynn, Early*	ball	25.00
	index card	6.00
	picture	12.00
Yastrzemski, Carl*	ball	35.00
	picture	20.00
Yost, Ed	picture	8.00
Yount, Robin	ball	25.00
	picture	16.00
Yvars, Sal	ball	14.00
	picture	8.00
Zeile, Todd	ball	18.00
	picture	9.00

Ted Williams autographed card from dinner in Cooperstown. $25.00-30.00.

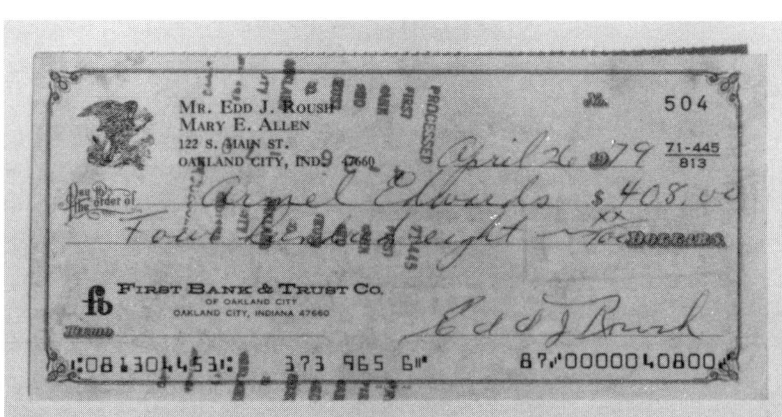

Cancelled check of Edd Roush from 1979. $20.00-25.00.

Paper baseball handed out by Casey Stengel to autograph seekers. $30.00-35.00.

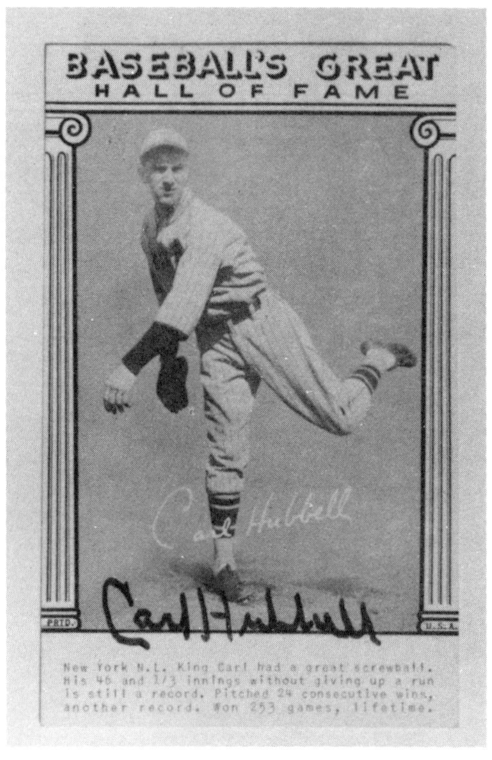

Exhibit card signed by Carl Hubbell. $15.00-20.00.

Autographed Baseball Cards

Many baseball card collectors would insist that a Mickey Mantle autograph on his perfectly centered 1953 Topps #82 card would **diminish** its value because it has been defaced by his signature.

An autograph by the player on card #53 in the 1933 Goudey set would belong to Babe Ruth and **add** significantly to the value of an already expensive baseball card.

Andy Cohen's card was #52 in the 1933 Goudey set. His autograph would make **little** difference in the value of the card.

Ruth's autograph is highly desirable and would add dramatically to the value of any item signed. Mantle's signature has been obtained at countless baseball card shows. Ruth died in 1948 and never faced long lines of autograph seekers at baseball card shows.

Since 1982 Donruss has produced a series of 26 Diamond King cards with each set. One player from each major league team is individually depicted in a painting or line drawing rather than a photograph on the card.

The cards are inexpensive and some collectors are attempting to complete each year's set with the autographs of every player on his card. To have a complete set of 700-900 Fleer, Topps, or Upper Deck cards autographed is a staggering proposition, but the diamond Kings with 26 cards each year are within reach. Several of the players (George Hendrick, Mario Soto) would be difficult to obtain.

The 1989 Fleer card #592 belongs to Tommy Gregg and has minimal value. Gregg's autograph on the card changes its value from 10¢ to a maximum of $1.00. It is important to keep in perspective that a "common" baseball card will not become a national treasure with the addition of the player's signature.

The list of autographed cards that follow was offered for sale in 1991. It is assumed that the cards are in a minimum of excellent to excellent-mint condition and the signatures are bold and legible.

The vast majority were secured through the mail, in hotel lobbies, parking lots, or at a major league stadiums. Few of the signatures were purchased at card shows or conventions.

The authors feel that the cards were priced very reasonably and there were many exceptional "buys" offered for sale. The autograph prices that follow should be considered "wholesale" rather than "retail."

* denotes member of the Hall of Fame

Hank Aaron*
- Donruss Champions 10.00
- 1957 Topps Milwaukee Braves teamcard 10.00
- Donruss Hall of Fame Heroes 6.00

Glenn Abbott
- 1975 Topps .... .50
- 1976 Topps .... .50
- 1979 Topps .... .50
- 1981 Topps .... .50
- 1982 Fleer .... .50
- 1982 Donruss .... .50
- 1982 Topps .... .50
- 1984 Fleer .... .50

Kyle Abbott
- 1990 Score 1.00
- 1990 Topps 1.00

Ted Abernathy
- 1966 Topps 1.00
- 1971 Topps .... .75

Shawn Abner
- 1985 Topps (#1 Draft Pick) 1.00

Tom Acker
- 1959 Topps 1.00

Bobby Adams
- 1952 Topps Reprint .... .50
- 1953 Bowman Reprint .... .50

1958 Topps 2.00
Buster Adams
1942-46 Cardinals .... .50
Earl "Sparky" Adams
1933 Goudey Reprint 1.00
Joe Adcock
1952 Topps Reprint 1.25
1953 Bowman Reprint 1.25
Hank Aguirre
1961 Topps 1.00
1964 Topps 1.00
Dale Alexander
1961 Fleer 1.00
Doyle Alexander
1973 Topps .... .75
1975 Topps .... .75
1976 Topps .... .75
Luis Alicea
1989 Topps 2.00
Ethan Allen
1933 Goudey Reprint 1.00
Neil Allen
1980 Topps .... .50
Billy Almon
1978 Topps .... .50
Sandy Alomar
1970 Topps 5.00
1972 Topps 5.00
Felipe Alou
1969 Topps 1.00
Jesus Alou
1970 Topps .... .75
1975 Topps .... .75
Walter Alston*
1957 Topps 10.00
1961 Topps 8.00
1964 Topps 6.00
1969 Topps 6.00
1970 Topps 6.00
1973 Topps 6.00
Max Alvis
1969 Topps 1.00
Joe Amalfitano
1963 Fleer 1.00
Ruben Amaro
1966 Topps 1.00
1968 Topps 1.00
Brady Anderson
1989 Fleer .... .75
1990 Topps .... .75
Craig Anderson
1962 Mets .... .50
Mike Anderson
1976 Topps .... .75
Sparky Anderson
1960 Topps 2.50
1982 Donruss 1.00
1983 Topps 1.00
1985 Fleer 1.00
Rob Andrews
1976 Topps .... .75
Bob Apodaca
1975 Topps .... .75
Luke Appling*
Donruss Hall of Fame Heroes 8.00
Baseball Legends 8.00
1984 Atlanta Braves Police Set 10.00
Hank Arft
1952 Topps Repring .... .50
Diamond Greats .... .50
Ed Armbrister
1976 Topps .... .75
Luis Arroyo
1961 Topps 1.50
1962 Topps 1.50
Richie Ashburn
1959 Topps 5.00
1960 Topps 4.00
Baseball's Greatest Hitters 3.00
Alan Ashby
1976 Topps .... .75
1982 Topps .... .75
Tucker Ashford
1978 Topps .... .50
1979 Topps .... .50
1984 Topps .... .50
Bob Aspromonte
1963 Topps 1.00
1960's Atlantic Richfield 2.00
Ken Aspromonte
1964 Topps 1.00
1974 Topps .... .75
Rick Auerbach
1972 Topps .... .75
Don August
1985 Topps (Olympics) 1.00
Rick Austin
1976 Topps .... .75
Earl Averill
1959 Topps 1.00
Joe Azcue
1964 Topps 1.00
Stan Bahnsen
1973 Topps .... .75
1975 Topps .... .75

Scott Bailes
1987 Topps 1.00
Ed Bailey
1957 Topps 2.00
Bob Bailor
1978 Topps .... .75
Harold Baines
1983 Fleer 1.00
Dusty Baker
1973 Topps .... .75
1975 Topps .... .75
Gene Baker
1957 Topps 2.00
Steve Balboni
1983 Topps .... .75
1983 Donruss .... .75
Rick Baldwin
1976 Topps .... .75
Chris Bando
1983 Topps .... .50
Ernie Banks*
Cracker Jack 7.50
All-Time Record Holder 7.00
1959 Topps 10.00
1961 Topps Checklist 8.00
1971 topps 11.00
1973 Topps 8.50
Alan Bannister
1978 Topps .... .75
1983 Topps .... .50
1983 Donruss .... .50
Steve Barber
1963 Topps 1.00
1970 Topps .... .75
Ray Bare
1976 Topps .... .75
Ray Barker
1966 Topps 1.00
Jim Barr
1975 Topps .... .75
1976 Topps .... .75
Steve Barr
1976 Topps .... .75
Red Barrett
1942-46 Cardinals .... .50
Hank Bauer
1952 Topps Reprint 1.50
1953 Bowman Reprint 1.50
TCMA 1.25
1961 Topps w/Jerry Lumpe 2.50
1965 Topps 3.00
Glen Beckert
Kelloggs .... .75
1972 Topps (In Action) 2.00
1973 Topps 2.00
Julie Becquer
1961 Topps 1.00
Fred Beene
1975 Topps .... .75
Tim Belcher
1985 Topps (#1 Draft Pick) .... .50
Gary Bell
1969 Topps 1.00
Gus Bell
1961 Topps 2.00
James "Coll Papa" Bell*
Donruss Hall of Fame Heroes 12.00
Jerry Bell
1973 Topps .... .75
Johnny Bench*
1969 Topps All-Star 12.50
1982 Donruss 8.00
1982 Donruss Diamond King 5.00
1983 Topps (Super Vet) 5.00
1984 Fleer 5.00
Donruss Champions 7.00
Bruce Benedict
1981 Topps .... .50
1983 Topps .... .50
Ray Benge
1933 Goudey Reprint 1.00
Wally Berger
Diamond Classics 5.00
1933 Goudey Reprint 3.00
Yogi Berra*
1952 Topps Reprint 5.00
1953 Bowman Reprint 5.00
Donruss Hall of Fame Heroes 5.00
1981 Donruss 5.00
1984 Topps Traded 5.00
Damon Berry hill
1988 Donruss 1.00
Dick Bertell
1965 Topps 1.00
Kurt Bevacqua
1974 Topps .... .75
1974 Topps Traded .... .75
Buddy Biancalana
1986 topps .... .50
Jim Bibby
1975 Topps .... .75
1976 Topps .... .75
Larry Biltner
1972 Topps .... .75
1973 Topps .... .75
1976 Topps .... .75

Jack Billingham
- 1969 Topps 1.00

Doug Bird
- 1974 Topps .... .75
- 1975 Topps .... .75
- 1976 Topps .... .75

Ewell Blackwell
- 1952 Topps Reprint 1.00

John Blanchard
- 1961 Topps 1.50
- 1964 Topps 2.00

Larvell Blanks
- 1974 Topps Traded .... .75
- 1975 Topps .... .75

Don Blasingame
- 1957 Topps 3.00
- 1959 Topps 2.00
- 1960 Topps 2.00

Wade Blasingame
- 1965 Topps 1.00

Buddy Blattner
- 1942-46 Cardinals .... .50

Ron Blomberg
- 1972 Topps .... .75

Vida Blue
- 1981 Fleer 2.50
- 1982 Donruss 2.50
- 1983 Topps 2.50
- 1983 Fleer 2.50

Bert Blyleven
- 1971 Topps 4.00
- 1976 Topps 3.50
- 1983 Topps 3.00
- 1984 Topps 3.00
- 1985 Topps 3.00
- 1985 Fleer Limited Edition 2.00
- 1986 Topps mini 2.00

John Boccabella
- 1970 topps .... .75

Bruce Bochte
- 1975 Topps .... .75
- 1976 Topps .... .75

Mike Bokkicker
- 1984 Topps 1.00
- 1984 Donruss 1.25
- 1985 Topps 1.00
- 1985 Topps (All Star) 1.00
- 1985 Donruss 1.00

Joe Boever
- 1990 Donruss .... .75
- 1990 Fleer .... .75

Wade Boggs
- 1984 Fleer 10.00
- 1985 Fleer 10.00

Frank Bolling
- 1959 Topps 1.00
- 1964 Topps 1.00

Bill Bonham
- 1972 Topps .... .75
- 1975 Topps .... .75

Bob Boone
- 1975 Topps .... .75
- 1983 Topps .... .75

Ray Boone
- 1952 Topps Reprint .... .75
- 1953 Bowman Reprint .... .75
- TCMA .... .50
- 1957 Topps 2.00

John Boozer
- 1964 Topps 1.00
- 1968 Topps 1.00

Pedro Borbon
- 1976 Topps .... .75

Glenn Borgmann
- 1974 Topps .... .75
- 1975 Topps .... .75

Tom Borland
- 1960 Topps 1.00

Steve Boros ....
- 1962 Topps 1.00

Thad Bosley
- 1978 Topps .... .75

Dick Bosman
- 1970 Topps .... .75
- 1975 Topps .... .75
- 1976 Topps .... .75

Ken Boswell
- 1975 Topps .... .75

Lou Boudreau*
- Donruss Hall of Fame Heroes 5.00
- All-Time Greats 6.00
- 1953 Bowman Reprint 6.00
- 1960 Fleer 7.00
- 1961 Fleer 7.00

Jim Bouton
- 1965 Topps (World Series) 2.50
- 1986 Big League Chew 1.50

Sam Bowens
- 1964 Topps 1.00

Bob Bowman
- 1959 Topps 1.00

Ernie Bowman
- 1963 Topps 1.00

Bob Boyd
- Sports Novelties 1.00
- 1957 Topps 2.00

Cloyd Boyer
1952 Topps Reprint..1.00
1953 Bowman Reprint 1.00
Phil Bradley
1985 Donruss 2.00
1985 Donruss Leaf...2.00
1985 Fleer 2.00
1986 Topps...2.00
1986 Donruss (Diamond King).........................2.00
Tom Bradley
1974 Topps 75
Bobby Bragan
1963 Topps 1.00
Ralph Branca
1952 Topps Repting 3.00
1953 Bowman Reprint (b/w) 3.00
Ron Brand
1969 Topps 1.00
Darrell Brandon
1968 Topps 1.00
Mickey Brantley
1988 Donruss 1.00
1988 Score..1.00
Steve Braun
1972 Topps 75
1975 Topps 75
1976 Topps 75
1979 Topps 50
1984 Topps 50
1986 Topps 50
Harry Brecheen
All-Time Cardinals 2.00
Hal Breeden
1974 Topps 75
Marv Breeding
1961 Topps...1.00
1962 Topps 1.00
Eddie Bressoud
1965 Topps 1.00
George Brett
1976 Topps...15.00
Ken Brett
1975 Topps 75
1976 Topps 75
Jim Brewer
1970 Tops 75
1973 Topps 75
1975 Topps 75
1976 Topps 75
Rocky Bridges
1952 Topps Reprint...50
1953 Bowman Reprint 50
Johnny Briggs
1959 Topps 1.00
Nelson Briles
1970 Topps 75
1971 Topps Traded 75
1974 Topps Traded 75
1975 Topps 75
1976 Topps 75
chuck Brinkman
1974 Topps 75
Dave Bristol
1973 Topps 75
Pete Broberg
1972 Topps 75
1975 Topps 75
Greg Brock
1983 Donruss 50
1983 Fleer 50
1983 Topps Traded...75
1984 Topps 50
1984 Fleer 50
1985 Topps 50
Lou Brock*
1967 Topps (Cards Clubbers) 7.50
1968 Topps (World Series) 7.50
1969 Topps (World Series)...............................7.50
1972 Topps 8.00
1975 Hostess 8.00
1975 Topps..6.50
1978 Topps (Record Breaker) 6.00
Dick Brodowski
1959 Topps 1.00
Ernie Broglio
1959 Topps 1.00
1961 Topps...1.00
Jack Brohamer
1973 Topps 75
1974 Topps 74
1975 Topps 75
1976 Topps 75
Mark Brouhard
1983 Donruss 50
1986 Topps 50
Chris Brown
1986 Donruss 2.00
1986 Fleer Limited Edition............................2.00
Jackie Brown
1971 Topps...75
Tom Browning
1986 Topps Mini 2.00
1986 Fleer (Baseball's Greatest Pitchers) ... 2.00
Bob Bruce
1963 Topps 1.00

1966 Topps 1.00
Tom Brunansky
1983 Fleer 2.50
1983 Donruss 2.50
1983 Topps 2.50
1984 Fleer 2.50
1987 Sportsflics 1.50
Bill Bryan
1965 Topps 1.00
Steve Brye
1974 topps 75
1975 Topps 75
1976 Topps 75
Bill Buckner
1972 Topps 5.00
1974 Topps 3.00
1975 Topps 3.00
1981 Donruss 2.50
1984 Topps Traded 2.50
Steve Buechele
1986 Topps 1.50
1986 Donruss 1.75
Jay Buhner
1987 International League All Star 2.00
1988 Donruss 1.50
Don Buford
1967 Topps 1.00
Al Bumbry
1974 Topps 75
1975 Tops 75
1976 Topps 75
1982 Fleer 50
Wally Bunker
1970 Topps 75
1971 Topps 75
Jim Bunning
1961 Topps 8.00
1970 Topps 7.00
Baseball's Greatest Pitchers 4.50
Bill Burbach
1970 Topps 75
Bob Burda
1970 Topps 75
1971 Topps 75
Lou Burdette
1953 Bowman Reprint 3.00
1958 Topps 6.50
1961 Topps 6.00
1963 Topps 6.00
1963 Jello 6.00
Fleer World Series 4.00
Smoky Burgess
1952 Topps Reprint 50
1953 Bowman Reprint 50
1963 Fleer 1.50
1966 Topps 1.00
Tom Burgmeier
1969 Topps 75
1970 Topps 75
1975 Topps 75
1976 Topps 75
Ellis Burks
1990 Donruss 2.50
Rick Burleson
1976 Topps 75
Britt Burns
1981 Topps 50
Pete Burnside
1963 Topps 1.00
Jeff Burrought
1974 Topps 75
Off-size card 50
Jim Burton
1976 Topps 75
Jim Busby
1959 Topps 1.00
Steve Busby
1975 Topps 75
Tom Buskey
1975 Topps 75
1976 Topps 75
John Buzhardt
1963 Topps 1.00
Bud Byerly
1942-46 Cardinals 50
1952 Topps Reprint 50
Tommy Byrne
TCMA 2.50
Bob Cain
1952 Topps Reprint 1.00
1953 Bowman Reprint 1.00
Diamond Greats 1.00
Ivan Calderon
1988 Donruss Diamond King 1.50
Mike Caldwell
1973 Topps 75
1974 Topps 75
1975 Topps 75
1983 Topps 75
Johnny Callison
1959 Topps 5.00
1973 Topps 1.00
Dolph Camilli
1961 Fleer 2.50
Rick Camp
1981 Topps 50

Bert Campaneris
1968 Topps 1.50
1970 Topps 1.50
1971 Topps 1.50
1975 Topps 1.25
1978 Topps 1.00
1982 Fleer .... .75
1982 Donruss .... .75

Jim Campanis
1967 Topps 1.00
1969 Topps 1.00

Bill Campbell
1976 Topps .... .75

Jim Campbell
1964 Topps 1.00

Casey Candaele
1987 Donruss 1.50

John Candelaria
1976 Topps .... .75

John Cangelosi
1986 Donruss Highlights 1.50
1987 Donruss 1.00
1987 Topps 1.00

Chris Cannizarro
1962 Mets 1.00
1965 Topps 1.00
1975 Topps .... .75

Jose Canseco
1986 McCrory's Sluggers vs. Pitchers 6.00
1986 Walgreens 6.00
1988 Topps 6.00
1988 Donruss 6.00

Bernie Carbo
1976 Topps 1.00
1979 Topps 1.00

Andy Cardenal
1972 Topps .... .75
1975 Topps .... .75
1976 Topps .... .75

Don Cardwell
1969 Topps 1.00

Rod Carew
1981 Topps 7.00
1981 Donruss (Baseball's Best Hitters) 7.00

Andy Carey
Yankee Diamond Greats .... .50

Martk Carreon
1987 International League All Star 1.00
1987 Fleer .... .50

Don Carrithers
1973 Topps .... .75
1974 Topps .... .75

Clay Carroll
1969 Topps .... .75
1975 Topps .... .75

Gary Carter
1982 Donruss 4.00
1982 Donruss Diamond King 5.00
1982 Fleer 4.00
1982 Fleer (Special) 4.00

Rico Carty
1970 Topps 2.00
1971 Topps 2.00
1972 Topps 2.00
1975 Topps 2.00
1976 Topps 2.00

Norm Cash
1972 Topps 3.50

Bill Castro
1976 Topps .... .75

Danny Cater
1973 Topps .... .75

Wayne Causey
1964 Topps 1.00
1966 Topps 1.00

Phil Cavaretta
1952 Topps Reprint .... .75
1953 Bowman Reprint .... .75

Art Ceccarelli
1959 Topps 1.00
Photo 1.00

Cesar Cedeno
1975 Topps 1.00

Orlando Cepeda
1962 Post 7.00
1972 Topps 8.00
1974 Topps 7.00

Dave Chalk
1975 Topps .... .75

Chris Chambliss
1976 Topps .... .75

Billy Champion
1975Topps .... .75

Dean Chance
1964 Topps 1.50

A.B. Happy Chandler*
Magazine photos 5.00

Spud Chandler
Yankee Diamond Greats 3.50

Darrel Chaney
1971 Topps .... .75
1972 Topps .... .75
1974 Topps .... .75
1976 Topps .... .75
1976 Topps Traded .... .75

Ben Chapman
- Yankee Diamond Greats 3.00
- Original All Stars 5.00
- 1933 Goudey Reprints 4.50

The Chicken
- 1982 Donruss 2.50
- 1983 Donruss 2.50
- 1982 Donruss and 1983 Donruss signed "Ted Guannoules", each 25.00

Rich Chiles
- 1972 topps .... .75

Neil Chrisley
- 1959 Topps 1.00

Larry Christenson
- 1974 Topps .... .75
- 1975 Topps .... .75

Bubba Church
- 1952 Topps Reprint 1.00
- 1953 Bowman Reprint 1.00

Galen Cisco
- 1963 Topps 1.00
- 1964 Topps 1.00

Dave Clark
- 1988 Donruss 1.00
- 1988 Score 1.00

Will Clark
- 1988 Score 6.00
- 1988 Topps (Leaders) 6.00

Horace Clark
- 1971 Topps .... .75

Roger Clemens
- 1985 Donruss-Leaf 10.00
- 1986 OPC 8.00

Reggie Cleveland
- 1974 Topps Traded .... .75
- 1975 Topps .... .75

Gene Clines
- 1971 Tops .... .75
- 1972 Topps .... .75

Lou Clinton
- 1963 Topps 1.00

Tony Cloninger
- 1966 Topps 1.00

Bryan Clutterbuck
- 1987 Topps .... .50

Jaime Cocanower
- 1985 Topps .... .50
- 1986 Topps .... .50
- 1986 Donruss .... .50

Andy Cohen
- 1933 Goudey Reprint 1.00

Rocky Colavito
- 1958 Topps 4.50
- 1960 Topps w/ Tito Francona 4.00
- 1961 Topps 4.00
- 1962 Topps 4.00

Jim Colborn
- 1971 Topps .... .75
- 1975 Topps .... .75

Rich Coggins
- 1974 Topps .... .75

Nate Colbert
- 1970 Topps .... .75

Gordy Coleman
- 1963 Topps 1.00

Jerry Coleman
- 1952 Topps Reprints .... .50
- TCMA .... .50

Vince Coleman
- 1986 Fleer Limited Edition 4.50

Bob Colliccio
- 1975 Topps .... .75
- 1976 Topps .... .75

Wayne Comer
- 1969 Topps 1.00

Dave Concepcion
- 1971 Topps 3.25
- 1976 Topps 3.00
- 1983 Topps (All Star) 2.50
- 1985 Fleer 2.00
- 1986 Donruss 2.00

Jocko Conlan*
- Baseball Legends 7.50

Bob Conley
- 1959 Topps 1.00

Chuck Connors
- Baseball Legends 6.25

Dennis Cook
- 1990 Donruss 2.00
- 1990 Score 2.00

Cecil Cooper
- 1974 Topps 5.00
- 1975 Topps 4.00
- 1976 Topps 4.00

Walker Cooper
- Diamond Greats .... .50
- TCMA .... .50
- 1942-46 Cardinals .... .50

Pat Corrales
- 1974 Topps .... .75

Ray Corbin
- 1973 Topps .... .75
- 1976 Topps .... .75

Ed Correa
- 1987 Topps 1.25
- 1987 Donruss 1.25

Vic Correll
1975 Topps .75
Mike Cosgrove
1975 Topps .75
Stanley Coveleski*
1961 Fleer 12.50
Renata Galasso 12.50
Billy Cowan
1971 Topps .75
1972 Topps .75
Al Cowens
1975 Topps .75
1976 Topps .75
Casey Cox
1969 Topps .75
1972 Topps .75
Danny Cox
1986 Topps Mini 2.00
1987 Donruss 2.00
Roger Craig
1958 Topps 5.00
1962 Mets 3.00
1963 Topps 4.00
1987 Topps 1.00
1989 Topps 1.00
Roger "Doc" Cramer
Diamond Classics 5.00
Del Crandall
1952 Topps Reprint 2.00
1955 Bowman 6.25
1958 Topps 6.00
1959 Topps 5.00
1960 Topps 5.00
1962 Topps 4.50
1965 Topps 4.00
Cliff Crawford
1934 Cardinals 1.00
Jim Crawford
1974 Topps .75
Willie Crawford
1974 Topps .75
1975 Topps .75
1976 Topps .75
Frank "Creepy" Crespi
Diamond Greats .75
1942-46 Cardinals 1.00
Tim Crews
1988 Donruss 1.00
Frank Crosetti
1933 Goudey Reprint 5.00
1952 Topps Reprint 4.00
Jeff Cross
1942-46 Cardinals .50

Jose Cruz
1975 Topps 2.50
Mike Cubbage
1976 Topps .50
1980 Topps .50
1981 Topps .50
1982 Topps .50
Tony Cuccinello
1933 Goudey Reprints 4.00
Original All Stars 5.00
Tim Cullen
1970 Topps .75
Joe Cunningham
Diamond Greats 1.25
TCMA 1.25
John Curtis
1973 Topps .75
1974 Topps .75
1975 Topps .75
1976 Topps .75
Babe Dahlgren
Yankee Diamond Greats 5.00
Bruce Dal Canton
1970 Topps .75
1975 Topps .75
Clay Dalrymple
1964 Topps .75
1970 Topps .75
1971 Topps .75
Bennie Daniels
1959 Topps 1.00
Kal Daniels
1987 Topps 3.00
1987 Donruss 3.00
1987 Fleer 3.00
Pat Darcy
1976 Topps .75
Alvin Dark
TCMA 1.25
1952 Topps Reprint 1.25
1953 Bowman Reprint 1.25
1962 Topps 2.50
1970 Topps (light) .50
Ron Darling
1984 Topps Taded 5.00
1985 Topps 4.50
Bobby Darwin
1973 Topps .75
Darren Daulton
1986 Topps .50
1986 Donruss .50
Jim Davenport
1960 Topps 1.00

- 1962 Topps 1.00
- 1963 Topps 1.00
- 1966 Topps 1.00

Alvin Davis
- 1985 Fleer 3.00
- 1985 Fleer Limited Edition 3.00
- 1986 Walgreens 3.00
- McCrory's Pitchers vs. Sluggers 2.50

Bob Davis
- 1976 Topps .... .75

Brock Davis
- 1972 Topps .... .75

Chili Davis
- 1982 Topps 4.00
- 1984 Donruss 2.00
- 1984 Topps 2.00

Glenn Davis
- 1985 Fleer 5.00
- 1986 Donruss 4.00
- 1986 Topps 4.00

Ron Davis
- 1969 Ropps 1.00

Jerry DaVonan
- 1976 topps .... .75

Tommy Davis
- 1971 Topps 3.00

Andre Dawson
- 1984 Fleer 4.50
- 1986 Donruss Diamond King 4.50

Tommy Dean
- 1970 Topps .... .75

Doug DeCinces
- 1976 Topps .... .75

Rod Dedeaux
- 1985 Topps (Olympics) 1.50

Rob Deer
- 1985 Fleer 3.00
- 1986 Topps 2.50

Bruce Carlton
- 1970 Topps .... .75

Ike Delock
- 1958 Topps 2.00
- 1959 Topps 1.00

Jim Delsing
- 1959 Topps 1.00

Joe DeMaestri
- 1961 Topps 1.00

John Demerit
- 1962 Topps 1.00

Don Demeter
- 1964 Topps 1.00

Rick Dempsey
- 1974 Topps .... .75
- 1975 Topps .... .75
- 1983 Topps .... .50

Jim Deshaies
- 1986 Donruss Highlights 1.25
- 1987 Topps 1.50
- 1987 Topps (Record Breaker) 1.00

Rob Dibble
- 1990 Fleer 3.50
- 1990 Donruss 3.50

Bill Dickey*
- Baseball Legends 12.00
- Donruss Hall of Fame Heroes 12.00
- Original All Stars 12.00
- TCMA 12.00
- Baseball's Greatest Hitters 12.00
- 1933 Goudey Reprint 12.00

Murry Dickson
- 1959 Topps 1.00

Bob Didier
- 1970 Topps .... .75

Larry Dierker
- 1969 Topps 1.00

Dick Dietz
- 1970 Topps .... .75

Don Dillard
- 1959 Topps 1.00
- 1961 Topps 1.00

Dom DiMaggio
- 1946 Play Ball Reprint 7.50

Joe DiMaggio
- Baseball Legends 12.00
- Yankee Diamond Greats 12.00
- TCMA Mini 12.00
- Baseball's Greatest Hitters 12.00
- All-Time Greats 12.00

Vince DiMaggio
- Diamond Classics 7.50

Pat Dodson ....
- 1987 Donruss .... .75
- 1987 Topps .... .75

Bobby Doerr*
- 1947 Play Ball Reprint 5.00
- 1986 Donruss Highlights 5.00

Atley Donald
- Yankee Diamond Greats 1.00

Dutch Dotterer
- 1959 Topps 1.00

Al Downing
- 1968 Topps 1.25
- 1974 Topps 1.00

Brian Downing
- 1975 Topps 75.00

Denny Doyle
- 1972 Topps .75
- 1975 Topps .75
- 1976 Topps .75

Moe Drabowsky
- 1959 Topps 1.00
- 1961 Topps 1.00

Dick Drago
- 1970 Topps .75

Walt Dropo
- 1958 Topps 2.00
- 1959 Topps 1.00
- 1952 Topps Reprint .50
- 1953 Bowman Reprint .50

Don Drysdale*
- 1958 Topps 15.00
- TCMA (The 60's) 6.00
- TCMA 6.00
- 1962 Topps (Leaders) 8.00
- 1962 Topps All Star 8.00
- 1963 Fleer 8.00
- 1967 Topps 7.00
- K-Mart 5.00

Frank Duffy
- 1975 Topps .75

Bob Duliba
- 1963 Topps 1.00

Dave Duncan
- 1974 Topps .75
- 1975 Topps .75

Mariano Duncan
- 1986 Topps 2.00
- 1986 Donruss 2.00
- 1986 Walgreen 2.00

Shawon Dunston
- 1985 Topps (#1 Draft Pick) 3.00
- 1986 Topps 2.00

Ryne Duren
- 1963 Topps 3.00
- 1964 Topps 3.00
- TCMA 2.50

Leo Durocher
- Baseball Legends 4.00
- Diamond Greats 4.00
- TCMA 4.00
- 1933 Goudey Reprint 5.00
- 1934 St. Louis Cardinals 5.00
- 1952 Topps Reprint 4.00
- 1953 Bowman Reprint 4.00
- 1969 Topps 5.00
- 1973 Topps 5.00

Erv Dusak
- 1952 Topps Reprint .50
- TCMA .50

Duffy Dyer
- 1971 Topps .75
- 1972 Topps .75
- 1973 Topps .75
- 1974 Topps .75
- 1976 Topps .75

Rawley Eastwick
- 1976 Topps .75

Dennis Eckersley
- 1976 (Leaders) 1.00
- 1989 Topps 1.00
- 1990 Fleer 1.00
- 1990 Score 1.00

Jim Eisenreich
- 1988 Topps 1.00
- 1988 Donruss 1.00
- 1988 Score 1.00

Don Elston
- 1958 Topps 2.00

Bill Endicott
- 1942-46 Cardinals .50

Woody English
- Original All Stars 4.00
- 1933 Goudey Reprint 3.00

Del Ennis
- 1952 Topps Reprint .50
- 1953 Bowman Reprint .50
- 1959 Topps .75
- TCMA .50

Carl Erskine
- 1952 Topps Reprint 3.00
- 1953 Bowman Reprint 3.00
- 1959 Topps 4.00

Sammy Esposito
- 1960 Topps 1.00
- 1961 Topps 1.00

Chuck Essegian
- 1958 Topps 2.00

Dwight Evans
- 1974 Topps 3.50
- 1975 Topps 3.00

Hoot Evers
- 1952 Topps Reprint .75
- 1953 Bowman Reprint .75
- TCMA .50

Elroy Face
- 1957 Topps 3.50
- 1960 Topps 3.00
- 1961 Topps 3.00
- 1961 Topps (Buc Hill Aces) 2.75
- 1962 Topps 3.00
- 1967 Topps 2.50

Baseball's Greatest Pitchers 2.00

Bill Fahey
- 1973 Topps .... .75
- 1976 Topps .... .75

Ferris Fain
- 1952 Topps Reprint 2.00
- Baseball's Greatest Hitters 2.00

Pete Falcone
- 1976 Topps .... .75

George Fallon
- 1942-46 Cardinals .... .50

Carmen Fanzone
- 1973 Topps 1.00
- 1974 Topps 1.00

John Farrell
- 1988 Topps 1.00
- 1988 Donruss 1.00
- 1988 Score 1.00

Monty Fariss
- 1989 Topps (#1 Draft Pick) 1.00

Bob Feller*
- Baseball Legends 5.00
- Cracker Jack 6.00
- Baseball's Greatest Pitchers 5.00
- Doug West Set 7.00
- 1946 Play Ball Reprint 5.00
- 1953 Bowman Reprint 5.00
- 1955 Bowman 10.00
- Donruss Hall of Fame Heroes 5.00
- All-Time Greats 5.00

Chico Fernandez
- 1961 Topps 1.00

Tony Fernandez
- 1987 Topps 1.00
- 1988 Fleer 1.00
- 1988 Donruss 1.00

Rick Ferrell*
- Original All Stars 5.00
- 1933 Goudey Reprint 5.00
- 1944 Play Ball Reprint 5.00

Mark Fidrych
- 1977 Topps (Leaders) 1.50
- 1981 Topps 3.00

Ed Figueroa
- 1975 Topps .... .75

Rollie Fingers
- 1972 Topps 8.00
- 1975 Topps 7.00
- 1976 Topps 7.00

Eddie Fisher
- 1963 Topps 1.00
- 1970 Topps 1.00
- 1971 Topps 1.00

Carlton Fisk
- 1973 Topps 8.00
- 1974 Topps 7.00
- 1975 Topps 7.00
- 1976 Topps 7.00
- 1985 Topps (Record Breaker) 5.00
- 1986 Fleer Limited Edition 4.00

Ed Fitzgerald
- 1959 Topps 1.00

Doug Flynn
- 1976 Topps .... .75

Hank Foiles
- 1959 Topps 1.00
- 1960 Topps 1.00

Tim Foli
- 1973 Topps .... .75
- 1976 Topps .... .75

Rich Folkers
- 1974 Topps .... .75
- 1975 Topps .... .75

Lew Fonseca
- 1933 Goudey Reprint 1.00
- 1961 Fleer 2.00

Barry Foote
- 1975 Topps .... .75

Whitey Ford*
- TCMA 7.00
- Record Holder 7.00
- Baseball's Greatest Pitchers 7.00

Mike Fornieles
- 1963 Topps 1.00

Bob Forsch
- 1975 Topps 1.00

Ken Forsch
- 1976 Topps 1.00

Dan Ford
- 1976 Topps .... .75

Terry Forster
- 1975 Topps .... .75

Ray Fosse
- 1970 Topps .... .75
- 1971 Topps .... .75
- 1973 Topps .... .75
- 1974 Topps .... .75
- 1975 Topps .... .75
- 1976 Topps .... .75

Alan Foster
- 1971 Topps .... .75
- 1973 Topps .... .75
- 1974 Topps .... .75
- 1975 Topps .... .75

George Foster
- 1972 Topps 6.00

1975 Topps 6.00
1976 Topps 6.00
1981 Topps 3.00
1981 Fleer 3.00
1981 Donruss 3.00
1982 Fleer 3.00

Terry Fox
1963 Tops 1.00

Joe Foy
1969 Topps 1.00

Paul Foytack
1962 Topps 1.00

Ken Fruiling
1975 Topps .... .75

Earl Francis
1964 Topps 1.00

John Franco
1985 Donruss 3.00
1985 Fleer 3.00
1986 Fleer 3.00
1985 Topps 3.00

Tito Francona
1957 Topps 2.00
1958 Topps 2.00

Fred Frankhouse
1933 Goudey Reprint 1.00

Will Fraser
1987 Donruss (Rated Rookie) 1.00

George Frazier
1983 Topps .... .50

Jim Fregosi
1964 Topps 1.00
1974 Topps 1.00
1975 Topps 1.00

Dave Freisleben
1975 Topps .... .75
1976 Topps .... .75

Jim French
1969 Topps 1.00

Pepe Frias
1975 Topps .... .75

Bob Friend
1952 Topps Reprint 2.00
1953 Bowman Reprint 2.00
1957 Topps 3.00
1958 Topps (All Star) 3.00
1959 Topps 2.50
1961 Topps (Leader) 2.50

Woody Fryman
1969 Topps 1.00

Tito Fuentes
1970 Topps .... .75
1972 Topps (In Action) .... .75
1973 Topps .... .75

Jim Fuller
1975 Topps .... .75

Frank Funk
1961 Topps 1.00

Carl Furillo
1953 Bowman Reprint 3.50
1957 Topps 5.00
1958 Topps 5.00
1960 Topps (World Series) 4.00

Len Gabrielson
1964 Topps 1.00

Phil Gagliano
1970 Topps .... .75

Andres Galarraga
1987 Topps 3.00
1987 Donruss 3.00
1990 Donruss 3.00

Bob Gallagher
1974 Topps .... .75
1975 Topps .... .75

Dave Gallagher
1990 Donruss 2.00
1990 Fleer 2.00

Oscar Gamble
1975 Topps .... .75

Joe Garagiola
1952 Topps Reprint 5.00
1942-46 Cardinals 5.00
NBC Card 10.00

Gene Garber
1974 Topps .... .75

Wayne Garland
1976 Topps .... .75

Ralph Garr
1973 Topps .... .75

Adrian Garrett
1976 Topps .... .75

Wayne Garrett
1972 Topps .... .75
1973 Topps .... .75
1974 Topps .... .75
1975 Topps .... .75
1976 Topps .... .75

Ned Garver
1958 Topps 2.00

Steve Garvey
1978 Topps 5.00
1981 Fleer 4.00
1981 Donruss 4.00
1982 Donruss 4.00
1984 Topps 3.50
1984 Fleer 3.50

1985 Topps (Record Breaker) 3.50
1986 Walgreens 3.00
1987 Topps 3.50
Donruss Champions 3.50
Off-sized card 3.50

Milt Gaston
1933 Goudey Reprints 1.00

Geddess
1973 Topps .75

Charlie Gehringer*
Original All Stars 7.00
Doug West Set 7.00
Donruss Hall of Fame Heroes 5.00
Baseball's All Time Greats 5.00
Baseball's Greatest Hitters 5.00
1933 Goudey Reprint 6.00
1960 Fleer 7.00

Gary Geiger
1961 Topps 1.00

Jake Gibbs
1969 Topps 1.00

Paul Giel
1958 Topps 2.00

Rod Gilbreath
1974 Topps .75

Jim Gilliam
Sports Novelties 5.00

Dave Giusti
1974 Tops .75

Fred Gladding
1969 Topps 1.00

Tom Glavine
1988 Donruss 1.00
1988 Score 1.00

Ed Glynn
1981 Topps .50

Jim Golden
1961 Topps 1.00

Dave Goltz
1974 Topps .75
1975 Topps .75
1976 Topps .75

Lefty Gomez*
Original All Stars 10.00
Original All Stars (Team) 8.00
Yankee Diamond Greats 10.00
Baseball's Greatest Pitchers 10.00
1961 Fleer 10.00

Preston Gomez
1974 Topps .75

Fernando Gonzales
1974 Topps Traded .75

Tony Gonzalez
1963 Topps 1.00

Tom Gorman
1957 Topps 2.00

John Goryl
1958 Topps 2.00

Goose Gossage
1974 Topps 7.00
1983 Topps 4.00
1983 Topps (Super Veteran) 3.50
1983 Fleer 4.00
1985 Fleer 4.00

Mark Grace
1988 Donruss (Rated Rookie) 6.00

Wayne Granger
1970 Topps .75

Dick Green
1967 Topps 1.00

Gary Green
1985 Topps (Olympics) 1.00

Lenny Green
1961 Topps 1.00
1963 Topps 1.00

Hank Greenberg*
Baseball's Greatest Hitters 20.00
Donruss Hall of Fame Heroes 20.00

Tom Grieve
1971 Topps .75
1975 Topps .75
1976 Topps .75

Derrell Griffith
1965 Topps 1.00

Doug Griffin
1975 Topps .75

Tom Griffin
1975 Topps .50

Bob Grim
1959 Topps 1.00

Burleigh Grimes*
Renata Galasso 10.00
Baseball Legends 10.00
Baseball's Greatest Pitchers 10.00
Donruss Hall of Fame Heroes 10.00
1960 Fleer 12.00
1961 Fleer 12.00

Charlie Grimm
Renata Galasso 10.00

Ross Grimsley
1974 Topps .75
1974 Topps Traded .75
1976 Topps .75

Dick Groat
1954 Topps 5.00

1966 Topps 3.50
Johnny Grodzicki
1942-46 Cardinals .... .50
Greg Gross
1975 Topps .... .75
1976 Topps .... .75
Jerry Grote
1967 Topps 1.00
Johnny Groth
1959 Topps 1.00
TCMA .... .50
Johnny Grubb
1976 Topps .... .75
1978 Topps .... .75
Off-sized card .... .50
Pedro Guerrero
1988 Donruss 2.00
1990 Donruss 2.00
1990 Donruss MVP 2.00
Ron Guidry
1983 Donruss 5.00
Don Gullett
1972 Topps .... .75
1974 Topps .... .75
Eric Gunderson
1990 Bowman .... .75
Larry Gura
1976 Topps .... .75
Don Gutteridge
1970 Topps .... .75
Tony Gwynn
1986 Donruss 4.00
1986 McCrory's Sluggers vs. Pitchers 3.00
1986 Topps Mini 3.50
1985 Fleer 4.00
Harvey Haddix
1959 Topps 3.00
1961 Topps 3.00
1964 Topps 2.50
1965 Topps 2.50
Don Hahn
1974 Topps .... .75
John Hale
1976 Topps .... .75
Ed Halicki
1975 Topps .... .75
1976 Topps .... .75
Tom Hall
1970 Topps .... .75
1975 Topps .... .75
Tom Haller
1963 Topps 1.00
1971 Topps .... .75

1972 Topps (In Action) .... .75
1972 Topps .... .75
Dave Hamilton
1975 Topps .... .75
1976 Topps .... .75
Jeff Hamilton
1987 Topps 1.00
Rich Hand
1974 Topps .... .75
Bill Hands
1975 Topps .... .75
Larry Haney
1976 Topps .... .75
Larry Hardy
1975 Topps .... .75
Steve Hargan
1975 Topps .... .75
1976 Topps .... .75
Mike Hargrove
1975 Topps .... .75
1978 Topps .... .75
Mike Harkey
1987 Fleer 3.00
1989 Donruss 3.00
Terry Harmon
1975 Topps .... .75
Toby Harrah
1972 Topps .... .75
1975 Topps .... .75
1976 Topps .... .75
Billy Harrell
1961 Topps 1.00
Billy Harris
1969 Topps 1.00
Donald Harris
1990 Score (1st round pick) 1.00
Lum Harris
1970 Topps .... .75
Vic Harris
1975 Topps .... .75
Bob Hartman
1959 Topps 1.00
Fred Hatfield
1952 Topps Reprint .... .50
1953 Bowman Reprint .... .50
Dave Heaverlo
1976 Topps .... .75
Rich Hebner
1976 Topps .... .75
Mike Hegan
1969 Topps 1.00
1970 Topps .... .75
1976 Topps .... .75

1976 Topps (Father-son) .75
Jack Heidemann
1971 Topps .75
Bobby Heise
1974 Topps Traded .75
1975 Topps .75
Al Heist
1961 Topps 1.00
Woody Held
1960 Topps 1.00
1961 Topps 1.00
1964 Tops 1.00
Tommy Helms
1972 Topps .75
Solly Hemus
1961 Topps 2.00
Bob Hendley
1962 Topps 1.00
Elrod Hendricks
1975 Topps 1.00
Tom Henke
1987 Fleer 1.00
1988 Donruss 1.00
1988 Topps 1.00
Bob Henrich
1958 Topps 2.00
Tommy Henruch
TCMA 3.00
Bill Henry
1961 Topps 1.00
Ray Herbert
1959 Topps 1.00
Babe Herman
Baseball's Greatest Sluggers 6.00
Billy Herman*
Baseball Legends 6.00
1933 Goudey Reprint 6.00
1952 Topps Reprint 6.00
1966 Topps 6.00
Gene Hermanski
Diamond Greats .75
TCMA .75
Enzo Hernandez
1974 Topps .75
1976 Topps .75
Keith Hernandez
1976 Topps 10.00
Tommy Herr
1981 Topps 1.25
1985 Donruss 1.00
1987 Fleer 1.00
1987 Donruss 1.00
1990 Donruss (DK) 1.00
1990 Donruss 1.00
Mike Hershberger
1963 Topps 1.00
Whitey Herzog
1958 Topps 3.50
1960 Topps 3.00
1961 Topps 3.00
1990 Topps 1.00
Teddy Higuera
1986 Tops 2.00
1986 Donruss 2.00
Tom Hilgendorf
1975 Topps .75
Marc Hill
1976 Topps .75
Shawn Hilegas
1988 Donruss 1.00
1988 Score 1.00
Chuck Hiller
1962 Topps 1.00
Dave Hilton
1975 Topps .75
Larry Hisle
1975 Topps .75
Billy Hitchcock
Diamond Greats .75
1952 Topps Reprint .75
Ed Hobaugh
1962 Topps 1.00
Glen Hobaugh
1962 Topps 1.00
Glen Hobbie
1958 Topps 2.00
1960 Topps 1.00
1961 Topps 1.00
1961 Topps (Batter Bafflers) 1.00
Ron Hodges
1974 Topps .75
Joe Hoerner
1969 Topps 1.00
1974 Topps .75
1975 Topps .75
Brian Holman
1990 Fleer 1.00
1990 Topps 1.00
Gary Holman
1969 Topps 1.00
Don Hood
1974 Topps .75
1975 Topps .75
1976 Topps .75
Jay Hook
1960 Topps 1.00

1961 Topps 1.00
1962 Mets 1.00

Johnny Hopp
Diamond Greats 1.00
1942-46 Cardinals 1.00
1952 Topps Reprint 1.00

Bob Horner
1981 Topps 2.00
1982 Donruss 2.00

Charlie Hough
1974 Topps .... .75
1976 Topps .... .75
1986 Topps (Leaders) .... .75

Ralph Houk
1968 Topps 3.00
1973 Topps 3.00
1982 Donruss 2.00
1983 Topps 2.00
1984 Topps 2.00
1985 Topps 2.00

Tom House
1975 Topps .... .75

Art Houtteman
1956 Topps 2.00

Bruce Howard
1965 Topps 1.00

Elston Howard
1966 Topps 5.00
1975 Topps w/Sandy Koufax 10.00

Roy Howell
1976 Topps .... .75

Dick Howser
1983 Donruss 3.00
1985 Topps 3.00
1987 Topps 3.00

Lamarr Hoyt
1981 Donruss .... .50

Waite Hoyt*
Renata Galasso 10.00
1960 Fleer 10.00

Kent Hrbek
1984 Topps 3.00
1985 Fleer 3.00
1987 Topps 3.00

Walter Kriniak
1970 Topps .... .75

Glenn Hubbard
1981 Topps .... .50

Carl Hubbell*
Donruss Champions 6.00
TCMA mini 6.00
Original All Stars 7.00
Baseball's Greatest Pitchers 6.00
Donruss Hall of Fame Pitchers 6.00
Original All Stars (Team) 6.00
1933 Goudey Reprint 7.00
1961 Fleer 7.00

Willis Hudlin
1933 Goudey Reprint 1.00

Dick Hughes
1969 Topps .... .75

Jim Hughes
1976 Jtopps .... .75

Billy Hunter
1958 Topps 2.00
1959 Topps .... .75

Jim "Catfish" Hunter*
1976 Topps 7.50
Baseball's Greatest Pitchers 5.00

Steve Huntz
1972 Topps .... .75

Tom Hutton
1975 Topps .... .75

Pete Incaviglia
1987 Topps 4.00

Monte Irvin*
Donruss Hall of Fame Heroes 5.00
TCMA 5.00
1953 Bowman Reprint 5.00

Al Jackson
1967 Topps 1.00

Bo Jackson
1988 Score 4.00

Grant Jackson
1974 Topps .... .75
1976 Topps .... .75

Larry Jackson
1962 Topps 1.00

Reggie Jackson
1981 Donruss 12.50

Ron Jackson
1958 Topps 2.00

Sonny Jackson
1968 Topps 1.00
1969 Topps 1.00

Travis Jackson*
Diamond Classics 12.00
1933 Goudey Reprint 12.00
1935 National Chicle 28.00

Charley James
1963 Topps 1.00

Stan Javier
1987 Donruss 1.00

Mike Jeffcoat
1985 Topps .... .50
1985 Donruss .... .50

Stanley Jefferson
- 1987 Donruss 1.00

Ferguson Jenkins
- 1968 Topps 8.00
- 1976 Topps 6.50
- 1981 Fleer 5.00
- 1982 Fleer 5.00
- 1982 Donruss 5.00
- 1983 Donruss 5.00
- 1983 Topps 5.00
- 1983 Topps Super Veteran 5.00
- 1983 Fleer 5.00
- 1984 Topps 5.00
- 1984 Fleer 5.00

Sam Jethroe
- 1952 Topps (smeared) .... .50
- 1953 Bowman Reprint 1.00

Tommy John
- 1982 Donruss 3.00
- 1982 Fleer 3.00

Bart Johnson
- 1971 Topps .... .75
- 1974 Topps .... .75

Billy Johnson
- 1952 Topps Reprint .... .50
- TCMA .... .50

Bob Johnson
- 1967 Topps 1.00

Darrell Johnson
- 1960 Topps 1.00
- 1974 Topps 1.00

Dave Johnson
- 1970 Topps .... .75

Ken Johnson
- 1961 Topps 1.00
- 1969 Topps 1.00

Lance Johnson
- 1988 Donruss (Rated Rookie) 1.00

Randy Johnson
- 1990 Donruss 1.00

Tim Johnson
- 1975 Topps .... .75

Bobby Jones
- 1985 Donruss .... .50
- 1986 Topps .... .50

Cleon Jones
- 1968 Topps 3.00
- 1972 Topps In Actions 2.00

Dalton Jones
- 1967 Topps 1.00

Mack Jones
- 1962 Topps 1.00
- 1969 Topps 1.00
- 1970 Topps .... .75

Nippy Jones
- Diamond Greats .... .50
- 1942-46 Cardinals .... .50

Mike Jorgensen
- 1983 Fleer .... .75
- 1985 Topps .... .75

Von Joshua
- 1976 Topps .... .75

Wally Joyner
- Sluggers vs. Pitchers 5.00
- 1986 Donruss Diamond King 5.00
- 1988 Topps 5.00
- 1988 Score 5.00
- 1988 Topps (Leader) 5.00

Ed Jurak
- 1985 Topps .... .50
- 1985 Donruss .... .50
- 1986 Topps .... .50

Bill Jurges
- 1933 Goudey Reprint 1.00

Skip Jutze
- 1976 Topps .... .75

Jim Kaat
- 1961 Topps 7.00
- 1976 Topps 5.00
- 1982 Fleer 3.00
- 1983 Fleer 3.00

Al Kaline*
- 1958 Topps (Tigers' Big Bats) 9.00
- 1959 Topps (Baseball's Greatest Thrills) 10.00
- 1960 Topps 16.50
- 1961 Post 10.00
- 1962 Topps All Star 12.50
- 1964 Topps (Leader) 5.00
- 1965 Topps 14.00
- 1967 Topps 11.00
- 1967 Topps (Leader) 5.00
- 1967 Topps (Bengal Belters) 5.00
- 1971 Topps 9.00
- Cracker Jack 5.00
- Baseball's Greatest Hitters 5.00
- TCMA 5.00
- Doug West Set 6.50
- Donruss Hall of Fame Heoes 5.00

Willie Kamm
- 1933 Goudey Reprint 1.00

Rod Kanehl
- 1962 Mets 2.00
- 1963 Fleer 3.00

Ron Karkovice
- 1987 Donruss 1.00
- 1987 Topps 1.00

Bob Keegan
1957 Topps 3.00
George Kell*
1952 Topps Reprint 5.00
1953 Bowman Reprint 5.00
1946 Play Ball Reprint 5.00
1954 Red Heart 14.00
1956 Topps 12.00
1957 Topps 12.00
1958 Topps 12.00
TCMA 5.00
Fred Kendall
1973 Topps .... .75
John Kennedy
1965 Tops 1.00
Terry Kennedy
1982 Donruss .... .50
Kurt Kepshire
1985 Topps .... .50
1986 Topps .... .50
Charlie Kerfeld
1987 Topps .... .50
Johnny Kerr
1933 Goudey Reprint 1.00
Don Kessinger
1975 Topps 3.00
1976 Topps 3.00
Jimmy Key
1986 Donruss 2.00
1986 Topps mini 2.00
1987 Donruss 2.00
Harmon Killebrew*
1961 Topps 15.00
1972 Topps 10.00
1974 Topps 10.00
Jerry Kindall
1958 Topps 2.00
Ralph Kiner*
1961 Fleer 6.00
1977 Topps 6.00
Diamond Classics 6.,00
Donruss Hall of Fame Heroes 6.00
Clyde King
1983 Topps .... .50
Eric King
1987 Topps 1.00
1987 Donruss 1.00
1987 Fleer 1.00
Jeff King
2 1990 Topps 1.00
Jim King
1961 Topps 1.00
1965 Topps 1.00

Dave Kingman
1973 Topps 5.00
1975 Topps 5.00
Don Kirkwood
1976 Topps .... .75
Bruce Kison
1972 Topps .... .75
Ron Kittle
1984 Fleer .... .75
Billy Klaus
1961 Topps 1.00
Lou Klimchock
1970 Topps .... .75
Ron Klimlowski
1971 Topps .... .75
Steve Kline
1973 Topps .... .75
1975 Topps .... .75
Johnny Klippstein
1959 Topps 1.00
1960 Topps 1.00
Darold Knowles
1966 Topps 1.00
1970 Topps .... .75
Kevin Kobel
1975 Topps .... .75
Mark Koenig
1933 Goudey 1.50
Gary Kolb
1964 Topps 1.00
Cal Koonce
1971 Topps .... .75
Jerry Koonce
1976 Topps 4.00
Howie Koplitz
1964 Topps 1.00
Joe Koppe
1961 Topps 1.00
1962 Topps 1.00
Steve Korcheck
1960 Topps 1.00
Andy Kosco
1970 Topps .... .75
1974 Topps .... .75
Sandy Koufax*
1958 Topps 30.00
1962 Topps 20.00
TCMA 8.00
Diamond Greats 8.00
Baseball's Greatest Pitchers 6.00
Ed Kranepool
1971 Topps 1.00
1972 Topps 1.00

1972 Topps In Action 1.00
1973 Topps 1.00
1974 Topps 1.00
1975 Topps 1.00
1976 Topps 1.00

Lew Krause
1975 Topps 75

Chad Kreuter
1989 Topps 75
1990 Topps 75
1990 Fleer 75

Howie Krist
Diamond Greats 75
1942-46 Cardinals 75

Dick Kryhoski
1952 Topps Reprint 50
1953 Bowman Reprint (b/w) 50

Mike Kurkow
1986 Donruss Highlights 50

Tony Kubek
1958 Topps 8.00
1965 Topps 5.00
Yankee Diamond Greats 4.00

Ted Kubiak
1972 Topps 75

Johnny Jucks
1961 Topps 1.25
Yankee Diamond Greats 75

Harvey Kuenn
1958 Topps 4.00

Duane Juiper
1976 Topps 75

Whitey Kurowski
1942-46 Cardinals 50

Craig Kusick
1975 Topps 75

Jose Laboy
1970 Topps 75

Marcel Lachemann
1971 Topps 75

Pete LaCock
1975 Topps 75

Lee Lacy
1974 Topps 75
1975 Topps 75
1976 Topps 75

Lack Lamabe
1963 Topps 1.00

Ray Lamb/Bob Stinson
1970 Topps 75

Keith Lampard
1970 Topps 75

Les Lancaster
1987 Donruss 1.00
1988 Topps 1.00
1988 Donruss 1.00
1988 Score 1.00

Jim Landis
1959 Topps 1.00
1961 Topps 1.00

Ken Landreaux
1982 Donruss 50

Hobie Landrith
1959 Topps 1.00

Don Landrum
1958 Topps 2.00
1966 Topps 1.00

Dick Lange
1975 Topps 75

Hal Lanier
1967 Tops 1.00
1973 Topps 75

Max Lanier
Diamond Greasts 50
1942-46 Cardinals 50

Norm Larker
1962 Topps 1.00

Barry Larkin
1987 Topps 3.00
1987 Donruss 3.00
1987 Fleer 3.00
1988 Topps 3.00
I 1988 Donruss 3.00
I 1988 Score 3.00
I 1990 Score 3.00

Dave LaRoche
1975 Topps 75
1976 Topps 75
1983 Topps 75

Don Larsen
1957 Topps 8.00
1961 Topps 5.00

Frank Lary
Baseball's Greatest Pitchers 75
1963 Fleer 1.25

Gary Lavelle
1976 Topps 75

Vernon Law
1952 Topps Reprint 2.00

Bill Lee
1971 Topps 75
1974 Topps 75
1975 Topps 75

Bob Lee
1965 Topps 1.00

Don Lee
1963 Fleer 2.00
1965 Topps 1.00
Leron Lee
1973 Topps .... .75
1975 Topps .... .75
Jim Lefebvre
1966 Topps 1.00
Al Leiter
1988 Donruss (Rated Rookie) 2.00
International League All Star 2.00
Denny Lemaster
1963 Topps 1.00
1971 Topps .... .75
Dick Leman
1962 Topps 1.00
Bob Lemon*
1952 Topps Reprint 5.00
1953 Bowman Reprint (b/w) 5.00
1957 Topps 10.00
1971 Topps 7.00
1982 Donruss 5.00
TCMA 5.00
Donruss Hall of Fame Heroes 5.00
Jim Lemon
1958 Topps 2.00
Dave Lemonds
1973 Topps .... .75
Bob Lennon
1957 Topps 2.00
Eddie Leon
1975 Topps .... .75
Maximino Leon
1976 Topps .... .75
Dennis Leonard
1976 Topps .... .75
Dutch Leonard
1961 Fleer 3.00
Don Leppert
1963 Topps 1.00
Johnny Lewis
1967 Topps 1.00
Nick Leyva
1989 Topps .... .75
1990 Topps .... .75
Bob Lillis
1959 Topps 1.00
Paul Lindblad
1968 Topps 1.00
1969 Topps 1.00
Johnny Lindell
Yankee Diamond Greats 1.00

Phil Linz
1966 Topps 1.00
1968 Tops 1.00
Frank Linzy
1971 Topps .... .75
1972 Topps .... .75
Mark Littell
1976 Topps .... .75
Winston Llenas
1974 Topps .... .75
1975 Topps .... .75
Don Lock
1963 Topps 1.00
Bobby Locke
1960 Topps 1.00
Bob Locker
1975 Topps .... .75
Gene Locklear
1975 Topps .... .75
Whitey Lockman
1973 Topps .... .75
Skip Lockwood
1972 Topps .... .75
1974 Topps .... .75
1975 Topps .... .75
1976 Topps .... .75
Johnny Logan
1960 Topps 1.00
1963 Topps 1.00
TCMA .... .75
Mickey Lolich
1976 Topps 2.50
1976 Topps (Record Breaker) 2.50
Tim Lollar
1984 Donruss .... .50
1984 Fleer .... .50
Jim Lonborg
1966 Topps 1.25
Baseball's Greatest Pitchers 1.00
1972 Topps 1.00
1974 Topps 1.00
1976 Topps 1.00
Ed Lopat
1952 Topps Reprint 4.00
TCMA 4.00
Diamond Greats 4.00
1963 Topps 4.00
Stan Lopata
1957 Topps 2.00
Davey Lopes
1976 Topps (Record Breaker) 1.00
1974 Topps 1.00
1975 Topps 1.00

1983 Donruss 1.00
1983 Fleer 1.00

Al Lopez*
Diamond Greats 5.00
1960 Topps 8.00
1961 Topps 8.00
1962 Topps 8.00

Hector Lopez
TCMA 2.50
1957 Topps 5.00
1960 Topps 3.00
1961 Topps 3.00
1963 Topps 3.00

John Lowenstein
1973 Topps .... .75
1974 Topps .... .75
1975 Topps .... .75
1967 Topps .... .75
1983 Donruss .... .50
1983 Fleer .... .50

Turk Lown
1952 Topps Reprint .... .75
1953 Bowman Reprint .... .75
1957 Topps 2.00
1958 Topps 2.00
1961 Topps 1.00

Mike Loynd
1987 Topps .... .50

Red Lucas
Diamond Classics 1.50
1933 Goudey Reprints 1.50

Jerry Lumpe
1961 Topps 1.00
1964 Topps 1.00

Greg Luzinski
1974 Topps .... .75

Jerry Lynch
1961 Topps 1.00
1963 Topps 1.00
1965 Topps 1.00

Barry Lyons
1987 Topps Update 1.00

Ted Lyons*
1961 Fleer 8.00
Renata Galasso 7.50

Shane Mack
1985 Topps (Olympics) 2.00

Pete Mackanin
1976 Topps .... .75

Ken MacKenzie
1962 Mets .... .50

Sal Maglie
1958 Topps 5.00

Joe Magrane
1988 Donruss 3.00
1988 Score 3.00

Bob Malkmus
1959 Topps 1.00

Frank Malzone
1958 Topps 4.00
1960 Topps All-Star 3.00

Felix Mantilla
1958 Topps 3.00
1960 Topps 2.00
1962 Mets .... .75

Marty Marion
TCMA 3.50
Diamond Classics 3.50
1942-46 Cardinals 3.50
1960 Fleer 5.00

Roger Maris
1962 Topps (61st Home Run) 40.00

Dave Marshall
1969 Topps 1.00

Mike Marshall
1983 Topps 3.00
1984 Topps 3.00
1985 Donruss (Diamond Kings) 4.00

Willard Marshall
Diamond Greats .... .50
1952 Topps Reprint .... .50
1953 Bowman Reprint .... .50

Billy Martin
1971 Topps 5.00
1972 Topps (In Action) 5.00
1971 Topps 5.00
1974 Topps 5.00

J.C. Martin
1961 Topps 1.00
1962 Topps 1.00

Buck Martinez
1975 Topps .... .75

Dave Martinez
1988 Topps 2.00

Marty Martinez
1970 Topps .... .75
1971 Topps .... .75

Ramon Martinez
1990 Donruss 2.50
1990 Fleer 2.50
1990 Topps 2.50

John Marzano
1985 Topps (Olympics) 3.00

Eddie Mathews*
1958 Topps 9.00
1961 Topps 8.00

Greg Mathews
1987 Topps 1.00
Jon Matcack
1974 Topps .... .75
1975 Topps .... .75
1976 Topps .... .75
Gene Mauch
1974 Topps 3.00
Dal Maxvill
1972 Topps .... .75
Charlie Maxwell
1961 Topps 1.00
1963 Topps 1.00
Rudy May
1972 Topps .... .75
1983 Topps .... .75
Ed Mayer
1958 Topps 2.00
Willie Mays*
K-Mart 7.00
Baseball's Greatest Hitters 7.00
Record Holder 7.00
Baseball's All-Time Greats 7.00
Willie Mays Story 8.00
Renata Galasso 7.00
Baseball Legends 7.00
1985 Woolwroth 7.00
Cracker Jack 8.00
Baseball's Greatest Sluggers 7.00
1960 Topps 30.00
1961 Topps 25.00
1963 Fleer 25.00
1972 Topps 15.00
Bill Mazeroski
1962 Topps 5.00
1962 Topps All-Star 5.00
1965 Topps 4.00
Dick McAuliffe
1974 Topps .... .75
Tim McCarver
1971 Topps 1.50
1972 Topps 1.50
1974 Topps 1.50
1976 Topps 1.50
Denny McClain
TCMA 2.50
Mike McCormick
1961 Topps 1.00
Tom McCraw
1967 Topps 1.00
Lance McCullers
1986 Topps 2.00
1986 Donruss (Rated Rookie) 2.00

LIndy McDaniel
1959 Topps 1.00
1970 Topps 1.00
1973 Topps 1.00
1974 Topps 1.00
1974 Topps Traded 1.00
1975 Topps 1.00
Ben McDonald
1990 Topps (#1 Draft Pick) 3.50
Gil McDougald
TCMA 3.00
1952 Topps Reprint 3.00
1953 Bowman Reprint 3.00
Oddibe McDowell
1985 Topps (Olympics) 4.00
1986 Walgreens 3.00
1986 Topps 3.00
Willie McGee
1984 Topps 3.00
1984 Donruss 3.00
1985 Fleer 3.00
Tug McGraw
1981 Topps (World Series) 3.50
1982 Fleer 3.00
1984 Fleer 3.00
1984 Topps 3.00
Mark McGwire
1988 Topps (Record Breaker) 5.00
1988 Donruss 5.00
1988 Donruss (Diamond King) 5.00
Don McMahon
1964 Topps 1.00
Roy McMillan
TCMA .... .75
1952 Topps Reprint .... .75
1953 Bowman Reprint .... .75
1963 Topps 1.25
1965 Topps 1.25
Ken McMullen
1973 Topps .... .75
1975 Topps .... .75
1976 Topps .... .75
Dave McNally
1970 Ropps 1.00
Jerry McNertney
1969 Topps 1.00
Mike McQueen
1972 Topps .... .75
Hal McRae
1971 Topps 1.00
1972 Topps 1.00
1975 Topps 1.00
1976 Topps 1.00

Kevin McReynolds
Las Vegas Stars 5.00
Padres Police Set 5.00
1985 Donruss-Leaf 4.50
George Medich
1974 Topps 1.00
Sam Mele
1965 Topps 1.25
1966 Topps 1.25
Mario Mendozo
1975 Topps .... .75
Dennis Menke
1970 Topps .... .75
1971 Topps .... .75
Rudy Meoli
1975 Topps .... .75
Jim Merritt
1974 Topps .... .50
1975 Topps .... .50
Andy Messersmith
1972 Topps 1.00
1976 Topps .... .75
1979 Topps .... .75
Off-sized card .... .50
Charlie Metro
1970 Topps .... .75
Roger Metzger
1972 Topps .... .75
Dan Meyer
1976 Topps .... .75
Russ Meyer
TCMA .... .50
1953 Bowman Reprint .... .50
Gene Michael
1970 Topps .... .75
1975 Topps .... .75
Felix Millan
1970 Topps All-Star .... .75
1976 Topps .... .75
Bruce Miller
1975 Topps .... .75
1976 Topps .... .75
Keith Miller
1987 International League Future Star 2.00
1988 Donruss 2.00
Rick Miller
1976 Topps .... .75
Stu Miller
1958 Topps 2.00
1959 Topps 1.00
1967 Topps 1.00
Randy Milligan
1987 Score 2.00
1987 Tidewater Tides 2.00
1987 International Leaague All-Stars 2.00
John Milner
1974 Topps .... .75
1975 Topps .... .75
Don Mincher
1972 Topps .... .75
Minnie Minoso
1963 Topps 8.00
George Mitterwald
1971 Topps .... .75
1974 Topps .... .75
1974 Topps Traded .... .75
1975 Topps .... .75
1976 Topps .... .75
Johnny Mize*
1961 Fleer 6.00
Baseball Legends 5.00
Donruss Hall of Fame Heroes 5.00
Vinegar Bend Mizell
1957 Topps 3.50
1962 Mets 2.50
Dave Moates
1976 Topps .... .75
Randy Moffitt
1973 Topps .... .75
1975 Topps .... .75
Paul Molitor
1982 Donruss 1.00
1982 Fleer 1.00
Bil Monbouquette
1963 Fleer 3.50
1965 Topps 2.00
Don Money
1976 Topps .... .75
John Montague
1975 Topps .... .75
Bob Montgomery
1975 Topps .... .75
Wally Moon
1958 Topps 3.00
1960 Topps 2.00
Barry Moore ....
1967 Topps 1.00
Charlie Moore
1975 Topps .... .75
Joe Moore
1933 Goudey Reprint 1.00
Randy Moore
1933 Goudey Reprint 1.00
Terry Moore
1942-46 Cardinals 2.00

Jerry Morales
1975 Topps .75
Rich Morales
1974 Topps .75
Al Moran
1964 Topps 1.00
Billy Moran
1963 Topps 1.00
Dave Morehead
1970 Topps .75
1971 Topps .75
Keith Moreland
1981 Donruss 1.00
1981 Fleer 1.00
1986 Walgreens 1.00
Joe Morgan
1982 Fleer 5.00
Tom Morgan
1958 Topps 2.00
Joe Morhardt
1962 Topps 1.00
Jack Morris
1981 Donruss 3.00
1983 Fleer 3.00
1984 Fleer 3.00
1982 Donruss (Diamond King) 3.50
1985 Fleer 3.00
1985 Donruss-Leaf 3.00
1986 Fleer (Baseball's Best) 3.00
John Morris
1975 Topps .75
John Morris
1987 Topps 1.00
Walt Moryn
1961 Topps 1.00
TCMA .50
Diamond Greats .50
Don Mossi
1964 Topps 1.00
Manny Mota
1970 Topps 1.00
1974 Topps 1.00
Jamie Moyer
1988 Donruss 2.00
1988 Score 2.00
Ray Mueller
1961 Fleer 1.00
Billy Muffett
1959 Topps 1.00
Bobby Murcer
1982 Topps .50
Dale Murphy
1982 Donruss 5.00
1987 Topps 5.00
Rob Murphy
1987 Donruss 2.00
1987 Topps 2.00
Tom Murphy
1974 Topps Traded .75
Dale Murray
1975 Topps .75
Eddie Murray
1982 Fleer 7.00
1983 Topps 7.00
Danny Murtaugh
1970 Topps 10.00
1974 Topps 10.00
Tony Muser
1974 Topps .75
1975 Topps .75
1976 Topps .75
Stan Musial*
Doug West Set 8.00
TCMA 7.00
Donruss Hall of Fame Heroes 7.00
Topps All-Time Record Holder 7.00
All-Time Cardinals 7.00
1942-46 Cardinals w/Johnny Hopp 7.00
1953 Bowman Reprint 7.00
1958 Topps All Star 12.50
1961 Topps 20.00
Mike Nagy
1970 Topps .75
Dan Napoleon
1966 Topps 1.00
Hal Naragon
1958 Topps 2.00
Sam Narron
1942-46 Cardinals .50
Craig Nettles
1981 Donruss 5.00
1981 Fleer 5.00
1983 Topps 5.00
Don Newcombe
Sports Novelties .400
Baseball's Greatest Pitchers 4.00
Don Newhauser
1974 Topps .75
Hal Newhouser
Baseball's Greatest Pitchers 3.00
Diamond Classics 3.00
1944 Play Ball Reprint .300
1960 Fleer 5.00
1961 Fleer 5.00
Joe Niekro
1970 Topps 3.00

1972 Topps....3.00
1973 Topps....3.00
1974 Topps....3.00
1975 Topps....3.00
1979 Topps....2.00
1983 Donruss Action All Star....2.00

Phil Niekro
1969 Topps....6.00
1972 Topps....6.00
1975 Topps....6.00
1982 Donruss....5.00
1982 Donruss (Niekro Brothers)....5.00
1983 Donruss....5.00
1983 Fleer....5.00
1983 Topps....5.00
1985 Fleer....5.00
1985 Topps....5.00
1983 Donruss Action All Star....5.00

Russ Nixon
1958 Topps....2.00

Paul Noce
1988 Score....1.00
1988 Donruss....1.00

Gary Nolan
1969 Topps....1.00

Fred Norman
1974 Topps....75

Jim Northrup
1973 Topps....75
1974 Topps....75

Joe Nuxall
1952 Topps Reprint....1.50
1953 Bowman Reprint....1.50
1957 Topps....4.00
1958 Topps....4.00
1965 Topps....2.00

Billy O'Dell
1958 Topps....2.00
1963 Topps....1.00

John "Blue Moon" Odom
1970 Topps....75

Bob O'Farrell
1933 Goudey Reprint....1.00

Ben Ogilvie
1979 Topps....75
1982 Donruss....75

Tony Oliva
Baseball's Greatest Hitters....4.00
1967 Topps....5.00
1974 Topps....4.50
1976 Topps....4.50

Gene Oliver
1967 Topps....1.00

1969 Topps....1.00

Gregg Olson (Orioles)
1990 Donruss....2.50
1990 Fleer....2.50

Karl Olson
1957 Topps....2.00

Jose Oquendo
1988 Donruss....1.00
1988 Score....1.00
1990 Fleer....1.00

Jim O'Toole
1961 Topps....2.00
1963 Topps....2.00
1963 Topps (Leaders)....1.50

Andy Pafko
1952 Topps Reprint....1.00
1953 Bowman Reprint (b/w)....1.00
1957 Topps....3.00
1958 Topps....3.00

Jim Pagliaroni
1959 Topps....1.00
1964 Topps....1.00

Tom Pagnozzi
1988 Topps....1.00
1988 Donruss....1.00

Rafael Palmeiro
1987 Topps....3.00

Jim Palmer*
1974 Topps....10.00
1983 Donruss....5.00
1984 Topps....5.00
1984 Fleer....5.00

J.A. Paparella
1955 Bowman....8.00

Milt Pappas
1960 Topps....2.50
1961 Topps....2.50
1962 Topps....2.50
1964 Topps....2.50

Dave Parker
1975 Topps....6.00
1982 Topps All Star....4.00
1982 Donruss (Diamond King)....4.00
1983 Fleer....4.00
1986 Walgreens....4.00
1986 Fleer Limited Edition....4.00

Lance Parrish
1983 Donruss....3.00
1983 Topps....3.00

Mel Parnell
1953 Bowman Reprint....3.50

Camilio Pascual
1970 Topps....1.25

Freddie Patek
1976 Topps ..... .75
Marty Pattin
1969 Topps 1.00
1970 Topps ..... .75
Don Pavletich
1969 Topps 1.00
Albie Pearson
1960 Topps 2.00
1963 Topps 2.00
1965 Topps 1.50
1966 Topps 1.50
Tony Pena
1982 Donruss 2.00
1984 Fleer 2.00
1985 Donruss 2.00
1985 Donruss (Diamond King) 2.50
1986 Donruss 2.00
Terry Pendleton
1986 Donruss 3.00
1986 Fleer 3.00
1989 Topps 2.50
1990 Donruss 2.50
1990 Score 2.50
Dick Perez
1983 Donruss 5.00
Marty Perez
1972 Topps ..... .75
Tony Perez
1976 Topps 5.00
1982 Topps (In Action) 4.00
1983 Topps (Super Veteran) 4.00
1984 Topps Traded 4.00
1986 Topps (Record Breaker) 4.00
1986 Donruss (DiamondKing) 4.50
Gaylord Perry*
1962 Topps 25.00
1976 Topps 8.00
1979 Topps 6.00
1981 Topps 5.00
1981 Donruss 5.00
1981 Fleer 5.00
1983 Topps 5.00
1984 Fleer (Special) 5.00
Jim Perry
1975 Topps 1.00
Johnny Pesky
1952 Topps Reprint 3.50
1964 Topps 3.50
Gary Peters
1961 Topps 1.00
Fritz Peterson
1972 Topps ..... .75
Harding Peterson
1958 Topps 2.00
Dave Philley
1961 Topps 1.00
Bubba Phillips
1959 Topps 1.00
1961 Topps 1.00
Taylor Phillips
1960 Topps 1.00
Ron Piche
1961 Topps 1.00
Billy Pierce
1952 Topps Reprint 1.25
1953 Bowman Reprint 1.25
TCMA 1.25
1963 Topps 2.00
Joe Pignatano
1961 Topps 1.00
Al Pilarcik
1959 Topps 1.00
1961 Topps 1.00
Duane Pillette
Diamond Greats ..... .50
1952 Topps Reprint ..... .50
1953 Bowman Reprint (b/w) ..... .50
Lou Pinella
1975 Topps 5.00
1982 Donruss 4.00
George Pipgras
1933 Goudey Reprint 8.00
Dan Plesac
1987 Topps 3.00
Johnny Podres
1958 Topps 4.00
1961 Topps 3.00
Paul Popovich
1967 Topps (Joe Niekro rookie) 3.50
Darrell Porter
1974 Topps 1.00
1981 Donruss 1.00
Mark Portugal
1987 Topps ..... .50
1987 Donruss ..... .50
Ted Power
1990 Donruss ..... .75
1990 Topps ..... .75
John C. Powers
1959 Topps 1.00
Bob Purkey
1958 Topps 3.00
Dan Quisenberry
1982 Fleer 4.00

Charley Rabe
1958 Topps 2.00
Doug Rader
1973 Tops 1.00
Tom Ragland
1975 Topps .... .75
Tim Raines
1982 Fleer 3.00
1982 Donruss 3.00
1984 Topps All-Star 3.00
1985 Topps 3.00
1985 Donruss 3.00
1985 Donruss (Canadian Greats) 5.00
1986 Topps 3.00
1986 Topps Mini 3.00
1987 Topps 3.00
1988 Donruss 3.00
1988 Donruss (AS) 3.00
1990 Donruss (MVP) 3.00
Len Randle
1975 Topps 1.50
Merritt Ranew
1964 Topps 1.00
Vic Raschi
TCMA 3.00
Paul Ratliff
1971 Topps .... .75
Johnny Ray
1982 Topps 2.50
1982 Fleer 2.50
1983 Fleer 2.00
1984 Topps 2.00
1984 Topps All Star 2.00
1986 Donruss Highlights 2.00
1986 Donruss 2.00
1986 Donruss (Diamond Kings) 2.50
Jeff Reardon
1986 Donruss Highlights 2.00
Jody Reed
1988 Score 3.00
Pee Wee Reese*
Baseball Legends 7.50
1952 Topps Reprint 7.50
1953 Bowman Reprint 7.50
1953 Red Man Chewing Gum 18.00
1955 Bowman 15.00
1957 Topps 15.00
1958 Topps 12.50
Phil Regan
1968 Topps 1.00
1971 Topps .... .75
Mike Remlinger
1990 Bowman .... .75
Rick Renick
1970 Topps .... .75
Hal Reniff
1966 Topps 1.00
Steve Renko
1970 Topps .... .75
Bill Renna
1958 Topps 2.00
Rick Reuschel
1975 Topps 1.00
Jerry Reuss
1983 Topps 2.00
Allie Reynolds
TCMA 3.50
Baseball's Greatest Pitchers 3.50
1952 Topps Reprint 3.50
1953 Bowman Reprint 3.50
1961 Fleer 5.00
Bob Reynolds
1974 Topps .... .75
Tommie Reynolds
1965 Topps 1.00
Jim Rice
1982 Fleer 4.00
1983 Fleer 4.00
1985 Topps 4.00
Off-sized card 3.00
Bobby Richardson
1958 Topps 6.00
1961 Topps 5.00
1963 Fleer 5.00
Bill Rigney
Diamond Greats 1.50
1952 Topps Reprint 1.50
1953 Bowman Reprint (b/w) 1.50
1961 Topps 2.00
1965 Topps 2.00
Earnie Riles
1986 Topps 1.00
1986 Kaybee 1.00
Billy Ripken
1988 Donruss 2.00
1988 Score 2.00
1987 International League Star 2.50
Cal Ripken, Jr.
1982 Fleer 12.00
1983 Topps 10.00
1985 Topps All Star 7.00
1985 Fleer w/Cal Ripken, Sr. 8.00
Cal Ripken, Sr.
1982 Donruss 1.50
Mickey Rivers
1972 Topps 1.00

Phil Rizzuto
- 1952 Bowman 15.00
- 1952 Topps Reprint 5.00
- 1953 Bowman Reprint 5.00
- 1954 Topps 7.00
- 1961 Topps 7.00
- TCMA (Large) 6.00

Bip Roberts
- 1987 Donruss 1.00
- 1987 Topps 1.00

Dave Roberts
- 1975 Topps (Astros) 75

Dave Roberts
- 1975 Topps (Padres) 75

Robin Roberts*
- Baseball Legends 6.00
- Donruss Hall of Fame Heroes 6.00
- 1957 Topps 11.00
- 1961 Topps 8.00
- 1964 Topps 7.50
- 1965 Topps 7.50

Andre Robertson
- 1983 Topps 50

Brooks Robinson*
- Diamond Classics 6.00
- Baseball Legends 5.00
- K-Mart 5.00
- Sports Novelties 5.00
- TCMA mini 5.00
- Cracker Jack 6.00
- Doug West Set 6.00
- Arkansas Traveler Appreciation Night Card ..5.00
- 1960 Topps 14.00
- 1962 Topps 12.00
- 1967 Topps 7.50
- 1968 Topps 7.50
- 1969 Topps All Star 7.50
- 1970 Topps 7.00
- 1969 Deckle Edge 6.00
- 1975 Topps 6.00
- 1976 Topps 6.00

Frank Robinson*
- 1961 Topps 12.00
- 1968 Topps All Star 8.50
- 1971 Topps 10.00
- 1974 Topps 6.00
- 1975 Topps 6.00
- 1982 Donruss 5.00

Ron Robinson
- 1985 Fleer 2.50

Preacher Roe
- Diamond Greats 3.50
- 1945 Play Ball Reprint 3.50
- 1952 Topps Reprint 3.50
- 1953 Bowman Reprint (b/w) 3.50

Billy Rogell
- 1933 Goudey Reprint 1.00

Kenny Rogers
- 1990 Donruss 75
- 1990 Topps 75

Steve Rogers
- 1975 Topps 75
- 1975 Topps 75
- 1976 Topps 75
- 1978 Topps 75
- 1979 Topps 75
- 1981 Topps 75
- 1982 Donruss Diamond King 1.00
- 1985 Donruss 75

Cookie Rojas
- 1976 Topps 1.00

Rich Rollins
- 1967 Topps 1.25

Johnny Romano
- 1963 Topps 1.00

John Romonosky
- 1960 Topps 1.00

Phil Roof
- 1966 Topps 1.00
- 1969 Topps 1.00
- 1973 Topps 75
- 1974 Topps 75
- 1975 Topps 75

Jim Rooker
- 1974 Topps 75

Buddy Tosar
- Yankee Diamond Greats 1.50

Pete Rose
- 1982 Fleer 5.00
- 1983 Fleer (Fountain of Youth) 5.00
- 1985 Topps 5.00
- 1986 Topps Record Breaker 5.00

John Roseboro
- 1958 Topps 3.50
- 1961 Topps 3.00
- 1962 Topps 3.00
- 1963 Topps 3.00
- 1964 Topps 3.00
- 1966 Topps 3.00
- 1968 Topps 3.00

Al Rosen
- Diamond Classics 2.00
- TCMA 2.00
- 1953 Bowman Reprint 2.00
- 1953 Red Man Chewing Tobacco 8.50
- 1975 Topps (1953 MVP) 3.50

Edd Roush*
Diamond Classics 15.00
Bruce Ruffin
1987 Topps 1.00
1987 Donruss 1.00
Red Ruffing*
Donruss Hall of Fame Heroes 12.00
Vern Ruhle
1976 Topps 75
Pete Runnels
1953 Bowman Reprint 2.50
1957 Topps 4.00
1959 Topps 3.00
1960 Topps 3.00
1964 Topps 3.00
Jeff Russell
1989 Donruss 1.00
1990 Rleer 1.00
Bill Russell
1974 Topps 75
1975 Topps 75
1976 Topps 75
Jack Russell
1933 Goudey Reprint 1.00
Marius Russo
Yankee Diamond Greats 1.00
Connie Ryan
1952 Topps Reprint 75
1953 Bowman Reprint 75
1953 Bowman 3.00
Mike Ryan
1974 Topps 75
Nolan Ryan
1975 Topps 12.00
Ray Sadecki
1974 Topps 1.00
Mike Sadek
1976 Topps 75
Ed Sadowski
1960 Topps 1.00
Ron Samford
1959 Topps 1.00
Juan Samuel
1984 Fleer 4.00
1985 Topps (Record Breaker) 3.00
1986 Walgreens 3.00
1986 Fleer Limited Edition 3.00
Ken Sanders
1975 Topps 75
Scott Sanderson
1982 Topps 50
Manny Sanguillen
1970 Tops 1.00
Andres Santana
1990 Bowman 75
Ron Santo
1961 Topps 9.00
1965 Topps 6.00
1968 Topps All-Star 6.00
1970 Topps 5.00
1973 Tops 5.00
1974 Topps 5.00
Nelson Santovenia
1990 Donruss 75
1990 Fleer 75
1990 Topps 75
Tom Satriano
1971 Topps 75
Hank Sauer
TCMA 1.50
1952 Topps Reprint 1.50
1953 Bowman Reprint 1.50
Bobby Saverine
1966 Topps 1.00
Mac Scarce
1974 Topps 75
Paul Schaal
1972 Topps (In Action) 50
Jimmie Schaffer
1963 Topps 1.00
Fred Scherman
1972 Topps 75
1974 Topps Traded 75
1975 Topps 75
Chuck Schilling
1966 Topps 1.00
Bob Schmidt
1958 Topps 2.00
1963 Topps 1.00
Mike Schmidt
1986 Fleer Limited Edition 5.00
1986 Sluggers vs. Pitchers 5.00
Willard Schmidt
1959 Topps 1.00
Red Schoendienst*
All-Time Cardinals 5.00
1942-46 Cardinals 5.00
1952 Topps Reprint 5.00
1953 Bowman Reprint 5.00
1960 Topps 6.00
1969 Topps 6.00
1971 Topps 6.00
1981 Donruss 5.00
Ron Schueler
1974 Topps 75

Dick Schofield
1963 Topps 1.00
1970 Topps .... .75
Rick Schu
1986 Fleer 1.00
Barney Schultz
1962 Topps 1.00
1965 Topps 1.00
Hal Schumacher
Original All Stars 3.50
1933 Goudey Reprints 3.50
Don Schwall
1967 Topps 1.00
Webb Schultz
Photograph 1.00
Herb Score
1957 Topps 5.00
1961 Topps 3.50
Mickey Scott
1976 Topps .... .75
Tom Seaver
1977 Topps (Leaders) 6.00
1981 Donruss 5.00
1982 Fleer 5.00
1982 Fleer Dynamic Duo 5.00
1982 Donruss Diamond King 6.00
1983 Donruss 5.00
1984 Topps 5.00
1984 Fleer 5.00
1985 Ralston Purina 5.00
1985 Fleer Limited Edition 5.00
1985 Fleer 5.00
1986 Sluggers vs. Pitchers 5.00
Diego Segui
1970 Topps .... .75
1975 Topps .... .75
George Selkirk
Yankee Diamond Greats 10.00
Walter Sessi
1942-46 Cardinals .... .50
Joe Sewell
Diamond Classics 5.00
Yankee Diamond Greats 5.00
1961 Fleer 6.00
Luke Sewell
Diamond Classics 2.00
1933 Goudey Reprint 1.00
1961 Fleer 2.50
Art Shamsky
1967 Topps 1.00
Bobby Shantz
TCMA 3.00
1952 Topps Reprint 3.00
1953 Bowman Reprint 3.00
1957 Topps 5.00
1958 Topps 5.00
1958 Topps w/Lou Burdette 7.00
1960 Topps 4.00
Bill Sharp
1974 Topps .... .75
Bob Shaw
1959 Topps 1.00
Frank "Spec" Shea
1952 Topps Reprint 1.25
1953 Bowman Reprint 1.25
Roland Sheldon
1966 Topps 1.25
Norm Sherry
1961 Topps 1.25
Joe Shipley
1959 Topps 1.00
Tom Shopay
1970 Topps .... .75
Norm Siebern
1958 Topps 3.00
Roy Sievers
TCMA 1.00
Diamond Greats 1.00
1957 Topps 4.00
1958 Topps 3.00
1959 Topps (Baseball Thrills) 3.00
1960 Topps 2.50
1963 Topps 2.00
Charlie Silvera
TCMA .... .50
1952 Topps Reprint .... .50
Curt Simmons
1952 Topps Reprint .... .50
1953 Bowman Reprint .... .50
1958 Topps 2.00
19670 Topps 1.00
1961 Topps 1.00
1961 Topps 1.00
1963 Topps 1.00
1967 Topps .... .75
Ted Simmons
1971 Topps 1.00
1972 Topps 1.00
1974 Topps 1.00
1975 Topps 1.00
1976 Topps 1.00
1989 Fleer 1.00
Ken Singleton
1975 Topps 1.00
1975 Topps 1.00

Dick Sisler
- TCMA .50
- Diamond Greats .50
- 1942-46 Cardinals .50
- 1952 Topps Reprint .50
- 1953 Bowman Reprint (b/w) .50

Ted Sizemore
- 1973 Topps .75
- 1975 Topps .75

Bill "Moose" Skowron
- TCMA 3.00
- 1957 Topps 5.00
- 1964 Topps 4.00

Enos Slaughter*
- Diamond Classics 5.00
- TCMA 5.00
- Baseball Legends 5.00
- 1942-46 Cardinals 5.00
- 1953 Topps 10.00
- 1953 Bowman Reprint 5.00
- Fleer World Series card 5.00

Roy Smalley (father)
- Diamond Greats .50
- 1952 Topps Reprint .50
- 1953 Bowman Reprint (b/w) .50

Roy Smalley (son)
- 1976 Topps .75

Al Smith
- 1959 Topps 1.00
- 1963 Topps 1.00

Charlie Smith
- 1969 Topps 1.00

Hal Smith
- 1958 Topps 2.00
- 1959 Topps 1.00

Lee Smith
- 1986 Fleer Limited Edition 3.00
- 1986 Walgreens 3.00

Lonnie Smith
- 1982 Donruss 1.00

Ozzie Smith
- 1983 Topps 5.00
- 1984 Topps 5.00

Duke Snider*
- Baseball Legends 5.00
- TCMA Mini 5.00
- TCMA Group 5.00
- Donruss Hall of Fame Heroes 5.00
- 1952 Topps Reprint 5.00
- 1953 Bowman Reprint 5.00
- 1960 Topps 15.00

Cory Snider
- 1987 Topps 3.50
- 1987 Donruss 3.50

Warren Spahn*
- TCMA 5.00
- TCMA (Cy Young Award) 5.00
- Baseball Legends 5.00
- Baseball's Greatest Pitchers 5.00
- Doug West Set 6.00
- Play Ball Reprint 5.00
- 1952 Topps Reprint 5.00
- 1953 Bowman Reprint 5.00
- 1953 Topps 10.00
- 1953 Red Man Chewing Tobacco 15.00
- 1957 Topps 12.50
- 1962 Topps 9.00

Al Spangler
- Sports Novelties .50
- 1963 Topps 1.00

Chris Speier
- 1974 Topps .75
- 1974 Topps Traded .75
- 1975 Topps .75
- 1976 Topps .75
- Off-sized card .50

Darryl Spencer
- 1960 Topps 1.00
- 1961 Topps 1.00

Jim Spencer
- 1972 Topps .75
- 1981 Fleer .75

Rob Sperring
- 1976 Topps .75

Charlie Spikes
- 1975 Topps .75
- 1976 Topps .75

Dan Spillner
- 1975 Topps .50
- 1983 Topps .50
- 1983 Fleer .50

Paul Splittorff
- 1972 Topps .75
- 1975 Topps .75

Bill Stafford
- 1961 Topps 1.00

Larry Stahl
- 1973 Topps .75

Jerry Staley
- 1958 Topps 2.00

Fred Stanley
- 1972 Topps .75
- 1974 Topps .75

Leroy Stanton
- 1973 Topps .75
- 1976 Topps .75

Willie Stargell*
- 1981 Topps 7.00
- 1981 Fleer 7.00
- 1982 Fleer 7.00

Dave Stenhouse
- 1963 Topps 1.00
- 1963 Fleer 1.00

Gene Stephens
- 1962 Topps 1.00

Johnny Stephenson
- 1966 Topps 1.00

Riggs Stephenson
- Baseball's Greatest Hitters 8.50

Dave Stieb
- 1982 Fleer 3.00
- 1982 Donruss Diamond King 3.50
- 1983 Donruss 3.00
- 1983 Topps 3.00
- 1985 Fleer 3.00

Dick Stigman
- 1959 Topps 1.00

Bob Stinson
- 1970 Topps w/Ray Lamb 1.00
- 1975 Topps 75
- 1976 Topps 75

Wes Stock
- 1961 Topps 1.00
- 1963 Topps 1.00
- 1965 Topps 1.00

Jeff Stone
- 1985 Donruss 50
- 1987 Topps 50

Todd Stottlemyre
- 1988 Donruss 2.50
- 1989 Topps 2.50
- 1990 Fleer 2.50

Hal Stowe
- 1962 Topps 1.00

George Strickland
- 1960 Topps 1.00

Jake Striker
- 1960 Topps 1.00

John Strohmayer
- 1971 Topps 75

Brent Strom
- 1971 Topps 75
- 1976 Topps 75

Ken Suarez
- 1971 Topps 75

Gus Suhr
- 1933 Goudey Reprint 1.00

Clyde Sukeforth
- Diamond Greats 1.00
- 1952 Topps Reprint 1.00

Frank Sullivan
- 1962 Topps 1.00

Haywood Sullivan
- 1958 Topps 2.00

Champ Summers
- 1976 Topps 75

B.J. Surhoff
- 1987 Topps 3.00
- 1987 Donruss (Rated Rookie) 3.00
- 1988 Topps 3.00
- 1988 Donruss 3.00

Gary Sutherland
- 1972 Topps 75
- 1975 Topps 75
- 1976 Topps 75

Bruce Sutter
- 1982 Topps (AS) 4.00
- 1983 Topps 4.00
- 1983 Donruss (DK) 4.50
- 1983 Fleer 4.00
- 1986 Fleer 4.00
- 1989 Topps 4.00
- 1989 Donruss 4.00
- 1989 Fleer 4.00

Don Sutton
- 1976 Topps 6.00
- 1982 Topps 5.00
- 1983 Fleer 5.00
- 1984 Fleer 5.00

Craig Swan
- 1976 Topps 1.00

Greg Swindell
- 1987 Topps 3.00

Ron Swoboda
- 1967 Topps 1.25
- 1972 Topps 1.25

Pat Tabler
- 1985 Donruss 1.00
- 1986 Donruss 1.00
- 1987 Topps 1.00
- 1987 Donruss 1.00

Frank Tanana
- 1976 Topps 1.00

Chuck Tanner
- 1960 Topps 1.00
- 1972 Topps 1.00
- 1974 Topps 1.00

Bob Taylor
- 1964 Topps 1.00

Chuck Taylor
- 1970 Topps 75
- 1971 Topps 75

1975 Topps .75
Ron Taylor
1972 Topps .75
Sammy Taylor
1958 Topps 2.00
1963 Topps 1.00
Tony Taylor
1960 Topps 1.00
1961 Topps 1.00
1962 Topps 1.00
1967 Topps 1.00
1972 Topps .75
1976 Topps .75
Birdie Tebbetts
1952 Topps Reprint 2.50
1963 Topps 3.00
Kent Tekulve
1976 Topps 2.50
Gene Tenace
1975 Topps 1.00
Jerry Terrell
1976 Topps .75
Bill Terry*
Renata Galasso 6.00
Baseball Legends 6.00
Original All Stars 6.00
1933 Goudey Reprint 6.00
1960 Fleer 7.50
Ralph Terry
1959 Topps 2.50
1963 Topps 2.50
Wayne Terwilliger
1960 Topps 1.00
Bob Tewksbury
1987 Donruss .75
1987 Topps .75
Darrell Thomas
1973 Topps .75
1975 Topps .75
1976 Topps .75
Frank Thomas
1962 Mets 1.00
Gorman Thomas
1975 Topps 1.00
Lee Thomas
Topps 1.00
1966 Topps 1.00
A.L. "Tommy" Thomas
1933 Goudey Reprint 1.00
Gary Thommason
1976 Topps .75
Jason Thompson
1983 Donruss Action All Star .50
Milt Thompson
1990 Donruss .75
1990 Fleer .75
1990 Topps .75
Robbie Thompson
1987 Topps 1.00
Bobby Thomson
1953 Red Man Chewing Tobacco 12.00
1957 Topps 6.00
1958 Topps 6.00
Andre Thornton
1983 Topps .50
1983 Fleer .50
Marv Thornberry
1962 Topps 4.00
Gary Thurman
1988 Donruss 2.00
1988 Score 2.00
Luis Tiant
1976 Topps 3.50
1981 Topps 3.00
1981 Donruss 3.00
1981 Fleer 3.00
Dick Tidrow
1975 Topps .75
Bobby Tiefenauer
1959 Topps 1.00
Bob Tillman
1969 Topps 1.00
Jim Todd
1975 Topps .75
Bobby Tolan
1971 Topps .75
1972 Topps .75
Ron Tompkins
1966 Topps 1.00
Hector Torres
1971 Topps .75
1976 Topps .75
Rusty Torres
1973 Topps .75
Mike Torrez
1973 Topps 1.50
1975 Topps 1.50
Alan Trammell
1981 Fleer 3.00
1983 Fleer 3.00
1985 Fleer Limited Edition 3.00
1985 Topps 3.00
1985 Donruss 3.00
1987 Topps 3.00
1987 Donruss 3.00

Bill Travers
1976 Topps .75
Cecil Travis
Diamond Greats .50
1946 Play Ball Reprint .50
Tom Tresh
1962 Topps 5.00
1963 Topps (World Series) 4.50
1964 Topps 5.00
Coaker Triplett
1942-46 Cardinals .50
Virgil Trucks
Diamond Greats .75
TCMA .50
John Tudor
1986 Topps All Star 2.00
Bob Turley
Diamond Greats 2.50
TCMA 2.50
1957 Topps 5.00
1958 Topps All Star 5.00
1959 Topps 5.00
1960 Topps (light) 3.00
1961 Topps 5.00
Jim Turner
1952 Topps Reprint .75
Wayne Twitchell
1974 Topps .75
Del Unser
1975 Topps .75
Bill Valentine
1979 Travelers schedule 1.00
1980 Travelers schedule 1.00
Bobby Valentine
1972 Topps .75
Fernando Valenzuela
1981 Fleer 7.50
1983 Topps 3.00
1983 Donruss Diamond King 3.50
1983 Fleer 3.00
1984 Ralston Purina 3.00
1985 Donruss Leaf 3.00
1986 Topps Mini 3.00
1986 Topps Record Breaker 3.00
1986 Donruss Highlights 3.00
1986 McCrory Sluggers vs. Pitchers 3.00
Elmer Valo
1952 Topps Reprint 1.00
1957 Topps 2.50
1960 Topps 1.50
Russell Van Atta
1933 Goudey Reprint 1.00
Andy Van Slyke
1984 Donruss 4.00
Coot Veal
1961 Topps 1.00
Emil Verban
1942-46 Cardinals 5.00
Johnny Vergez
1933 Goudey Reprint 1.00
Mickey Vernon
1952 Topps Reprint 1.00
1958 Topps 2.00
1960 Topps 1.50
1963 Topps 1.50
Bill Virdon
Sports Novelties 1.50
1959 Topps 2.00
1961 Topps 2.00
1963 Topps 2.00
Ozzie Virgil
1961 Topps 1.00
Harry Walker
1942-46 Cardinals 3.00
Jerry Walker
1961 Topps 1.00
Ken Walters
1962 Topps 1.00
Lloyd Waner*
1961 Fleer 50.00
Pete Ward
1964 Topps 1.00
Dan Warthen
1976 Topps .75
Carl Warwick
1965 Topps 1.00
Claudell Washington
1976 Topps 1.00
Gary Waslewski
1969 Topps 1.00
Bob Watson
1971 Topps .75
1972 Topps .75
1973 Topps .75
1974 Topps .75
1976 Topps .75
Eddie Watt
1968 Topps 1.00
Earl Weaver
1970 Topps 1.25
1981 Fleer 1.00
1982 Donruss 1.00
Monte Weaver
1933 Goudey Reprint 1.00

Pete Whisemant
1958 Topps 2.00
Burgess Whitehead
1934 Cardinals 1.00
Fred Whitfield
1969 Topps 1.00
Lou Whitaker
1981 Fleer 3.00
1982 Fleer 3.00
1983 Fleer 3.00
1984 Fleer 3.00
1984 Topps All Star 3.00
1985 Fleer 3.00
1985 Donruss-Leaf Diamond King 3.50
1986 Topps 3.00
1986 Fleer Limited Edition 3.00
1987 Topps 3.00
Floyd Wicker
1971 Topps .... .75
Dave Wickersham
1965 Topps 1.00
Milt Wilcox
1975 Topps .... .75
Hoyt Wilhelm*
Bseball's Greatest Pitchers 6.00
1961 Post Cereal 8.00
1968 Topps 7.00
Calendar Photo 6.50
Carl Willey
1965 Topps 1.00
Billy Williams*
1962 Topps 11.00
1965 Topps 8.00
1974 Topps 7.00
1976 Topps 7.00
Baseball's Greatest Sluggers 6.00
Charlie Williams
1972 Topps .... .75
Dibrell Williams
1933 Goudey Reprint 1.00
Dick Williams
Diamond Greats .... .50
TCMA .... .50
1952 Topps Reprint .... .50
1958 Topps 2.00
1959 Topps 1.00
1969 Topps .... .75
1972 Topps .... .75
1973 Topps .... .75
Stan Williams
1963 Topps 1.00
1969 Topps 1.00
1971 Topps .... .75
1972 Topps .... .75
Ted Williams*
All-Time Greats 12.00
Donruss Hall of Fame Heroes 12.00
Mookie Wilson
1981 Donruss 2.00
Red Wilson
1958 Topps 2.00
1959 Topps 1.00
Steve Wilson
1990 Donruss .... .75
Willie Wilson
All-Time Record Holder 3.00
Rick Wise
1974 Topps .... .75
Jack Wisner
Photo w/handwritten note on back 1.00
Bobby Witt
1988 Donruss 1.00
1988 Score 1.00
Whitey Witt
Yankee Diamond Greats .... .50
Doley Womack
1967 Topps 1.00
Wilbur Wood
1975 Topps 1.00
Gene Woodling
1952 Topps Reprint 1.00
1953 Bowman Reprint (b/w) 1.00
TCMA 1.00
1962 Mets 1.00
Rob Woodward
1987 Topps 1.00
1987 Donruss 1.00
Woody Woodward
1969 Topps 1.00
Todd Worrell
1986 Donruss (Rated Rookie) 4.00
1987 Topps 2.50
1987 Topps Record Breaker 2.50
1987 Topps All Star 2.50
1989 Topps 2.50
1990 Donruss 2.50
1990 Fleer 2.50
Al Worthington
1958 Topps 2.00
Clyde Wright
1972 Topps .... .75
Early Wynn*
TCMA 6.00
Baseball's Greatest Pitchers 6.00
Donruss Hall of Fame Heroes 6.00

Jim Wynn
- 1964 Topps 1.00
- 1974 Topps 1.00
- 1974 Topps Traded 1.00
- 1976 Topps 1.00

Carl Yastrzemski*
- 1982 Fleer 12.00

Rich Yett
- 1987 Topps .... .50

Floyd Youmans
- 1988 Donruss 2.00

Gerald Young
- 1988 Donruss 1.00
- 1988 Score 1.00

CHAPTER III
Tobacco Related Collectibles

1952-55 Red Man - Last of the Tobacco Cards

by Lou Hagenbruch

The 1955 Red Man set marked the end of a practice that began in the early 1900's, baseball cards being issued with tobacco products. For a last hurrah the Red Man cards are very impressive. The players' pictures are not photographs, but artists' portraits. The artwork is superb - close facsimiles, life-like and colorful. With many players the background was simply a solid color, but a number of the players have ball fields and stands in the background. A number of the poses contain only the upper chest and head. However, many poses include much of the torso and show the individual players either bunting, throwing or catching.

The cards were included, one per package, with the Red Man chew. The card was packaged face out inside of the cellophane outer wrap. So, it was easy to ascertain which player was to be had with each tobacco purchase. As a result, collecting an entire set each year was not too difficult an accomplishment provided a person or his father chewed regularly.

On the front of each card a short biographical sketch was positioned on either side of the portrait. The back side of the card contained selection information and cap redemption procedures. Located at the bottom of each card was a tab that could be cut off and saved in pursuit of 50 in number which could be redeemed for a free baseball cap. So, a large portion of the 3½" x 4" cards ended up being 3½" x 3½" and worth a good deal less than those with tabs intact.

A case in point is my own situation, wherein my grandparents owned a tavern in a small, rural town in Southern Illinois. Many of the customers did not want the cards and would leave them with my grandparents. So, there was a small stack of Red Man cards waiting each time our family managed a visit (three or four times a baseball season). The tabs had already been removed because my grandparents wanted to make sure each of their four grandsons had at least one free cap. Then where did all the cards end up? Most of them went the way of the clip-type clothes pin and the bicycle fender support - as the rotating spokes came in contact with an attached card a noise similar to that of a running motor was produced. Which cards escaped this fate - only our favorite players!

The '52 and '53 sets each contained 52 cards - 26 American and 26 National league members. This number was reduced to 50 cards for the '54 and '55 sets, translating into 25 players from each league. The tab on the '52 set contained the players league and card number, thus detachment meant no number. The '53 set incorporated a change which alleviated the number problem – the league and number were found on the tab and in the "bio" above the name. League and numbers for the '54 and '55 sets were only found in the "bio." The 52 or 50 individuals included in the set varied each year. Some were big names, while others were not. Some players were found in all four sets, while others were included only once. For example the following two Hall of Famers: Ted Williams, '52 only, and Red Schoendienst, all four sets. J.G. Taylor Spink, editor of the Sporting News selected the players each of the four years, while the 1951 World Series managers also helped with the '52 set, as did the 1952 World Series managers with the '53 set. These managers were the first card in their respective leagues' list of players for the first two sets. Managers were not included in the last two sets, thus accounting for the drop to 50 cards.

The following lists include each years' players, the card numbers and two prices: Good-VG and Ex-Mint. The only known variations are found in the '54 set. Three traded American league players, Kell, Mele and Philley, appear in two different uniforms with the same pose. In the National league portion of the set that year, Slaughter, who was traded, was replaced by Bell, thus both cards have the same number.

A complete set of all four issues, including variations, in excellent to mint condition with tabs, excluding one common card, sold at the Copeland auction for $6,600.00 in 1991.

1952

Number	Name	Good/VG no tab/tab	EX/Mint no tab/tab
AL#1	Casey Stengel (Mgr)	13.00/33.00	33.00/83.00
AL#2	Roberto Avila	4.00/10.00	10.00/25.00
AL#3	Yogi Berra	15.00/40.00	40.00/100.00
AL#4	Gil Coan	4.00/10.00	10.00/25.00
AL#5	Dom DiMaggio	7.00/18.00	18.00/45.00
AL#6	Larry Doby	6.00/15.00	15.00/38.00
AL#7	Ferris Fain	4.00/10.00	10.00/25.00
AL#8	Bob Feller	15.00/40.00	40.00/100.00
AL#9	Nelson Fox	10.00/25.00	25.00/63.00
AL#10	Johnny Groth	4.00/10.00	10.00/25.00
AL#11	Jim Hegan	4.00/10.00	10.00/25.00
AL#12	Eddie Joost	4.00/10.00	10.00/25.00
AL#13	George Kell	12.00/30.00	30.00/75.00
AL#14	Gil McDougald	7.00/18.00	18.00/45.00
AL#15	Minnie Minoso	7.00/18.00	18.00/45.00
AL#16	Billy Pierce	6.00/15.00	15.00/38.00
AL#17	Bob Porterfield	4.00/10.00	10.00/25.00
AL#18	Eddie Robinson	4.00/10.00	10.00/25.00
AL#19	Saul Rogovin	4.00/10.00	10.00/25.00
AL#20	Bobby Shantz	6.00/15.00	15.00/38.00
AL#21	Vern Stephens	4.00/10.00	10.00/25.00
AL#22	Vic Wertz	4.00/10.00	10.00/25.00
AL#23	Ted Williams	40.00/100.00	100.00/250.00
AL#24	Early Wynn	13.00/33.00	33.00/83.00
AL#25	Eddie Yost	4.00/10.00	10.00/25.00

Number	Name	Good/VG No tab/tab	EX/Mint no tab/tab
AL#26	Gus Zernial	4.00/10.00	10.00/25.00
NL#1	Leo Durocher (Mgr)	12.00/30.00	30.00/75.00
NL#2	Richie Ashburn	11.00/28.00	28.00/70.00
NL#3	Ewell Blackwell	6.00/15.00	15.00/38.00
NL#4	Cliff Chambers	4.00/10.00	10.00/25.00
NL#5	Murray Dickson	4.00/10.00	10.00/25.00
NL#6	Sid Gordon	4.00/10.00	10.00/25.00
NL#7	Granny Hamner	4.00/10.00	10.00/25.00
NL#8	Jim Hearn	4.00/10.00	10.00/25.00
NL#9	Monte Irvin	11.00/28.00	28.00/70.00
NL#10	Larry Jansen	4.00/10.00	10.00/25.00
NL#11	Willie Jones	4.00/10.00	10.00/25.00
NL#12	Ralph Kiner	14.00/35.00	35.00/88.00
NL#13	Whitey Lockman	4.00/10.00	10.00/25.00
NL#14	Sal Maglie	7.00/18.00	18.00/45.00
NL#15	Willie Mays	32.00/80.00	80.00/200.00
NL#16	Stan Musial	32.00/80.00	80.00/200.00
NL#17	Pee Wee Reese	14.00/35.00	35.00/88.00
NL#18	Robin Roberts	13.00/33.00	33.00/83.00
NL#19	Al Schoendienst	12.00/30.00	30.00/75.00
NL#20	Enos Slaughter	12.00/30.00	30.00/75.00
NL#21	Duke Snider	20.00/50.00	50.00/125.00
NL#22	Warren Spahn	13.00/33.00	33.00/83.00
NL#23	Ed Stanky	6.00/15.00	15.00/38.00
NL#24	Bobby Thomson	7.00/18.00	18.00/45.00
NL#25	Earl Torgeson	4.00/10.00	10.00/25.00
NL#26	Wes Westrum	4.00/10.00	10.00/25.00

1953

Number	Name	Good/VG No tab/tab	EX/Mint no tab/tab
AL#1	Casey Stengel (Mgr)	13.00/33.00	33.00/83.00
AL#2	Hank Bauer	7.00/18.00	18.00/45.00
AL#3	Yogi Berra	15.00/40.00	40.00/100.00
AL#4	Walt Dropo	4.00/10.00	10.00/25.00
AL#5	Nelson Fox	10.00/25.00	25.00/63.00
AL#6	Jackie Jensen	7.00/18.00	18.00/45.00
AL#7	Eddie Joost	4.00/10.00	10.00/25.00
AL#8	George Kell	12.00/30.00	30.00/75.00
AL#9	Dale Mitchell	4.00/10.00	10.00/.25.00
AL#10	Phil Rizzuto	12.00/30.00	30.00/75.00
AL#11	Eddie Robison	4.00/10.00	10.00/25.00
AL#12	Gene Woodling	6.00/15.00	15.00/38.00
AL#13	Gus Zernial	4.00/10.00	10.00/25.00
AL#14	Early Wynn	13.00/33.00	33.00/83.00
AL#15	Joe Dobson	4.00/10.00	10.00/25.00
AL#16	Billy Pierce	6.00/15.00	15.00/38.00
AL#17	Bob Lemon	12.00/30.00	30.00/75.00
AL#18	Johnny Mize	13.00/33.00	33.00/83.00
AL#19	Bob Porterfield	4.00/10.00	10.00/25.00
AL#20	Bobby Shantz	6.00/15.00	15.00/38.00

Number	Name	Good/VG No tab/tab	EX/Mint no tab/tab
AL#21	Mickey Vernon	6.00/15.00	15.00/38.00
AL#22	Dom DiMaggio	7.00/18.00	18.00/45.00
AL#23	Gil McDougald	7.00/18.00	18.00/45.00
AL#24	Al Rosen	7.00/18.00	18.00/45.00
AL#25	Mel Parnell	6.00/15.00	15.00/38.00
AL#26	Bobby Avila	4.00/10.00	10.00/25.00
NL#1	Charlie Dressen (Mgr)	6.00/15.00	15.00/38.00
NL#2	Bobby Adams	4.00/10.00	10.00/25.00
NL#3	Richie Ashburn	11.00/28.00	28.00/70.00
NL#4	Joe Black	6.00/15.00	15.00/38.00
NL#5	Roy Campanella	20.00/50.00	50.00/125.00
NL#6	Ted Kluszewski	7.00/18.00	18.00/45.00
NL#7	Whitey Lockman	4.00/10.00	10.00/25.00
NL#8	Sal Maglie	7.00/18.00	18.00/45.00
NL#9	Andy Pafko	4.00/10.00	10.00/25.00
NL#10	Pee Wee Reese	14.00/35.00	35.00/88.00
NL#11	Robin Roberts	13.00/33.00	33.00/83.00
NL#12	Al Schoendienst	12.00/30.00	30.00/75.00
NL#13	Enos Slaughter	12.00/30.00	30.00/75.00
NL#14	Duke Snider	20.00/50.00	50.00/125.00
NL#15	Ralph Kiner	14.00/35.00	35.00/88.00
NL#16	Hank Sauer	4.00/10.00	10.00/25.00
NL#17	Del Ennis	4.00/10.00	10.00/25.00
NL#18	Granny Hamner	4.00/10.00	10.00/25.00
NL#19	Warren Spahn	13.00/33.00	33.00/83.00
NL#20	Wes Westrum	4.00/10.00	10.00/25.00
NL#21	Hoyt Wilhelm	12.00/30.00	30.00/75.00
NL#22	Murray Dickson	4.00/10.00	10.00/25.00
NL#23	Warren Hacker	4.00/10.00	10.00/25.00
NL#24	Gerry Staley	4.00/10.00	10.00/25.00
NL#25	Bobby Thomson	7.00/18.00	18.00/45.00
NL#26	Stan Musial	32.00/80.00	80.00/200.00

1954

Number	Name	Good/VG No tab/tab	EX/Mint no tab/tab
AL#1	Bobby Avila	4.00/10.00	10.00/25.00
AL#2	Jim Busby	4.00/10.00	10.00/25.00
AL#3	Nelson Fox	10.00/25.00	25.00/63.00
AL#4	George Kell (Boston)	13.00/33.00	33.00/83.00
AL#4	George Kell (Chicago)	18.00/45.00	45.00/133.00
AL#5	Sherman Lollar	4.00/10.00	10.00/25.00
AL#6	Sam Mele (Baltimore)	8.00/20.00	20.00/50.00
AL#6	Sam Mele (Chicago)	15.00/38.00	38.00/75.00
AL#7	Minnie Minoso	7.00/18.00	18.00/45.00
AL#8	Mel Parnell	6.00/15.00	15.00/38.00
AL#9	Dave Philley (Cleveland)	8.00/20.00	20.00/50.00
AL#9	Dave Philley (Philadelphia)	15.00/38.00	38.00/75.00
AL#10	Billy Pierce	6.00/15.00	15.00/38.00
AL#11	Jim Piersall	7.00/18.00	18.00/45.00
AL#12	Al Rosen	7.00/18.00	18.00/45.00

Number	Name	Good/VG No tab/tab	EX/Mint No tab/tab
AL#13	Mickey Vernon	6.00/15.00	15.00/38.00
AL#14	Sammy White	4.00/10.00	10.00/25.00
AL#15	Gene Woodling	6.00/15.00	15.00/38.00
AL#16	Whitey Ford	14.00/35.00	35.00/88.00
AL#17	Phil Rizzuto	12.00/30.00	30.00/75.00
AL#18	Bob Porterfield	4.00/10.00	10.00/25.00
AL#19	Chico Carrasquel	4.00/10.00	10.00/25.00
AL#20	Yogi Berra	15.00/40.00	40.00/100.00
AL#21	Bob Lemon	12.00/30.00	30.00/75.00
AL#22	Ferris Fain	4.00/10.00	10.00/25.00
AL#23	Hank Bauer	7.00/18.00	18.00/45.00
AL#24	Jim Delsing	4.00/10.00	10.00/25.00
AL#25	Gil McDougald	7.00/18.00	18.00/45.00
NL#1	Richie Ashburn	11.00/28.00	28.00/70.00
NL#2	Billy Cox	4.00/10.00	10.00/25.00
NL#3	Del Crandall	4.00/10.00	10.00/25.00
NL#4	Carl Erskine	6.00/15.00	15.00/38.00
NL#5	Monte Irvin	11.00/28.00	28.00/70.00
NL#6	Ted Kluszewski	7.00/18.00	18.00/45.00
NL#7	Don Mueller	4.00/10.00	10.00/25.00
NL#8	Andy Pafko	4.00/10.00	10.00/25.00
NL#9	Del Rice	4.00/10.00	10.00/25.00
NL#10	Al Schoendienst	12.00/30.00	30.00/75.00
NL#11	Warren Spahn	13.00/33.00	33.00/83.00
NL#12	Curt Simmons	6.00/15.00	15.00/45.00
NL#13	Roy Campanella	20.00/50.00	50.00/125.00
NL#14	Jim Gilliam	7.00/18.00	18.00/45.00
NL#15	Pee Wee Reese	14.00/35.00	35.00/88.00
NL#16	Duke Snider	20.0/50.00	50.00/125.00
NL#17	Rip Repulski	4.00/10.00	10.00/25.00
NL#18	Robin Roberts	13.00/33.00	33.00/83.00
NL#19	Enos Slaughter	22.00/55.00	55.00/138.00
NL#19	Gus Bell	15.00/38.00	38.00/75.00
NL#20	Johnny Logan	4.00/10.00	10.00/25.00
NL#21	John Antonelli	6.00/15.00	15.00/38.00
NL#22	Gil Hodges	13.00/33.00	33.00/83.00
NL#23	Eddie Mathews	14.00/35.00	35.00/88.00
NL#24	Lew Burdette	6.00/15.00	15.00/38.00
NL#25	Willie Mays	32.00/80.00	80.00/200.00

1955

Number	Name	Good/VG No tab/tab	EX/Mint No tab/tab
AL#1	Ray Boone	4.00/10.00	10.00/25.00
AL#2	Jim Busby	4.00/10.00	10.00/25.00
AL#3	Whitey Ford	14.00/35.00	35.00/88.00
AL#4	Nelson Fox	10.00/25.00	25.00/63.00
AL#5	Bob Grim	4.00/10.00	10.00/25.00
AL#6	Jack Harshman	4.00/10.00	10.00/25.00
AL#7	Jim Hegan	4.00/10.00	10.00/25.00
AL#8	Bob Lemon	12.00/30.00	30.00/75.00

Number	Name	Good/VG No tab/tab	EX/Mint No tab/tab
AL#9	Irv Noren	4.00/10.00	10.00/25.00
AL#10	Bob Porterfield	4.00/10.00	10.00/25.00
AL#11	Al Rosen	7.00/18.00	18.00/45.00
AL#12	Mickey Vernon	6.00/15.00	15.00/38.00
AL#13	Vic Wertz	4.00/10.00	10.00/25.00
AL#14	Early Wynn	13.00/33.00	33.00/83.00
AL#15	Bobby Avila	4.00/10.00	10.00/25.00
AL#16	Yogi Berra	15.00/40.00	40.00/100.00
AL#17	Joe Coleman	4.00/10.00	10.00/25.00
AL#18	Larry Doby	6.00/15.00	15.00/38.00
AL#!9	Jackie Jensen	7.00/18.00	18.00/45.00
AL#20	Pete Runnels	4.00/10.00	10.00/25.00
AL#21	Jim Piersall	7.00/18.00	18.00/45.00
AL#22	Hank Bauer	7.00/18.00	18.00/45.00
AL#23	Chico Carrasquel	4.00/10.00	10.00/25.00
AL#24	Minnie Minoso	7.00/18.00	18.00/45.00
AL#25	Sandy Consuegra	4.00/10.00	10.00/25.00
NL#1	Richie Ashburn	11.00/28.00	28.00/70.00
NL#2	Del Crandall	4.00/10.00	10.00/25.00
NL#3	Gil Hodges	13.00/33.00	33.00/83.00
NL#4	Brooks Lawrence	4.00/10.00	10.00/25.00
NL#5	Johnny Logan	4.00/10.00	10.00/25.00
NL#6	Sal Maglie	4.00/10.00	10.00/25.00
NL#7	Willie Mays	32.00/80.00	80.00/200.00
NL#8	Don Mueller	4.00/10.00	10.00/25.00
NL#9	Bill Sarni	4.00/10.00	10.00/25.00
NL#10	Warren Spahn	13.00/33.00	33.00/83.00
NL#11	Hank Thompson	4.00/10.00	10.00/25.00
NL#12	Hoyt Wilhelm	12.00/30.00	30.00/75.00
NL#13	John Antonelli	6.00/15.00	15.00/38.00
NL#14	Carl Erskine	6.00/15.00	15.00/38.00
NL#15	Granny Hamner	4.00/10.00	10.00/25.00
NL#16	Ted Kluszewski	7.00/18.00	18.00/45.00
NL#17	Pee Wee Reese	14.00/35.00	35.00/88.00
NL#18	Al Schoendienst	12.00/30.00	30.00/75.00
NL#19	Duke Snider	20.00/50.00	50.00/125.00
NL#20	Frank Thomas	4.00/10.00	10.00/25.00
NL#21	Ray Jablonski	4.00/10.00	10.00/25.00
NL#22	Dusty Rhodes	4.00/10.00	10.00/25.00
NL#23	Gus Bell	4.00/10.00	10.00/25.00
NL#24	Curt Simmons	4.00/10.00	10.00/25.00
NL#25	Marv Grissom	4.00/10.00	10.00/25.00

1952 Jim Hegan "with tab."

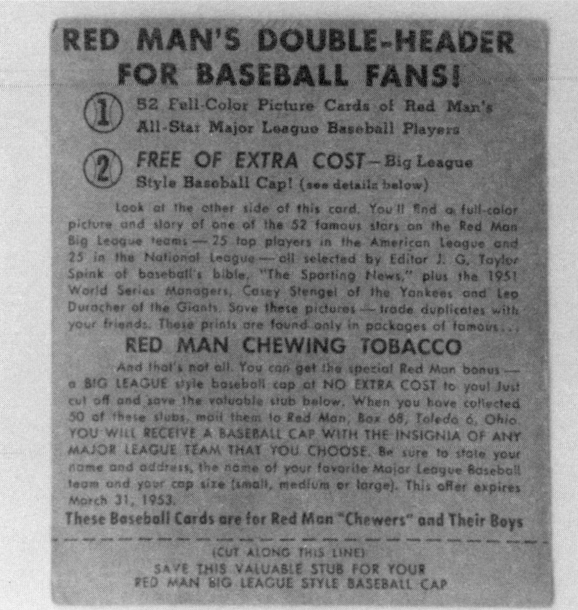

Backside of Hegan card that explains procedure to receive "Big League Style Baseball Cap" by saving tabs.

1954 Gus Bell with tab removed. There is also a #19 1954 card of fellow National League outfielder Enos Slaughter.

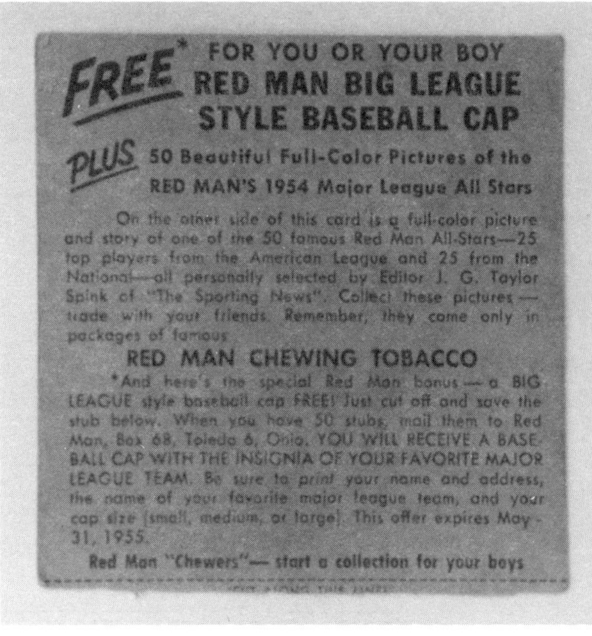

Backside of 1954 Bell card with explanation of how to obtain the baseball cap.

Three Pee Wee Reese cards from 1952, 1953, and 1955 with tabs removed.

1954 Roy Campanella.

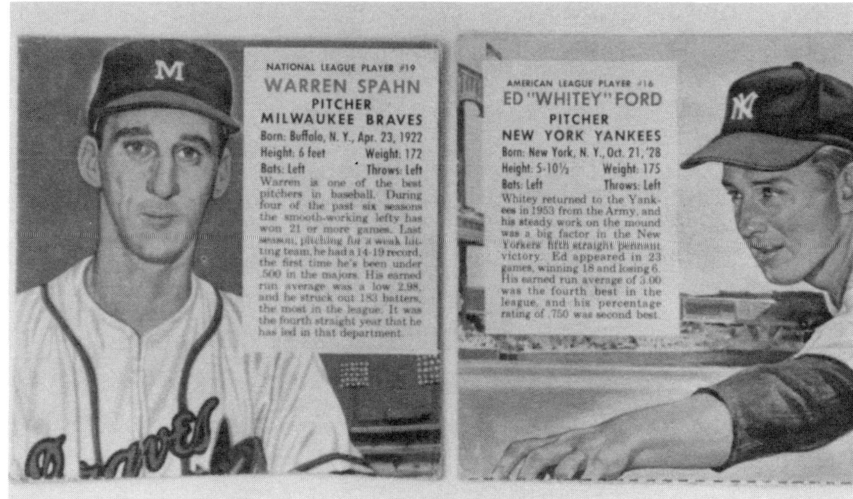

1953 Warren Spahn.
1954 Whitey Ford.

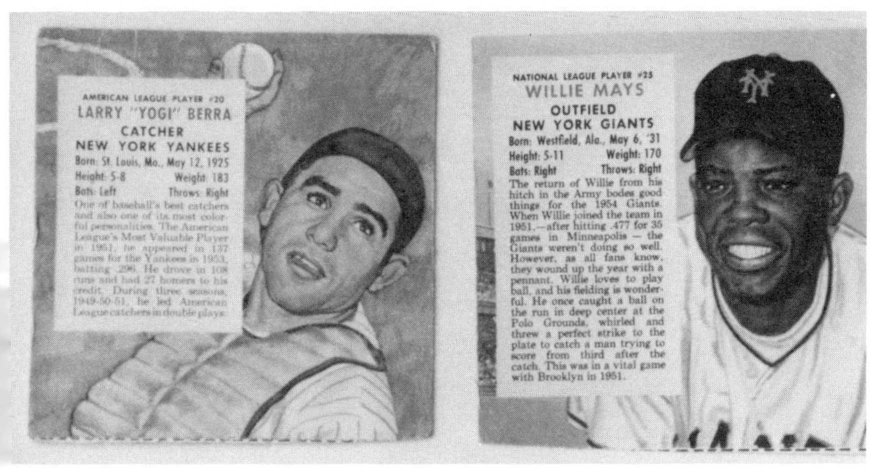

1954 Yogi Berra.
1954 Willie Mays.

1953 Jackie Jensen.
1955 Jackie Jensen.

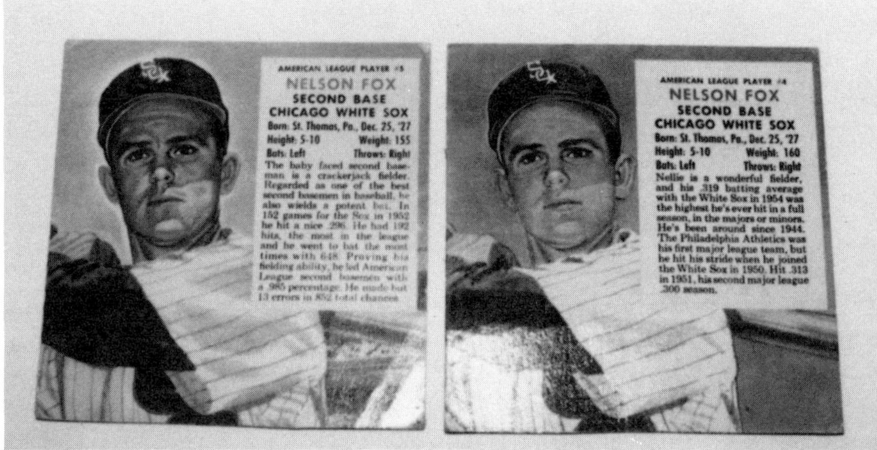

1953 Nelson Fox.
1955 Nelson Fox.

1914 Felt Blankets

by Lou Hagenbruch

This set of blankets contains felt-like squares that are approximately 5¼" per side. Each color-printed, cloth square is comprised of an infield surrounded by a base path with a centered player and two pennants. All blankets are printed on white, felt material with two or three varying colors depending whether or not the white is incorporated in the main color scheme. The infield, basepaths, and bases are each in one of the different colors. Dark brown or black is used for outlining and lettering. The pennants are colored the same as either the basepaths or the bases with the left one containing the name of the player's team and the right his league's initials. At the player's feet is his last name. Names are an item unto themselves - some are spelled incorrectly; instances of first name or initial being included exist; and names on dark blue infields are somewhat hard to see. Found on each base is a different baseball symbol: 1st - baseball, 2nd - mask, 3rd - glove, and home - crossed bats. The entire design is found in reverse on the backside. In the set are ten teams with nine players per team for a total of 90 different players.

The blankets were issued in 1914 only with several brands of tobacco, among them Egyptienne Straights Cigarettes (American Tobacco Company). After being folded into fourths, the individual felts were taped/fastened to the tobacco product, and as a result, fold and/or adhesive marks are found on some examples. These attractive little collectibles are found in various, distinctive, color combinations; each dependent upon the individual player's team. Portions of uncut sheets of blankets have been reported to exist. This coupled with a comparison of color combinations tend to show that one American and one National League team were printed together; the same colors with differing color arrangements. The color variations are listed below.

The distinguishing features of each team are capitalized.

Team	Infield	Basepaths	Bases
BOSTON Braves	WHITE/LT BROWN	Blue	Green
BROOKLYN Dodgers	DK BLUE/GREEN	Red	Tan
CLEVELAND Indians	White	GREEN/PURPLE	PURPLE/YELLOW
DETROIT Tigers	WHITE/LT BROWN	Green	Blue
NEW YORK Giants	White	TAN/GREEN	Red
NEW YORK Yankees	DK BLUE/GREEN	Tan	Red
PITTSBURGH Pirates	White	Gray	RED/PURPLE
ST. LOUIS Browns	White	RED/PURPLE	Gray
ST. LOUIS Cardinals	White	PURPLE/YELLOW	GREEN/PURPLE
WASHINGTON Senators	White	Red	TAN/GREEN

The values of these unique collectibles vary greatly and have escalated dramatically in recent years as more collectors discover them. Prices range from the inexpensive, a few dollars, to the expensive, hundreds of dollars, dependent upon: the individual player; the particular color combinations; sharpness, fading or bleeding of colors; overall centering of the design, its parts and the reverse; and straight or tattered edges. There exist a minute number of the Brooklyn and Detroit blankets that contain a red infield which drastically inflates the prices because of scarcity. It is thought that this color variation may be a result of a printing error as opposed to a planned color combination. In addition, two other player blankets are known to exist in a third color combination: Chance (N.Y. Yanks) with yellow basepaths and pennants on the blue infield; and Griffith (Boston) with red bases and pennants on the white infield.

The blankets are relatively hard to find, seldom found with dealers at card shows, and only occasionally listed in the regular baseball collectors publications. Some scattered dealers do have a few of the felts in their shops. Amassing a complete set, one blanket of each player, would be extremely difficult on a "few here, a couple there" basis. However, even a sampling of the felts is a nice, eye-catching addition to anyone's collection.

The blankets are unnumbered and are listed below alphabetically according to team name and player name. For evaluation purposes the following definitions are included: Good - blanket complete, slightly frayed, creased, mild discoloration, and outlines off-center; Excellent to Mint - close to condition when taken out of cigarette package in 1914, colors bright, no creases or frays, and distinct lines.

* signifies players with rare red infield

Team/Players	Color/Area	Good	EX/Mint
BOSTON BRAVES - Common Players: Connolly, Gowdy*, Griffith*, James, Mann*, Perdue, Tyler*, Whaling*.			
	WHITE INFIELD/GREEN BASES	5.00	25.00
	LT BROWN INFIELD	12.00	70.00
	RED INFIELD	200.00	1,000.00
	WHITE INFIELD/RED BASES	50.00	250.00
HOF Player: Maranville			
	WHITE INFIELD	8.00	50.00
	LT BROWN INFIELD	18.00	100.00
	RED INFIELD	400.00	1,500.00
BROOKLYN DODGERS - Common Players: Cutshaw, Daubert, Hummel, Miller, Rucker, Smith, Wagner			
	DK BLUE INFIELD	5.00	25.00
	GREEN INFIELD	5.00	25.00
HOF Player: Stengel			
	DK BLUE INFIELD	20.00	125.00
	GREEN INFIELD	20.00	125.00
HOF Player: Wheat			
	DK BLUE INFIELD	8.00	50.00
	GREEN INFIELD	8.00	50.00
CLEVELAND INDIANS - Common Players: Bassler, Chapman, Graney, Leibold, Mitchell, Olson, O'Neill, Turner			
	PURPLE BASES/GREEN PATHS	9.00	45.00
	YELLOW BASES/PURPLE PATHS	13.00	75.00
Noted Player: Jackson			
	PURPLE BASES/GREEN PATHS	100.00	500.00
	YELLOW BASES/PURPLE PATHS	125.00	600.00

Team/Players	Color/Area	Good	Ex/Mint
DETROIT TIGERS - Common Players: Baker*, Bauman* (Baumann), Burns*, Cavanaugh* (Kavanagh), Covelski*, Demmitt*, Gainor, Kavanaugh (white only) (Kavanagh), Moriarty*			
	WHITE INFIELD	5.00	25.00
	LT BROWN INFIELD	1200	70.00
	RED INFIELD	200.00	1,000.00
HOF Player: Ty Cobb			
	WHITE INFIELD	150.00	500.00
	LT BROWN INFIELD	200.00	600.00
	RED INFIELD	1,200.00	6,000.00
NEW YORK GIANTS - Common Players: Burns, Doyle, Fletcher, Grant, Meyers, Murray, Snodgrass, Tesreau, Wiltse			
	TAN PATHS	5.00	25.00
	GREEN PATHS	5.00	25.00
NEW YORK YANKEES - Common Players: Boone, Cole, Hartzell, Keating, Maisel, Peckinpaugh, Sweeney, Walsh			
	DK BLUE INFIELD	5.00	25.00
	GREEN INFIELD	5.00	25.00
HOF Player: Chance			
	DK BLUE INFIELD/TAN PATH	10.00	70.00
	GREEN INFIELD	10.00	70.00
	DK BLUE INFIELD/YELLOW PATH	40.00	200.00
PITTSBURGH PIRATES - Common Players: Adams, Gibson, Hyatt, Kelley (Kelly), Konetchy, Mowery, O'Toole, Viox			
	RED BASES	10.00	50.00
	PURPLE BASES	10.00	50.00
HOF Player: Carey			
	RED BASES	15.00	80.00
	PURPLE BASES	15.00	80.00
ST. LOUIS BROWNS - Common Players: Agnew, Austin, Hamilton, McAllister (McAllester), Pratt, Shotton, Walsh, Williams			
	RED PATHS	10.00	50.00
	PURPLE PATHS	10.00	50.00
HOF Player: Wallace			
	RED PATHS	15.00	80.00
	PURPLE PATHS	15.00	80.00
ST. LOUIS CARDINALS - Common Players: Doak, Dolan, Miller, Robinson, Sallee, Steele, Whitted, Wilson			
	PURPLE PATHS/GREEN BASES	8.00	40.00
	YELLOW PATHS/PURPLE BASES	12.00	70.00
HOF Player: Huggins			
	PURPLE PATHS/GREEN BASES	12.00	75.00
	YELLOW PATHS/PURPLE BASES	16.00	90.00
WASHINGTON SENATORS - Common Players: Ainsmith, Foster, Gandil, McBride, Milan, Moeller, Morgan, Shanks			
	TAN BASES	5.00	25.00
	GREEN BASES	5.00	25.00
HOF Player: Johnson			
	TAN BASES	70.00	350.00
	GREEN BASES	70.00	350.00

Top: Steele of the St. Louis Cardinals.

Left: Morgan of the Washington Senators.

Right: Cole of the N.Y. Yankees.

Hall of Fame outfielder Zach Wheat of the Brooklyn Dodgers.

Fletcher of the New York Giants.

Top: Hall of Fame outfielder Max Carey of the Pittsburgh Pirates.

Left: Viox of the Pittsburgh Pirates.

Right: Walsh of the St. Louis Browns.

Top: McAllister of the St. Louis Browns.

Left: Perdue of the Boston Nationals.

Right: Dolan of the St. Louis Cardinals.

Left: Gowdy of the Boston Braves.

Right: Grant of the New York Giants. Eddie Grant was the first major league player killed in World War I.

CHAPTER IV
Baseball Statues and Figurines

Hartland Statues

The Hartland Plastics Company of Hartland, Wisconsin produced molded plastic "authentic, detailed, and exact models" of horses, cattle, famous athletes, western television stars, and historical figures in the late 1950's and early 1960's.

Baseball memorabilia collectors are especially interested in the 18 major league player figures that were made from 1958 to 1963 and sold for $1.98 to $3.98 each in dime stores, shoe repair shops, baseball stadiums, and department stores across America.

The number of figures produced for each player ranged from 150,000 (Ruth, Mathews, Williams, Mays, Mantle, Berra, Aaron) to 5,000 (Groat) and 10,000 (Colavito).

In 1989-90 Hartland reproduced the original 18 players. The reproductions are slightly smaller than the originals and carry the anniversary logo on the players' backs. The anniversary edition figures were initially priced at $25.00 each and were produced in quanities of 10,000 of each player.

In 1990-91 Hartland began to manufacture a line of new baseball figures in quantities of approximately 10,000. They initially included Whitey Ford, Lou Gehirg, Roberto Clemente and Dizzy Dean. There were elaborate plans and orders were taken for figures of Carl Yastrzemski, Bob Feller, and a limited edition (3,000) two-figure set called "The Confrontation" that featured an umpire and a manager.

Subscribers to the "new" Hartland figures were informed in August of 1991 that due to the disappearance of its chief operating officer and financial difficulites, the corporation had been sold.

The Feller, Yastrzemski, and "The Confrontation" figures were not delivered and only a portion of the Cobb figures that had been ordered were ever mailed.

The Minor Leaguer and the Little Leaguer

The 6" tall Little Leaguer or "bat boy" was made in the early 1960's and was reported to have been discontinued when Hartland had difficulties with the Williamsport, Pennsylvania-based Little League Inc. There were approximately 25,000 of the Little Leaguers manufactured. The Little League was priced at 98¢ and described as "a cute little fellow that is every mother's all-American boy. Perfect for awards. 6¼" tall."

The 4" tall minor leaguer was made in similar numbers and was sold by many commercial bakeries for use on top of birthday cakes. Several sources mention that the minor leaguer was offered along with a 4" tennis player, bowler and golfer.

Evaluating Hartland Statues

In attempting to determine the approximate value of a vintage Hartland statue there are some obvious questions that must be asked.

1. What is the degree of "whiteness" of the figure? Has the white faded to a cream or yellow?
2. Does the figure stand by itself? Is it balanced?
3. Are the bats original to the figure? The bats originally came in three sizes.
   - Small: Banks, Groat, Maris, Musial, Snider
   - Medium: Colavito, Killebrew, Mantle, Williams
   - Large: Aaron, Ruth
4. Are the facial features without marks?
5. Is there still strong, original flesh color?
6. Is the original paint intact on the uniform?
7. Are the shoes scruffed?
8. Has the paint worn off the glove?
9. Are the seams of the figure tight?
10. Has any attempt at restoration with paint or nail polish been made?

Values of Hartland Statues

	Approx. # of orig. produced	White/N. White	Off White/Cream Color
Henry Aaron	150,000	300.00-325.00	150.00-175.00
Louie Aparicio	100,000	400.00-450.00	200.00-225.00
Ernie Banks	75,000	400.00-450.00	200.00-225.00
Yogi Berra (w/mask)	150,000	300.00-325.00	150.00-175.00
Yogi Berra (w/o mask)		200.00-225.00	100.00-125.00
Rocky Colavito	10,000	1,000.00-1300.00	625.00-725.00
Don Drysdale	75,000	500.00-550.00	275.00-300.00
Nellie Fox	100,000	300.00-375.00	175.00-200.00
Dick Groat	5,000	1,800.00-2,000.00	1,000.00-1,200.00
Harmon Killebrew	35,000	600.00-675.00	300.00-325.00
Mickey Mantle	150,000	375.00-400.00	200.00-225.00
Roger Maris	100,000	500.00-600.00	300.00-375.00
Eddie Mathews	150.000	150.00-225.00	75.00-100.00
Willie Mays	150,000	325.00-385.00	150.00-175.00
Stan Musial	100,000	300.00-350.00	150.00-200.00
Babe Ruth	150,000	250.00-325.00	125.00-175.00
Duke Snider	75,000	600.00-675.00	300.00-325.00
Warren Spahn	150,000	150.00-225.00	75.00-100.00
Ted Williams	150,000	300.00-375.00	175.00-225.00
Minor Leaguer (4")	25,000	150.00-175.00	50.00-75.00
Little Leaguer (6")	25,000	200.00-250.00	100.00-125.00

Hartland Statue Variations

There are several variations in the construction and decoration of the Hartland statues. Among the most significant are the following:

Nelson Fox and Louis Aparicio – On some of the figures the "Sox" on the front of the uniform is black instead of the more commonly found red. The Walgreen Drug chain was doing a Fox and Aparicio promotion and needed a large number of figures in a short time. An equipment malfunction at Hartland made it impossible to produce the red "Sox" and the black was substituted.

Henry Aaron – The early figures had Aaron's right foot up on his toes in a batting stance. This made it almost impossible for the figure to stand alone. The mold was altered to have his left foot stand flatter for a more solid balance.

Willie Mays – May's bat and glove were colored in a dye tank. The longer the individual pieces were left in the tank the darker they became. There are a variety of color variations found on the glove and bat of Willie's figure.

Williams, Aparicio, Drysdale, Colavito – The discs or standing platforms for these figures were originally dyed a dark purple. In an attempt to save a step in the manufacturing process the discs were eventually left white.

Aaron, Mantle, Mathews, Ruth, Spahn, Williams – These figures were offered with magnets for display on metal automobile dashboards. When car makers went to plastic or padded dashboards, magnets were no longer offered.

Hartland Boxes and Tags

Hartland packaged their figures in cardboard boxes, some of which had a cellophane-covered open front. The original box in "good" condition adds a minimum of $100.00-150.00 to the value of a figure. Each figure also had a "hang tag" on a string that can add $50.00-65.00 to the value of the piece.

"Shoes and Statues"

by Lou Hagenbruch

How did a junior-high aged baseball fan start collecting Hartland statues during the late 1950's? Money wasn't available in a family with five children. So, at most, a person had two pair of shoes – one everyday pair, and a Sunday pair that would eventually become the daily pair. As a result, most shoes were taken to the shoe repairman at least twice – once for heels, and a second time for soles and heels.

It was on one of the trips to Bill's Shoe Repair that I saw my first Hartland, Babe Ruth. Bill (Petroni) had a Ruth statue in his display case.

"How much are they? Are there any other players? Is there a Ted Williams statue?"

Bill, in his broken English, simply replied, "This one is $1.98, and I'll ask the salesman the next time he's in about any others."

When I returned to pick up my shoes, I bought the Ruth with change taken from a money can I had stashed in the corner of a bedroom drawer.

Bill got more statues, and Ted Williams, Stan Musial, Yogi Berra, Nellie Fox, Luis Aparicio, and Mickey Mantle were acquired over a period of months with money earned as a caddie at $1.50 for 18 holes and part-time work on the golf course grounds for $1.00 an hour.

My grandmother came through during a summer visit and trip to St. Louis that year. We found Hartlands for sale in Famous-Barr for $2.00 each in more generic, less decorative boxes. Warren Spahn, Henry Aaron, Eddie Mathews, and Ernie Banks were added to my collection as Grandma said, "Now this is for your birthday and part of Christmas in advance."

Obtaining more statues was somewhat forgotten for a couple of years. Then while Christmas shopping during the early 1960's, I found three more Hartlands in the local Gambles Department Store. Below the main floor was a small basement section containing a few toys and items that weren't selling well. Don Drysdale, Dick Groat, and Rocky Colavito statues were purchased for $3.00 each with no boxes available.

When the first few statues were acquired, I helped my father make and paint a 3' x 4' plywood baseball diamond on which to set the players. This board and the Hartlands ended up in the garage loft to be forgotten and eventually resurrected in the late 1970's. At that time, Willie Mays was purchased for $25.00 from a friend at work; Duke Snider was acquired through the mail for $50.00 from a former Hartland employee; Roger Maris was added through a trade for a 1959 Ted Williams Fleer card set (a set of 80 cards minus card #68) and a few 1957 and 1958 Topps cards; and the last, Harmon Killebrew, was obtained through the mail for $200.00 from a collector in Michigan.

Who would have known or even guessed that baseball statues originally selling for $1.98 to $3.98 would eventually be worth hundreds of dollars? A money-saving trip to the shoe repair shop ended in a big money proposition.

Pirate short-stop Dick Groat, the rarest Hartland.

Minnesota Twins Hall of Fame slugger Harmon Killebrew.

Yankee right fielder and home run hitter Roger Maris.

White Sox second baseman Nellie Fox.

Hall of Fame lefthanded pitcher Warren Spahn.

Original Hartland advertising booklet that lists baseball statues for $1.98 each.

1950's Ted Williams "stand-up" Moxie advertisement. $600.00-700.00.

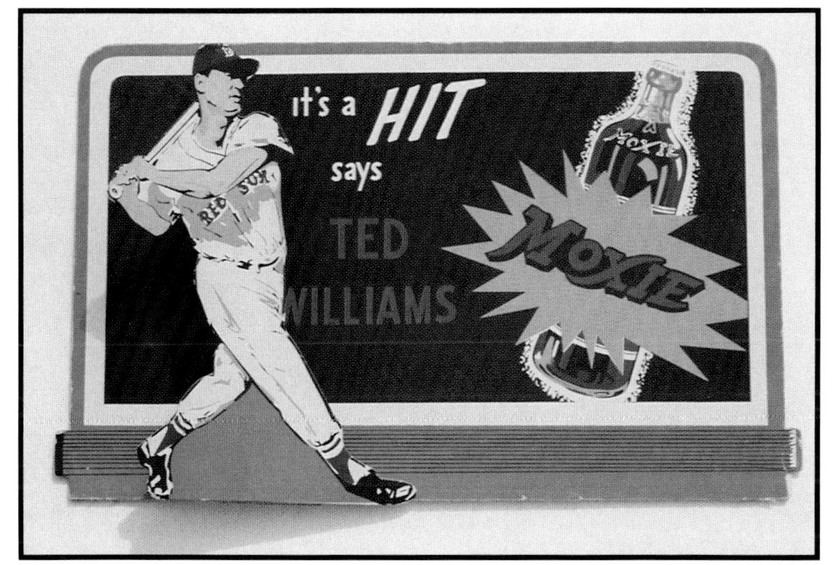

Early 1960's Ted Williams three-dimentional "stand-up." $700.00-950.00.

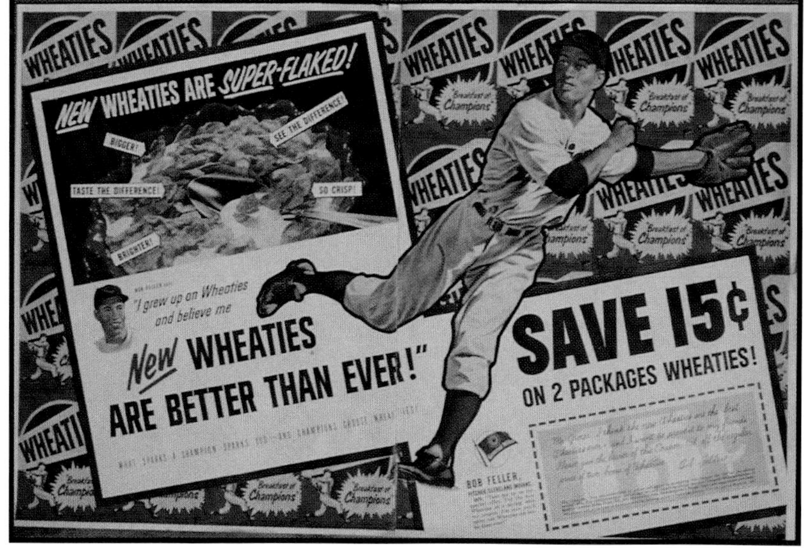

Bob Feller Wheaties magazine advertisement, c. 1950's. $4.00-6.00.

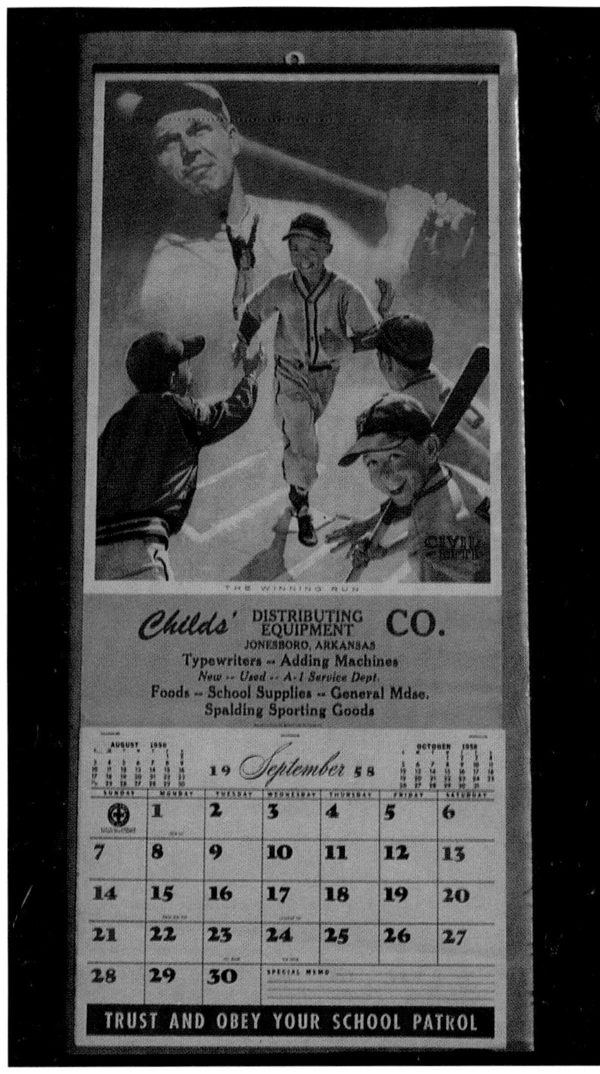

1958 Jimmy Foxx calendar from Brown and Bigelow. $150.00-185.00.

Dizzy Dean poster for the Denver Bears radio network by Medcalf. $100.00-125.00.

Autographed group photograph of 1987 Hall of Fame members attending the Induction in Cooperstown. $225.00-275.00.

1989 autographed group photograph of Hall of Fame members in Cooperstown. $200.00-225.00.

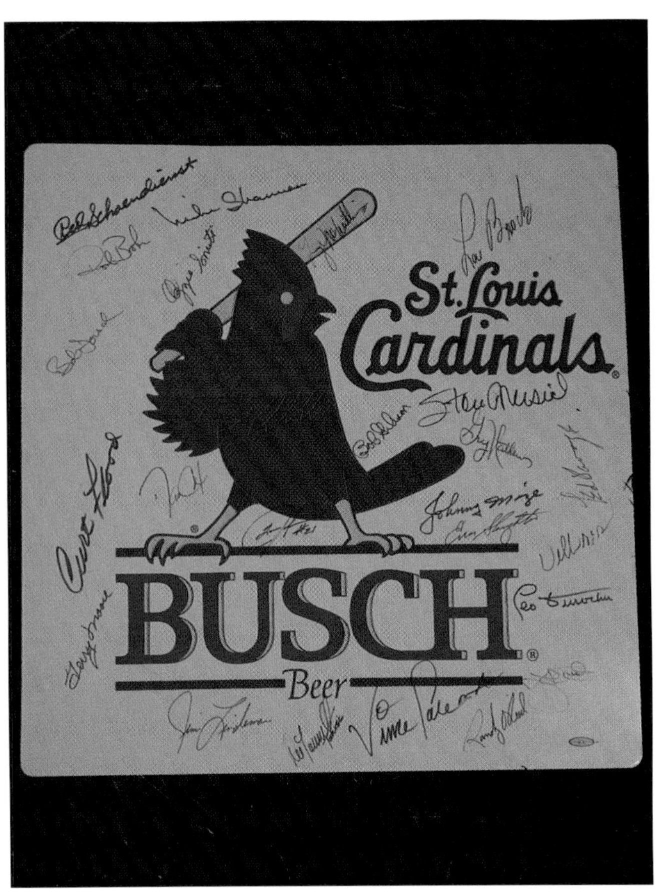

Cardboard Cardinal sign autographed by current and former team members. $75.00-100.00.

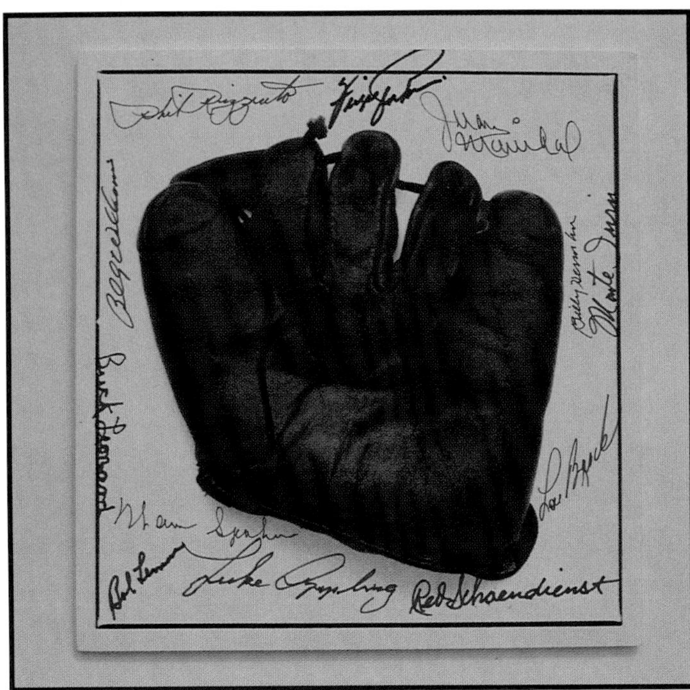

Photograph of fielder's glove autographed by members of the Hall of Fame. $75.00-95.00.

"Cub Power" album cover autographed by 10 1969 team members. $50.00-60.00.

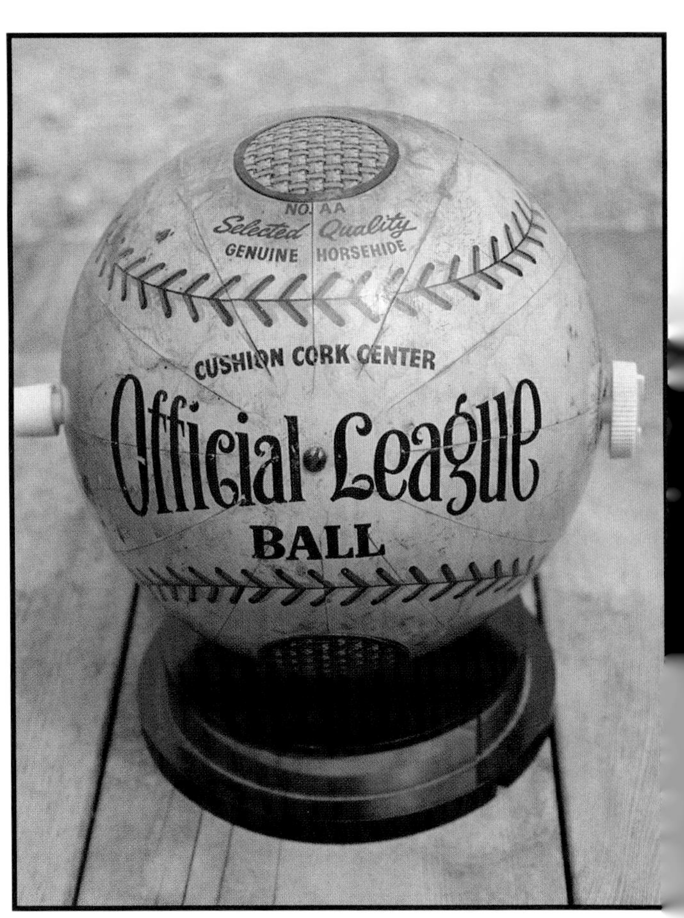

Baseball radio from the 1930's. $700.00-950.00.

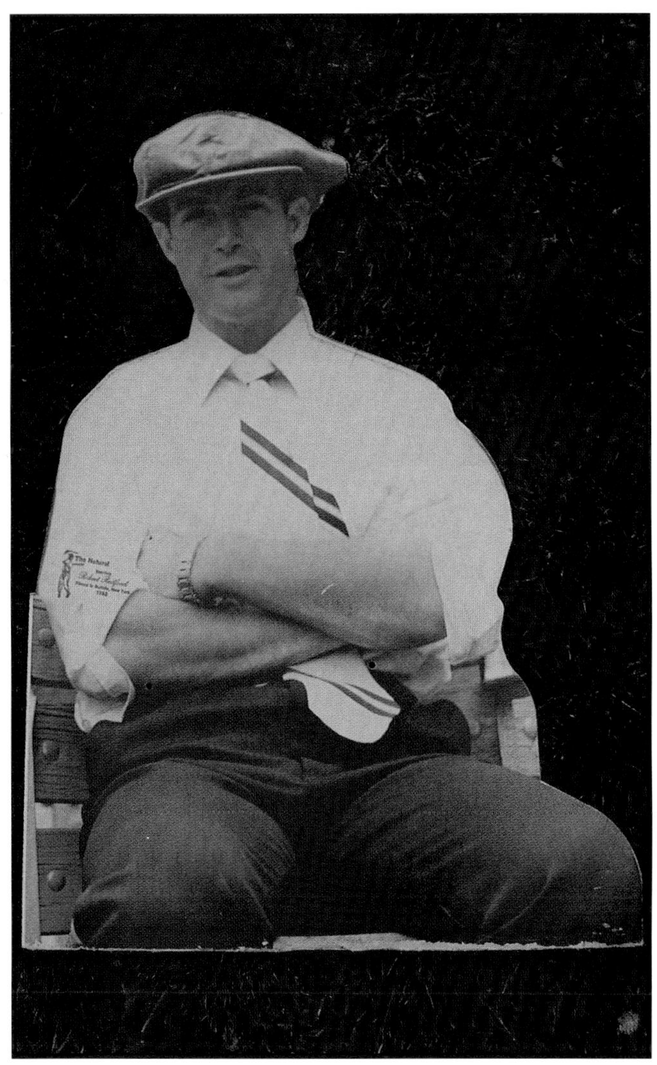

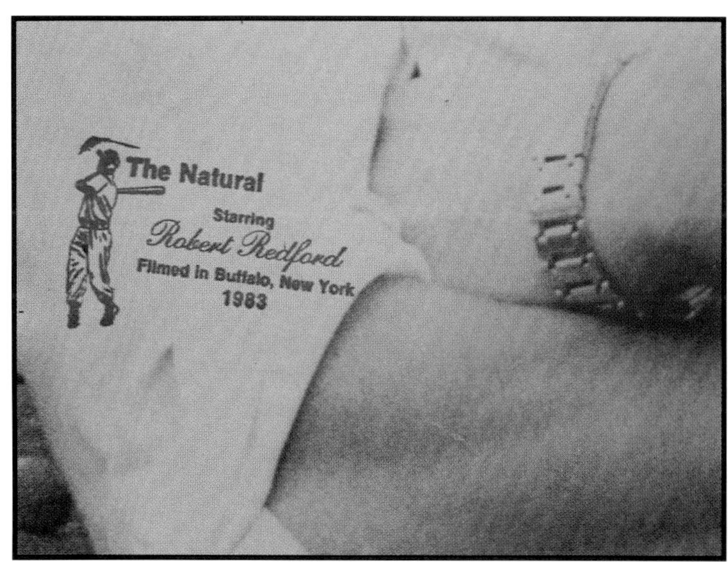

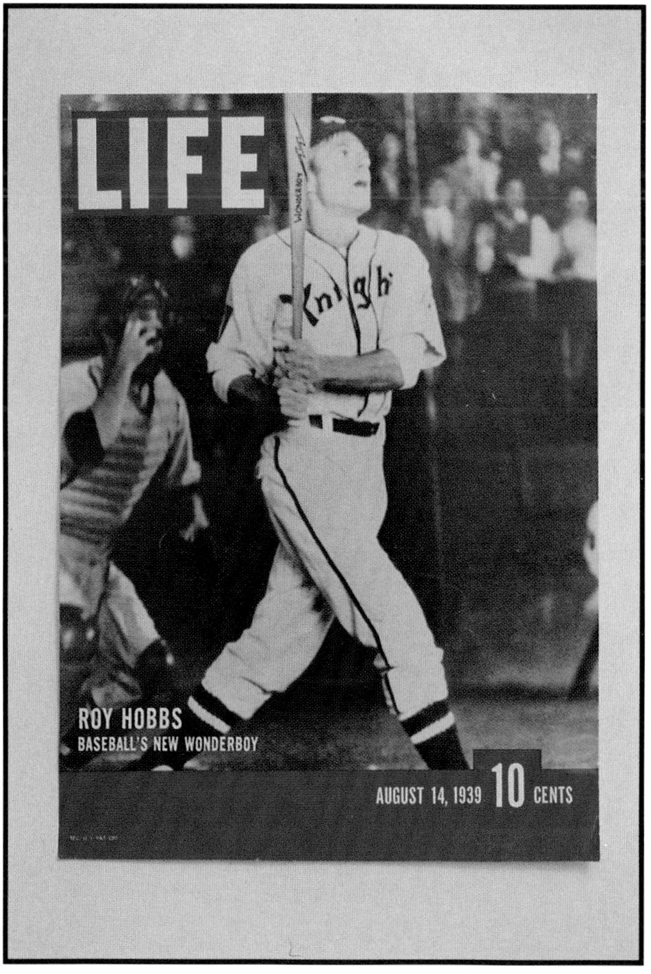

Above: Cardboard figure used to fill a seat during filming of *The Natural.* $65.00-75.00.

Right: Cover of Life Magazine made for *The Natural* with Roy Hobbs. $40.00-50.00.

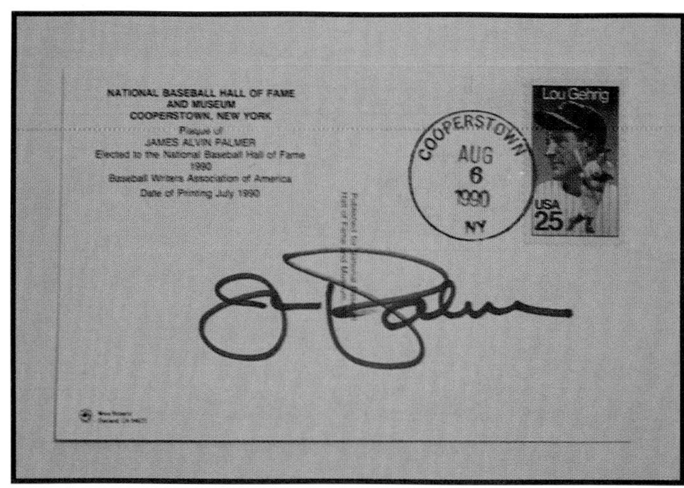

Left: Jim Palmer HOF postcard.

Above: Reverse of Palmer postcard autographed and postmarked on his Induction Day in Cooperstown. $20.00-25.00.

Below left: Autographed Sandy Koufax HOF postcard. $20.00-25.00.

Below right: Autographed Hank Aaron HOF postcard. $20.00-25.00.

Above left: Walter Johnson Hall of Fame bust, C. 1963. $75.00-100.00.

Above right: Honus Wagner Hall of Fame bust, C. 1963. $75.00-100.00.

Right: Error bust with Dickey plaque and Hornsby face. $115.00-130.00.

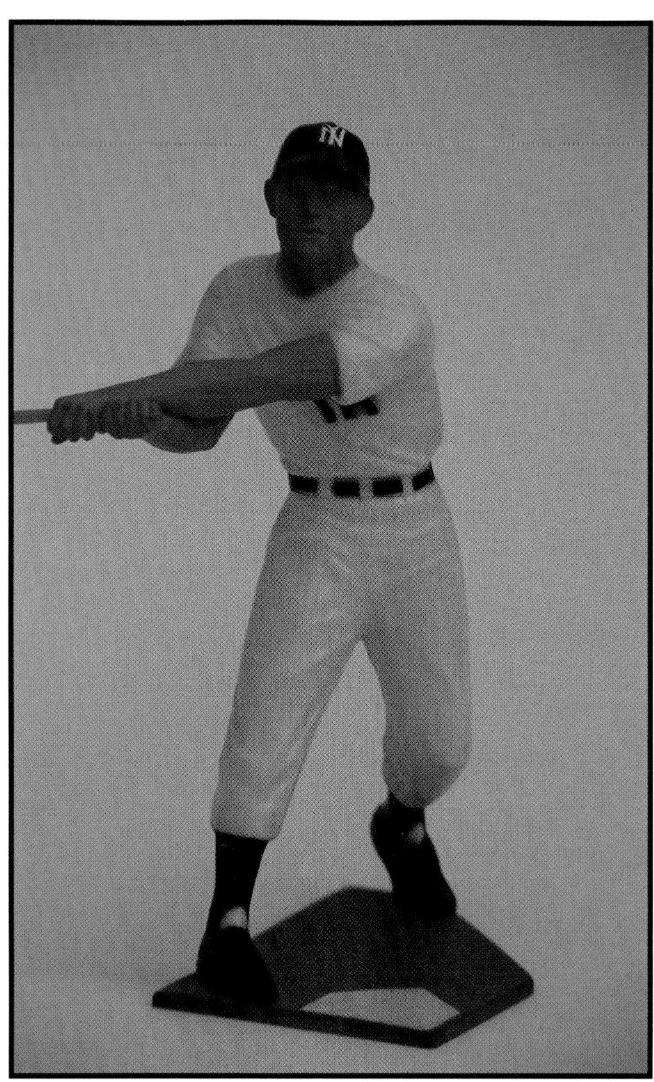

Original Roger Maris Hartland, C. 1960. $500.00-600.00.

Original and rare Rocky Colavito Hartland, c. 1960. $1,000.00-1,300.00.

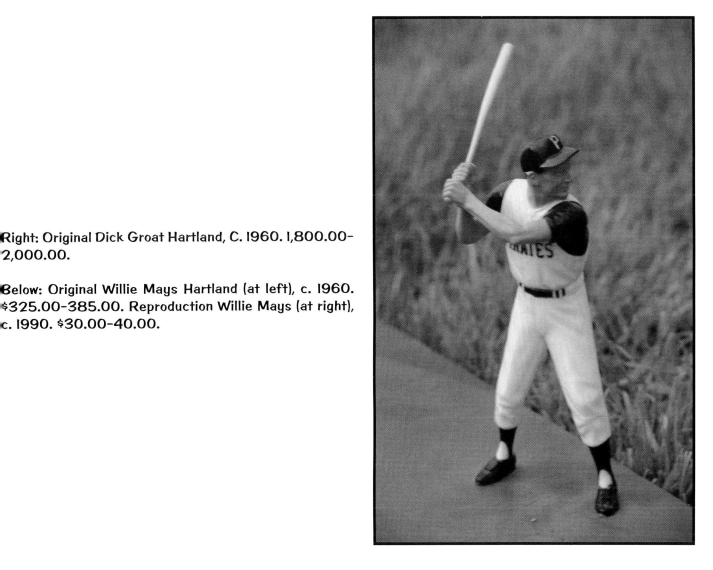

Right: Original Dick Groat Hartland, C. 1960. 1,800.00-2,000.00.

Below: Original Willie Mays Hartland (at left), c. 1960. $325.00-385.00. Reproduction Willie Mays (at right), c. 1990. $30.00-40.00.

Original Ted Williams Hartland, c. 1960. $375.00-450.00. Original Yogi Berra Hartland, c. 1960. $200.00-225.00.

Reproduction Hartland of Nelson Fox, c. 1990. $30.00-40.00. "New" Hartland of a sliding Ty Cobb, c. 1991. $75.00-100.00.

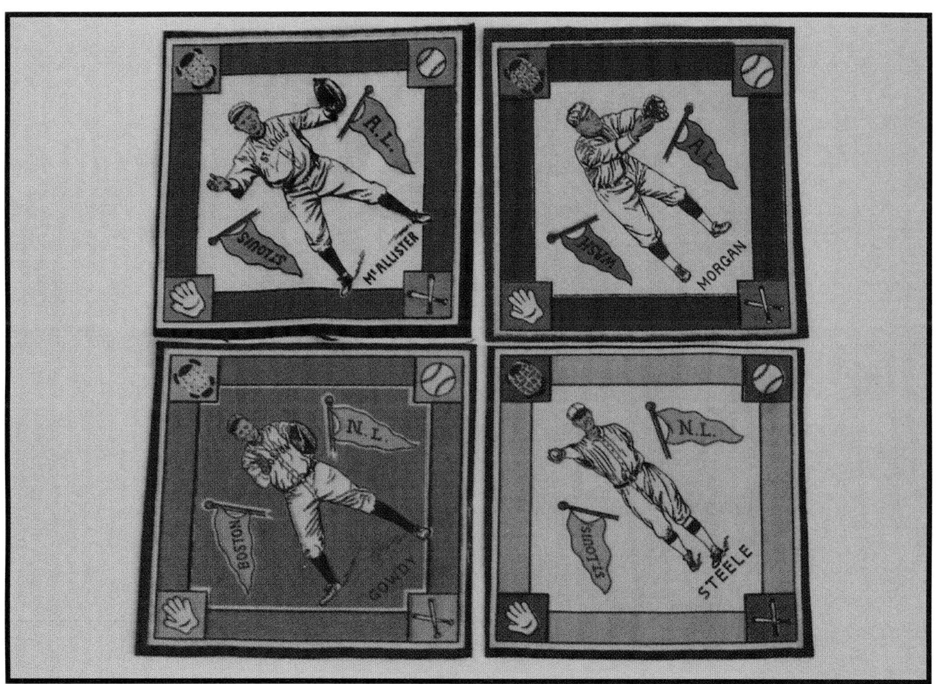

1914 "blankets" of Steele, Gowdy, Morgan, and McAllister. $25.00-70.00 each.

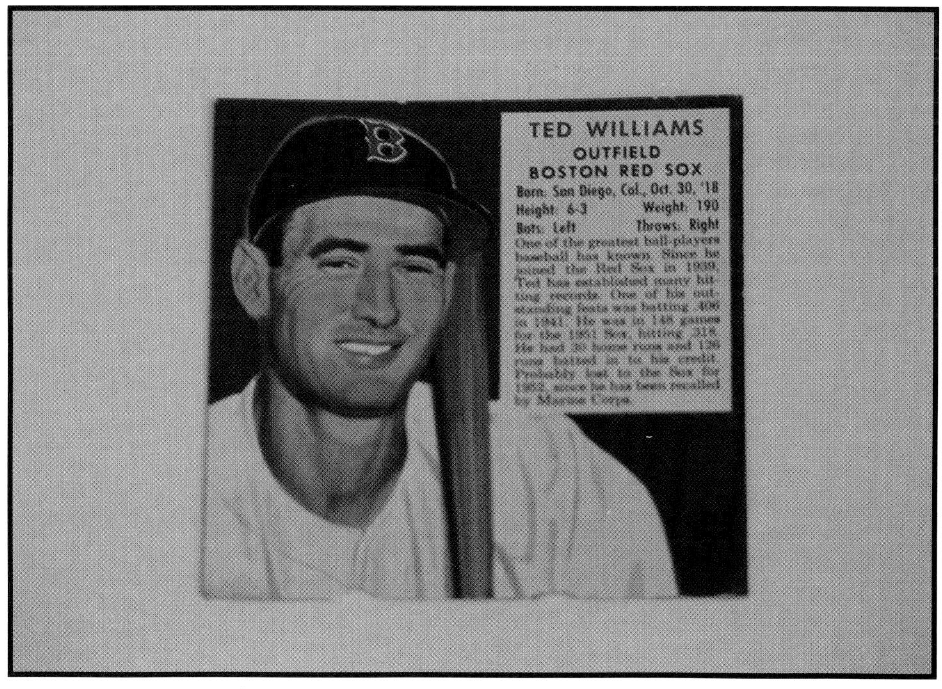

1952 Ted Williams Red Man Tobacco card without the "tab." $50.00-65.00.

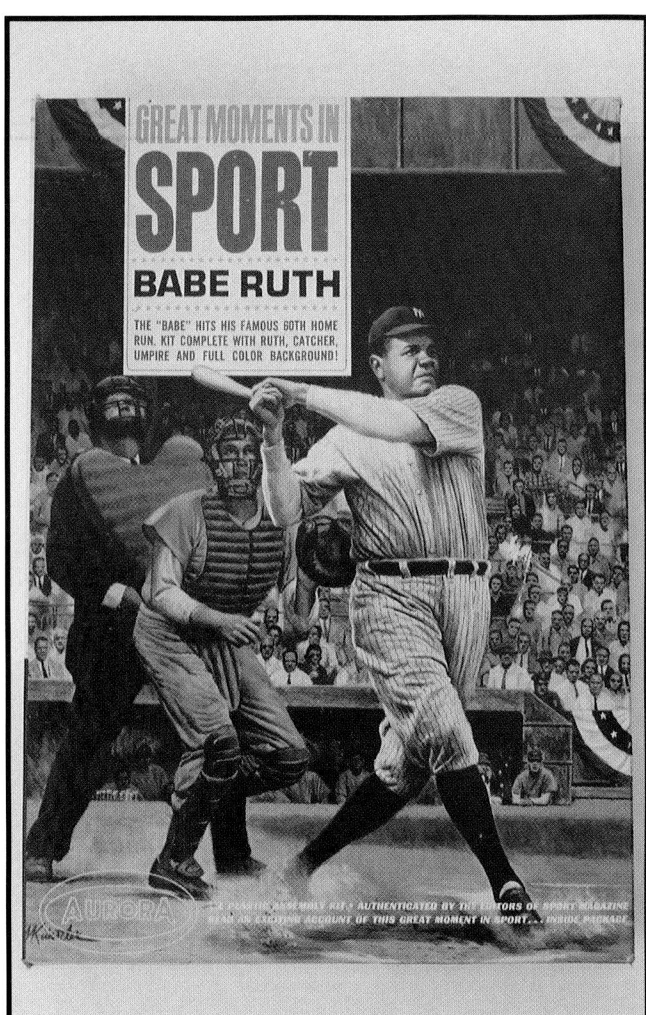

"Great Moments In Sports" plastic model of Babe Ruth, early 1960's, unopened. $150.00-300.00.

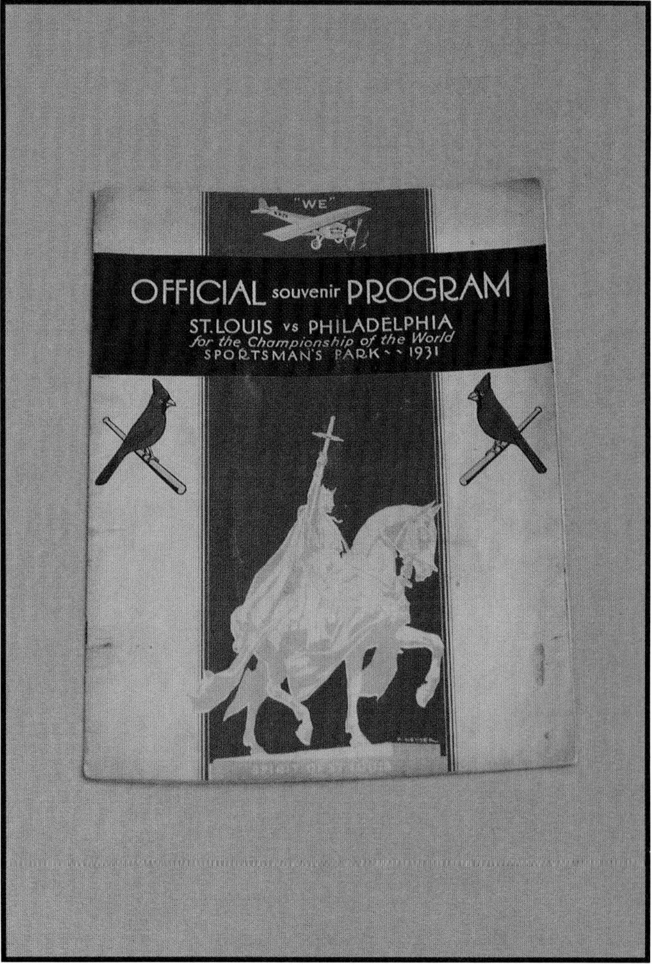

1931 World Series program from St. Louis, fair to good condition, unscored. $135.00-150.00.

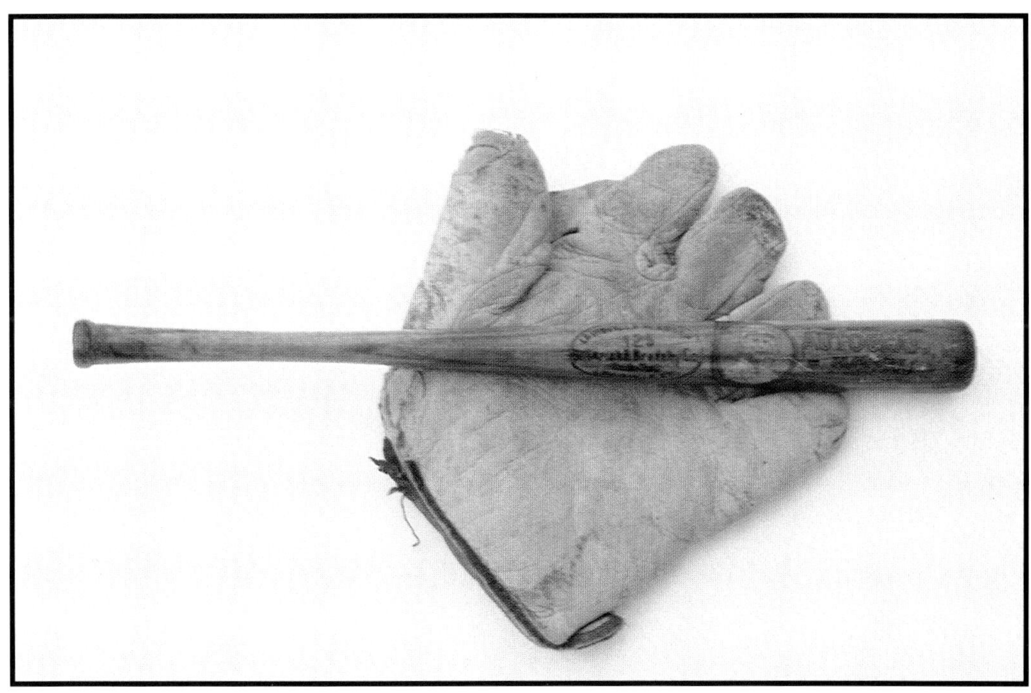

George Sisler model Louisville Slugger "decal" bat, 16" long, c. 1920's. $200.00-235.00.

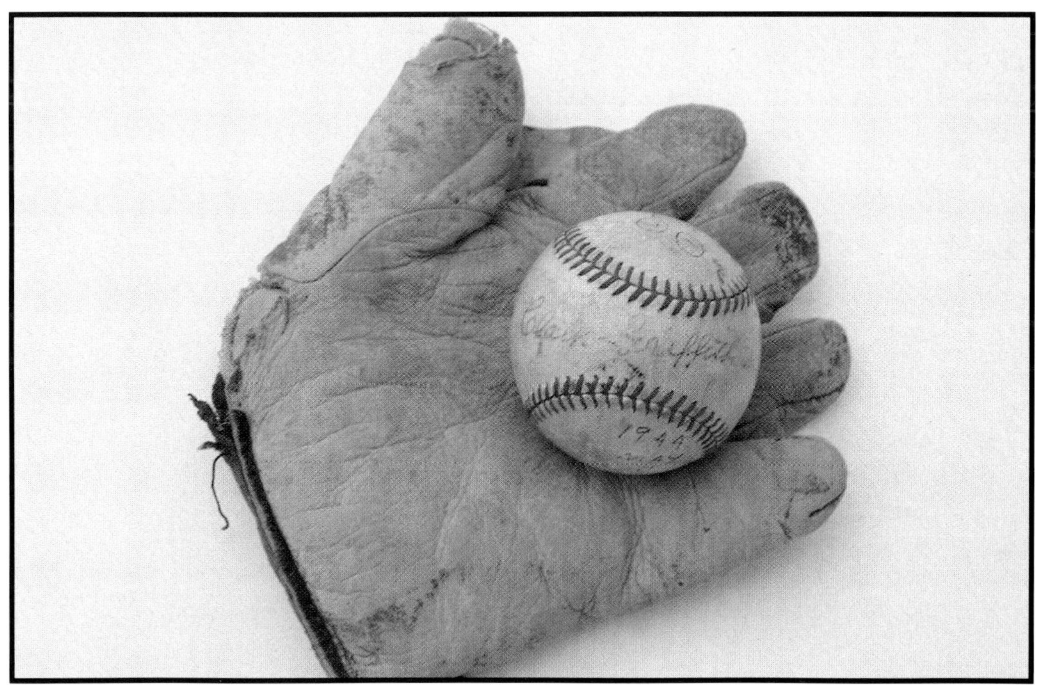

Child's baseball glove from the early 1920's. $30.00-35.00. Single-signed baseball autographed by Washington Senator owner and Hall of Famer Clark Griffith. $300.00-500.00.

Famous Slugger plastic bat rack and miniature player bats, c. late 1950's, ordered from Famous Slugger Yearbooks. $60.00-65.00 complete.

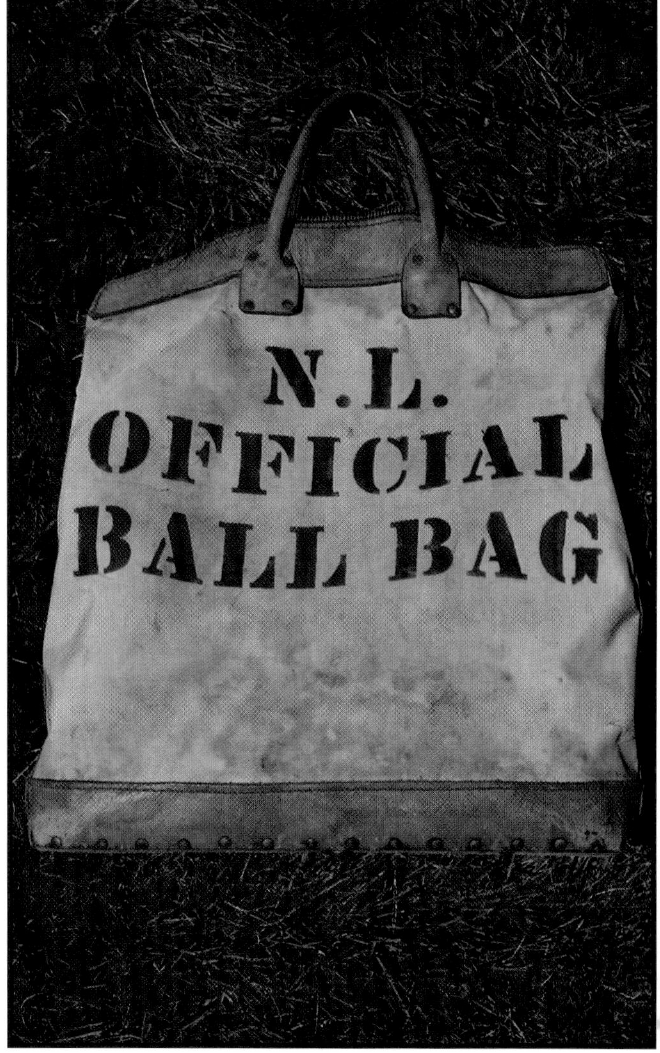

Leather and canvas ball bag used by National League umpires, c. early 1960's. $100.00-150.00.

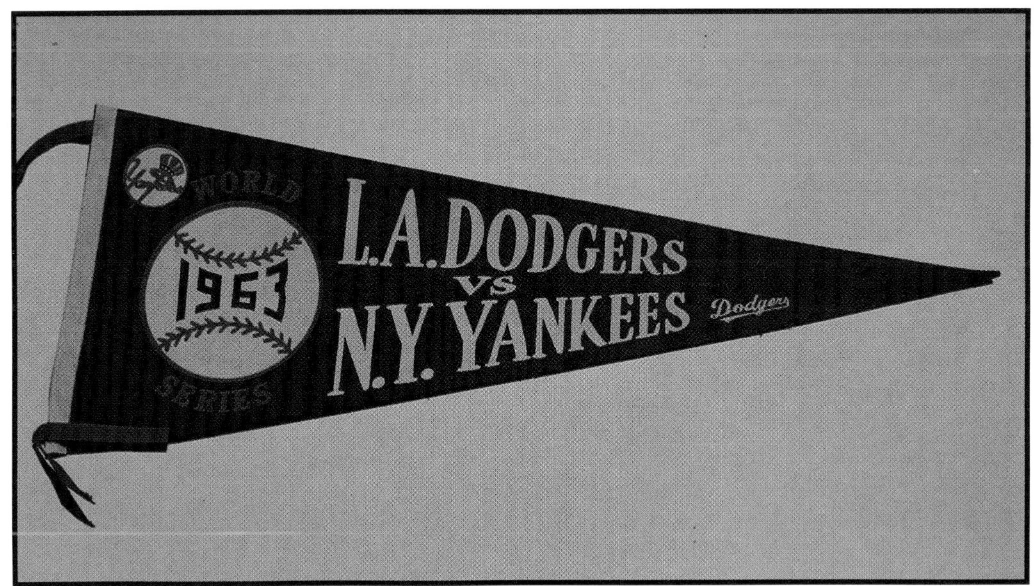

Top left: Gaylord Perry peanut bag, autographed. $12.00-15.00.

Top right: Donnie Moore's Chicago Cub road jersey, 1978 season. $200.00-250.00.

Above: World Series pennant, 1963. $45.00-55.00.

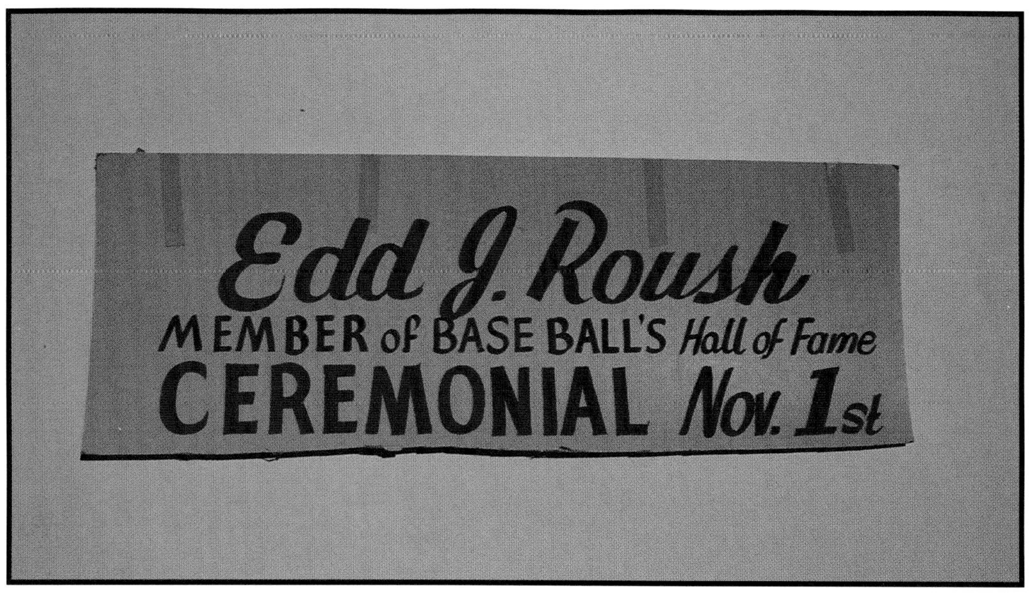

Edd Roush sign from side of convertible carrying Mr. Roush in 1962 parade in Oakland City, Indiana. $15.00-20.00.

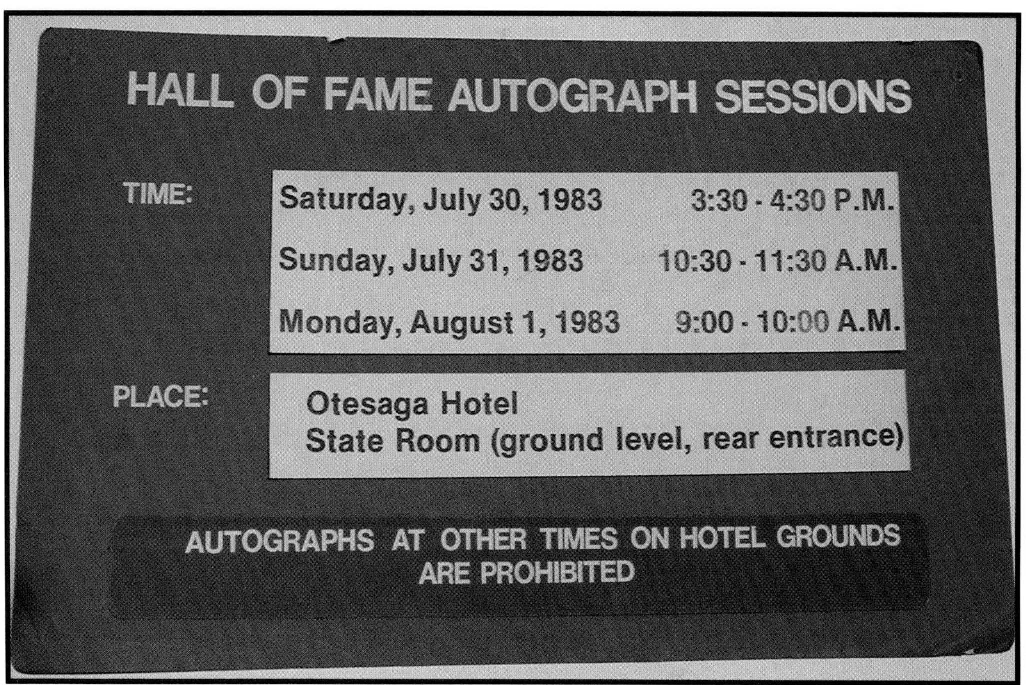

1983 sign announcing Hall of Fame autograph session hours in Cooperstown, NY. $25.00-40.00.

Kenner "Starting Lineup" Baseball Figures

The Kenner Company began producing 4" plastic statues or figures of major league baseball players in 1988. They were sold in toy stores, baseball card shops, and grocery stores for $4.00-6.00 each.

Collectors trying to put together the entire 1988 set (124 players) quickly found that many of the statues were distributed regionally rather than nationally. For example, Seattle outfielder Ken Phelps was readily available in Washington and Oregon but much more difficult to find in Illinois and New Hampshire. The rarest statue from the 1988 set is Nolan Ryan which was offered for sale primarily in Texas.

The 1989 Kenner "Starting Lineup" set included 167 players. In 1990 the number was reduced to 87 and in 1991 to 46. All the sets have continued to be offered generally on a regional basis.

The 167 player set from 1989 probably holds the least interest at this point for most collectors because it was a costly and time-consuming process to attempt to complete.

To secure maximum value and investment potential the "Starting Lineup" statue should be left in its original box. A figure that is not in its original packaging is worth no more than 20% of the value assigned to it in the lists below. The condition of the box is critical in establishing value. The values assigned to the statues that follow assume that the statue is in mint condition in the original packaging.

1988 Kenner Starting Lineup

Player	Value
Dale Murphy	20.00-25.00
Ken Oberkfell	13.00-15.00
Ozzie Virgil	15.00-17.00
Ken Griffey Sr.	35.00-40.00
Zane Smith	14.00-16.00
Eddie Murray	24.00-26.00
Cal Ripken	25.00-30.00
Fred Lynn	22.00-25.00
Mike Boddicker	14.00-16.00
Terry Kennedy	20.00-22.00
Wade Boggs	13.00-15.00
Roger Clemons	13.00-15.00
Jim Rice	20.00-22.00
Dwight Evans	20.00-22.00
Ellis Burks	55.00-60.00
Wally Joyner	14.00-16.00
Mike Witt	20.00-22.00
Brian Downing	20.00-22.00
Donnie Moore	18.00-22.00
Devon White	20.00-22.00
Leon Durham	13.00-15.00
Ryne Sandberg	32.00-36.00
Andre Dawson	20.00-24.00
Jody Davis	14.00-16.00
Rick Sutcliffe	14.00-16.00
Shawon Dunston	20.00-24.00
Harold Baines	13.00-15.00
Ozzie Guillen	20.00-24.00
Greg Walker	16.00-18.00
Gary Redus	20.00-24.00
Carlton Fisk	50.00-55.00
Eric Davis	13.00-15.00
Pete Rose	30.00-35.00
Kal Daniels	14.00-16.00
Buddy Bell	14.00-16.00
John Franco	14.00-16.00
Joe Carter	14.00-16.00
Mel Hall	13.00-15.00
Brett Saberhagen	16.00-20.00
Cory Snyder	15.00-17.00
Pat Tabler	14.00-16.00
Julio Franco	14.00-16.00
Jack Morris	13.00-15.00
Alan Trammell	14.00-15.00
Lou Whitaker	13.00-14.00
Willie Hernandez	15.00-18.00
Matt Nokes	14.00-16.00
Nolan Ryan	120.00-140.00
Mike Scott	12.00-14.00
Glenn Davis	15.00-17.00
Billy Hatcher	20.00-24.00
Kevin Bass	14.00-15.00
Alan Ashby	18.00-22.00
George Brett	20.00-24.00
Dan Quisenberry	17.00-20.00
Danny Tartabull	20.00-22.00
Kevin Seitzer	17.00-20.00
Pedro Guerrero	12.00-14.00
Fernando Valenzuela	12.00-13.00
Steve Sax	14.00-15.00
Mike Marshall	13.00-14.00
Franklin Stubbs	18.00-20.00
Robin Yount	55.00-60.00
Rob Deer	14.00-16.00
Paul Molitor	14.00-15.00
Ted Higuera	18.00-20.00
B.J. Surhoff	22.00-24.00
Kirby Puckett	14.00-16.00
Kent Hrbek	14.00-15.00
Gary Gaetti	13.00-14.00
Jeff Reardon	18.00-20.00
Tom Brunansky	26.00-28.00
Frank Viola	16.00-18.00
Tim Raines	20.00-24.00
Darryl Strawberry	13.00-15.00
Keith Hernandez	18.00-20.00
Gary Carter	12.00-14.00
Dwight Gooden	15.00-18.00
Len Dykstra	22.00-24.00
Kevin McReynolds	20.00-24.00
Howard Johnson	28.00-32.00
Rickey Henderson	30.00-35.00
Don Mattingly	20.00-24.00
Dave Winfield	15.00-17.00

Willie Randolph 18.00-20.00
Dave Righetti 18.00-20.00
Jack Clark 22.00-24.00
Jose Canseco 60.00-70.00
Mark McGwire 40.00-50.00
Carney Lansford 30.00-35.00
Dave Parker 40.00-45.00
Mike Schmidt..........35.00-40.00
Von Hayes 18.00-20.00
Juan Samuel 16.00-18.00
Shane Rawley 14.00-16.00
Steve Bedrosian 14.00-16.00
Sid Bream 16.00-20.00
Barry Bonds............24.00-28.00
Andy Van Slyke 25.00-30.00
Mike Dunne................12.00-14.00
Bobby Bonilla 22.00-25.00
Ozzie Smith 13.00-15.00
Vince Coleman 14.00-15.00
Tom Herr 14.00-15.00
Willie McGee.............14.00-15.00
Todd Worrell 18.00-20.00
Tony Gwynn 16.00-18.00
Benito Santiago 18.00-21.00
John Kruk 14.00-16.00
Chris Brown 18.00-20.00
Will Clark................40.00-50.00
Jeffrey Leonard.........13.00-15.00
Rick Reuschel 15.00-16.00
Candy Maldonado 16.00-18.00
Jim Presley 14.00-16.00
Alvin Davis 14.00-16.00
Mark Langston 18.00-20.00
Ken Phelps 15.00-20.00
Pete Incavigila............14.00-16.00
Pete O'Brian 13.00-15.00
Larry Parish 14.00-16.00
Charlie Hough 15.00-16.00
Ruben Sierra 40.00-50.00
George Bell 15.00-16.00
Ken Griffey, Jr. 45.00-65.00

1989 Kenner Starting Lineup

Dale Murphy..............11.00-13.00
Zane Smith 12.00-14.00
Gerald Perry 12.00-14.00
Dion James 12.00-14.00
Albert Hall 17.00-20.00
Bruce Sutter 14.00-16.00
Ron Gant 16.00-18.00
Cal Ripken 20.00-25.00
Larry Sheets 11.00-13.00
Pete Stanicek 9.00-11.00
Brady Anderson........12.00-15.00
Wade Boggs 9.00-10.00
Roger Clemons 9.00-10.00
Jim Rice 10.00-12.00
Ellis Burks.............20.00-22.00
Mike Greenwell 10.00-11.00
Lee Smith 10.00-11.00
Marty Barrett 10.00-12.00
Wally Joyner 10.00-11.00
Mike Witt 10.00-12.00
Devon White.............13.00-14.00
Johnny Ray 18.00-20.00
Chili Davis 14.00-16.00
Jack Howell 15.00-16.00
Dick Schofield 15.00-16.00
Ryne Sandberg 10.00-12.00
Andre Dawson 8.00-10.00
Greg Maddux 12.00-14.00
Rick Sutcliffe 10.00-12.00
Mark Grace............30.00-35.00
Shawon Dunston 9.00-11.00
Damon Berryhill......18.00-20.00
Harold Baines 14.00-16.00
Ozzie Guillen............12.00-14.00
Greg Walker 12.00-14.00
Ivan Calderon 14.00-16.00
Melido Perez.............16.00-18.00
Dan Pasqua 13.00-15.00
Bobby Thigpen 15.00-18.00
Eric Davis 11.00-13.00
Kal Daniels 11.00-13.00
John Franco 13.00-14.00
Danny Jackson 13.00-14.00
Bo Diaz 15.00-16.00
Barry Larkin 26.00-28.00
Jeff Treadway 28.00-34.00
Chris Sabo 20.00-24.00
Joe Carter 10.00-12.00
Mel Hall 10.00-12.00
Cory Snyder 12.00-13.00
Brook Jacoby.............13.00-14.00
Greg Swindell 12.00-13.00
Doug Jones 13.00-14.00
Jack Morris 11.00-12.00
Alan Trammell 12.00-14.00
Matt Nokes 12.00-13.00
Luis Salazar 18.00-20.00
Chet Lemon 9.00-10.00
Lou Whitaker..............9.00-10.00
Tom Brookens 17.00-19.00
Mike Henneman........10.00-12.00
Mike Scott 13.00-14.00
Glenn Davis 11.00-12.00
Billy Hatcher 11.00-12.00
Kevin Bass 8.00-9.00
Dave Smith.................10.00-11.00
Billy Doran 17.00-20.00
Gerald Young 11.00-12.00
George Brett..........22.00-24.00
Bret Saberhagen 12.00-13.00
Danny Tartabull..........11.00-12.00
Kevin Seitzer 11.00-12.00
Bo Jackson 65.00-75.00
Kurt Stillwell 12.00-13.00
Pat Tabler 10.00-11.00
Mark Gubicza 10.00-11.00
Fernando Valenzuela 12.00-13.00
Mike Marshall 8.00-10.00
Orel Hershiser 22.00-25.00
John Shelby 11.00-12.00
Kirk Gibson................8.00-10.00
Mike Scioscia 13.00-15.00
Robin Yount 30.00-35.00
Rob Deer 11.00-12.00
Paul Molitor..................7.00-9.00
Ted Higuera 9.00-10.00
B.J. Surhoff 11.00-12.00
Dan Plesac 11.00-12.00
Glenn Braggs 13.00-14.00
Kirby Puckett 8.00-10.00
Kent Hrbek 12.00-14.00
Gary Gaetti..................8.00-10.00
Jeff Reardon 12.00-13.00
Dan Gladden 8.00-10.00
Frank Viola 10.00-12.00
Tim Laudner 9.00-10.00
Tim Raines 10.00-11.00
Darryl Strawberry .20.00-22.00
Keith Hernandez 9.00-10.00
Gary Carter 15.00-16.00
Dwight Gooden 8.00-10.00
Len Dykstra 12.00-13.00

David Cone 20.00-22.00
Kevin Elster 10.00-11.00
Kevin McReynolds ...10.00-12.00
Randy Myers 18.00-20.00
Greg Jefferies 24.00-26.00
Rickey Henderson .20.00-22.00
Don Mattingly 10.00-13.00
Dave Winfield 8.00-10.00
Dave Righetti 10.00-12.00
MIke Pagilarulo.........10.00-12.00
Don Slaught 8.00-10.00
Al Leiter 10.00-12.00
Jose Canseco 22.00-2600
Mark McGwire 12.00-15.00
Dave Parker 18.00-20.00
Dave Stewart 14.00-17.00
Bob Welch 15.00-17.00
Terry Steinbach 30.00-40.00
Carney Lansford 16.00-19.00
Dennis Eckersley 13.00-15.00
Walt Weiss 24.00-28.00
Mike Schmidt 65.00-75.00

Von Hayes 10.00-12.00
Juan Samuel 13.00-14.00
Steve Bedrosian 10.00-12.00
Milt Thompson 17.00-20.00
Phil Bradley 28.00-35.00
Chris James 8.00-10.00
Barry Bonds..............10.00-12.00
Andy Van Slyke 13.00-15.00
Bob Walk 12.00-14.00
Bobby Bonilla 10.00-12.00
Mike LaValliere 10.00-12.00
Doug Drabek 10.00-12.00
Jose Lind 22.00-24.00
Tony Gwynn 28.00-32.00
Benito Santiago 18.00-21.00
Marvell Wynne 12.00-13.00
Mark Davis 15.00-18.00
Will Clark 18.00-20.00
Candy Maldonado 8.00-10.00
Brett Butler 13.00-14.00
Kevin Mitchell 20.00-22.00

Jose Uribe 12.00-13.00
Robby Thompson 12.00-13.00
Alvin Davis 13.00-14.00
Mark Langston 22.00-25.00
Harold Reynolds 18.00-22.00
Rey Quinones 20.00-25.-00
Mickey Brantley 18.00-21.00
Ozzie Smith 13.00-14.00
Vince Coleman 9.00-10.00
Tom Brunansky 11.00-12.00
Willie McGee 10.00-11.00
Todd Worrell..............13.00-15.00
Tony Pena 11.00-12.00
Terry Pendleton 16.00-19.00
Pedro Guerrero 11.00-13.00
Pete Incavigila 10.00-12.00
Ruben Sierra...........18.00-20.00
Scott Fletcher 9.00-11.00
Steve Buchele 13.00-15.00
Jeff Russell 10.00-12.00
George Bell 8.00-10.00

1990 Kenner Starting Lineup

Wade Boggs 8.00-10.00
Roger Clemons 8.00-10.00
Ellis Burks 10.00-12.00
MIke Greenwell 8.00-10.00
Jody Reed 11.00-12.00
Nick Esasky 35.00-40.00
Jim Abbott 15.00-20.00
Ryne Sandberg 12.00-13.00
Andre Dawson 10.00-11.00
Greg Maddux 10.00-11.00
Rick Sutcliffe 10.00-11.00
Mark Grace
(swinging) 25.00-30.00
Damon Berryhill 10.00-12.00
Mitch Williams 12.00-13.00
Jerome Walton 18.00-22.00
Eric Davis 8.00-9.00
Barry Larkin 14.00-15.00
Chris Sabo 10.00-12.00
Paul O'Neil 12.00-13.00
Todd Benzinger 10.00-11.00
Rob Dibble 17.00-19.00
Sandy Alomar 19.00-22.00
Alan Trammell 10.00-11.00
Matt Nokes 12.00-13.00
Gary Pettis 35.00-45.00

Lou Whitaker 10.00-11.00
Mike Scott 8.00-9.00
Bo Jackson 17.00-20.00
Orel Hershiser 8.00-11.00
Eddie Murray 12.00-13.00
Willie Randolph 12.00-13.00
Kirk Gibson 8.00-10.00
Robin Yount 24.00-27.00
Paul Molitor 9.00-11.00
Gary Sheffield 15.00-18.00
Chris Bosio 10.00-11.00
Kirby Puckett 8.00-10.00
Kent Hrbek 11.00-12.00
Gary Gaetti 11.00-12.00
Allan Anderson 11.00-12.00
Wally Backman 35.00-40.00
Andres Galarraga 9.00-10.00
Darryl Strawberry 8.00-10.00
(fielding) 14.00-16.00
Dwight Gooden 8.00-10.00
Kevin McReynolds 15.00-17.00
Gregg Jefferies 10.00-11.00
Ron Darling 10.00-11.00
Howard Johnson 15.00-17.00
Juan Samuel 13.00-14.00
Frank Viola 12.00-13.00

Don Mattingly
(swinging) 20.00-22.00
Dave Winfield 10.00-11.00
Dave Righetti 10.00-11.00
Steve Sax 8.00-10.00
Roberto Kelly 18.00-22.00
Jesse Barfield 9.00-10.00
Jose Canseco 10.00-11.00
Mark McGwire 10.00-11.00
Dave Stewart 14.00-16.00
Dennis Eckersley 18.00-20.00
Dave Henderson 13.00-15.00
Rickey Henderson .20.00-25.00
Von Hayes 10.00-11.00
Ricky Jordan 15.00-17.00
Tom Herr 10.00-11.00
Len Dykstra 20.00-23.00
Barry Bonds..............13.00-15.00
Andy Van Slyke 11.00-12.00
Bobby Bonilla 11.00-12.00
John Smiley 11.00-12.00
Ozzie Smith 8.00-10.00
Vince Coleman 8.00-10.00
Pedro Guerrero 10.00-11.00
Jose Oquendo 12.00-13.00
Joe Magrane 10.00-11.00

Joe Carter..............28.00-32.00
Will Clark (swinging) .18.00-22.00
Cal Ripken...................11.00-13.00
Kevin Mitchell 9.00-11.00
Steve Bedrosian 9.00-10.00
Rick Reuschel 11.00-12.00
Ken Griffey, Jr.
(sliding)...............50.00-55.00
(jumping) 38.00-42.00
Nolan Ryan 28.00-34.00
Fred McGriff...............9.00-11.00
Mickey Tettleton 13.00-17.00
Jeff Ballard 9.00-11.00
Ben McDonald 24.00-26.00

1991 Kenner Starting Lineup

Ben McDonald 12.00-13.00
Jim Abbot...................13.00-14.00
Mark Grace 8.00-11.00
Ryne Sandberg 8.00-10.00
Shawon Dunston........9.00-10.00
Andre Dawson 8.00-11.00
Ozzie Guillen.............14.00-15.00
Eric Davis...................10.00-12.00
Chris Sabo 7.00-9.00
Barry Larkin 8.00-11.00
Tom Browning 10.00-12.00
Jack Armstrong 10.00-11.00
Sandy Alomar Jr. 14.00-16.00
Alan Trammell 10.00-11.00
Cecil Fielder..............12.00-14.00
Bo Jackson 12.00-14.00
Ramon Martinez 14.00-17.00
Kirby Puckett 12.00-13.00
Delino Deshields.......12.00-15.00
Dwight Gooden 10.00-12.00
Frank Viola 10.00-12.00
Howard Johnson 12.00-13.00
Gregg Jefferies...........7.00-9.00
John Franco 10.00-12.00
Dave Madagan 12.00-14.00
Darryl Strawberry 10.00-12.00
Don Mattingly 8.00-9.00
Steve Sax 8.00-10.00
Roberto Kelly 12.00-14.00
Kevin Maas 18.00-22.00
Jose Canseco 8.00-10.00
Mark McGwire 7.00-8.00
Rickey Henderson 12.00-15.00
Dave Stewart 13.00-15.00
Len Dykstra................10.00-11.00
Bobby Bonilla 10.00-12.00
Barry Bonds..............10.00-12.00
Doug Drabek 10.00-12.00
Todd Zeile 18.00-20.00
Benito Santiago 10.00-12.00
Will Clark 8.00-10.00
Kevin Mitchell 7.00-8.00
Matt Williams.............15.00-17.00
Ken Griffey Jr. 22.00-24.00
Nolan Ryan.............22.00-26.00
Kelly Gruber 10.00-12.00

Angels' first baseman Wally Joyner, 1988. $3.00-4.00, $12.00-14.00 with original packaging in mint condition.

Bobbing Head Dolls

Collectible "bobbing head" dolls were made of papier-mache and sold at baseball parks, dime stores, and by mail for $1.00-4.00 from 1960-1972. Most of the dolls were 7" tall although several series of 4½" miniatures were also made available.

The Japanese-made bobbing heads were issued in numerous variations of round, square, or diamond-shaped bases that were painted green, gold, white, or black. A Japanese subsidiary of the Lego Company produced most of the dolls.

Bobbing Head Doll Chronology

1960-61	square bases painted green, light blue, red, blue, orange and gold
1961-62	Clemente, Mantle, Mays, Maris caricatures with round or square white bases
1961-62	white square bases
1961-62	4½" tall miniatures with white round bases with a magnet for use on automobile dashboards
1962-66	green round bases
1962-64	green round bases with black players
1967-72	gold round bases

Caricature Bobbing Head Dolls 1961-62

	7" reg. size	4½" miniature
Mickey Mantle	400.00-550.00	600.00-850.00
Roger Maris	400.00-575.00	700.00-900.00
Willie Mays	175.00-500.00	
Roberto Clemente	900.00-1,300.00	

The Clemente caricature is the rarest of the four dolls with some experts estimating that there are less than 200 in existence. The Clemente was sold without a box.

The Mantle can be found with a "Yankee" decal or embossed "N.Y." on his chest. The Mantle box is worth at least $50.00-100.00.

Of the four 1961-62 caricatures, Mays is the most commonly found. The Mays caricature with lighter flesh color is much more available than the Mays with darker flesh tone. The "darker" flesh tone adds $175.00-200.00 to the price of a Mays doll. The darker doll is worth $350.00-500.00 in "near mint" condition.

Henry Aaron, as a Milwaukee Brewer, was produced in large quantities in 1975 and is valued at $22.00-30.00 in mint condition. The Aaron caricature doll was made of plastic rather than papier-mache.

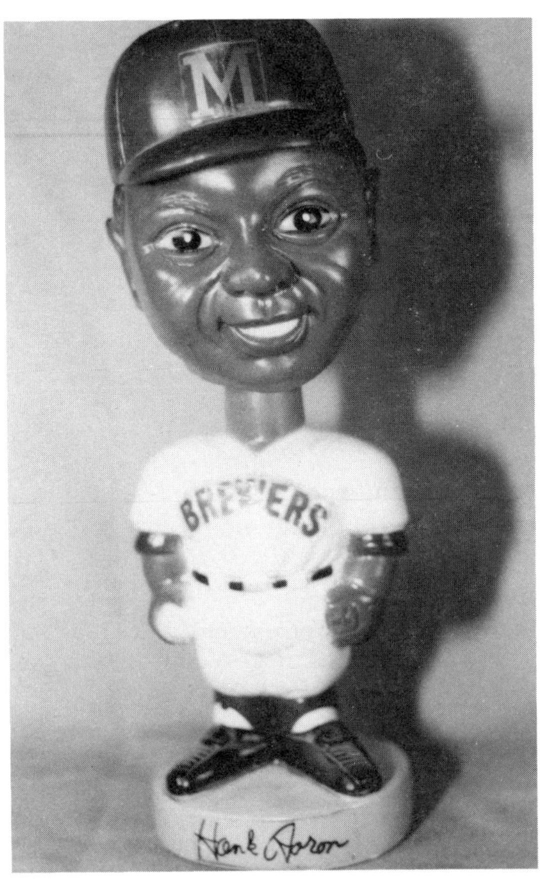

Henry Aaron bobbing head issued by the Milwaukee Brewers in large quantities. $25.00.

Left: 1962 Cleveland Indian made in Japan, green base. $65.00-75.00.
Right: 1970 Taiwan reproduction. $5.00-15.00.

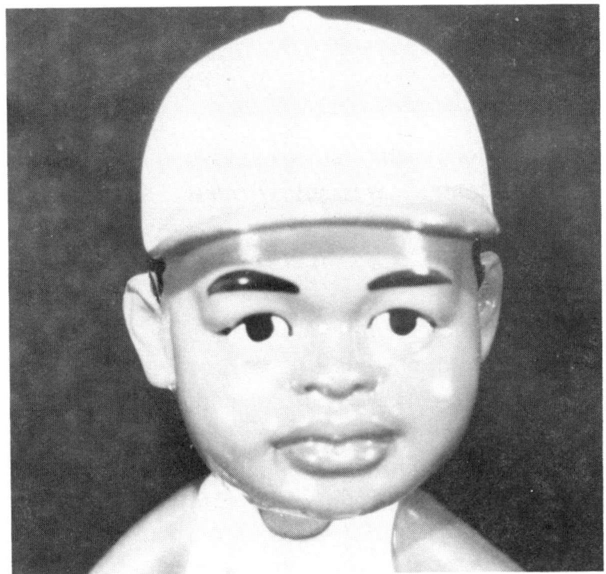

Head of 1962 black Cincinnati Red, green base. $350.00-500.00.

New York Yankee bobbing head, 1970's, imported from Taiwan. $5.00-15.00.

1962 green base Tiger bobbing head. $100.00-125.00.

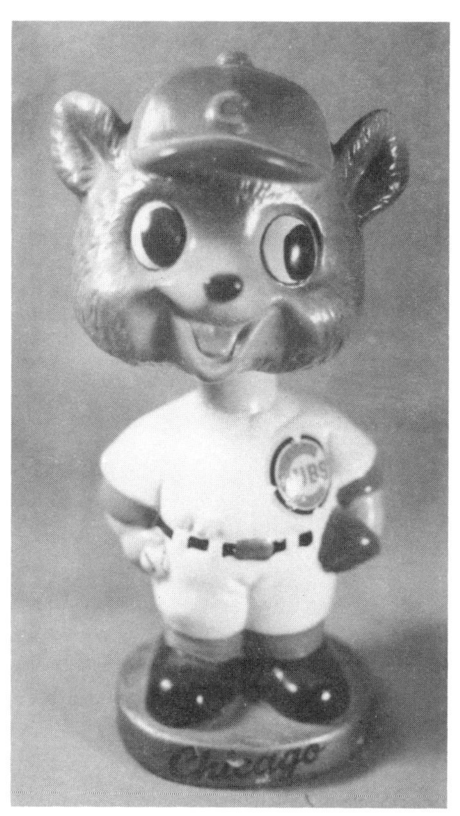

1967 Cub, gold base. $100.00-135.00.

1984 Cub, green base. $20.00-30.00.

1984 Cardinal, green base, made in Japan. $20.00-30.00.

1984 Philly, green base. $20.00-25.00.

1984 Pirate, green base. $20.00-30.00.

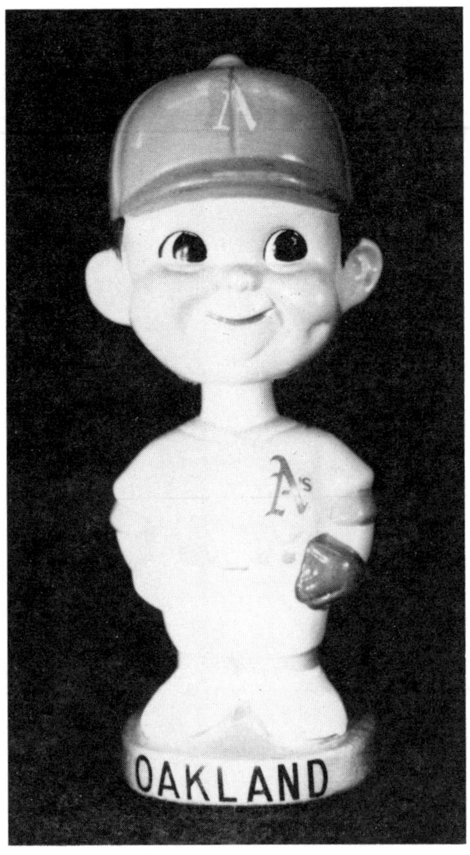

1967 Oakland A's, yellow uniform with gold base, made in Japan. $85.00-100.00.

1989 Babe Ruth, made in Taiwan, "Nodders." $20.00-30.00.

HOF Busts

by Lou Hagenbruch

This set of 20 plastic busts are described on their boxes as "sculptured statuettes of baseball immortals enshrined at the Baseball Hall of Fame and Museum in Cooperstown." The statuettes are approximately 6¾" tall with a white/ivory bust mounted on a dark brown base. The only part that is not plastic is the paper/foil plaque that is attached to the front of the base with adhesive. Sports Hall of Fame, Inc., Lynbrook, Long Island, New York, manufactured the busts in 1963. They could be purchased at Cooperstown, gift shops along the Pennsylvania Turnpike, and through mail order advertisements found in Sunday newspaper magazine sections. Originally they sold for $1.98 each, and could be had for as little as $5.00 each in the late 1970's.

The facial artwork on these statuettes is far superior to that of the original Hartlands. There is no question as to who each bust represents, even without the stick-on plaque. A number of variables go into the price of these busts, not the least of which are limited production and the particular player. Considerations that deal with condition are: the bust - white or yellowed; the base - unbroken (no cracks); and the plaque - readable and in good shape; and whether or not the bust is in its original box. The box is worth an additional $25.00. The busts are hard to find, seldom found at baseball cards shows, rarely listed in collectors publications, and definitely scarcer than the original Hartlands. At least one error is known to exist - a Hornsby bust with a Dickey plaque - but there are probably many others.

Ty Cobb 75.00-100.00
Mickey Cochrane ..75.00-100.00
Joe Cronin 60.00-90.00
Bill Dickey 75.00-100.00
Joe DiMaggio 75.00-125.00
Bob Feller 50.00-75.00
Jimmy Foxx 75.00-100.00
Lou Gehrig 125.00-200.00
Hank Greenberg 75.00-100.00
Rogers Hornsby 75.00-100.00
Walter Johnson......75.00-100.00
Christy Mathewson .75.00-100.00
John McGraw 75.00-115.00
Jackie Robinson ..115.00-200.00
Babe Ruth 125.00-200.00
George Sisler 60.00-90.00
Tris Speaker 75.00-100.00
Pie Traynor 60.00-90.00
Honus Wagner 75.00-100.00
Paul Waner 60.00-90.00

*Note: Special thanks to John Kressel, Kressel Sports Cards, Kenosha, Wisconsin, for his helpful input.

Rogers Hornsby.

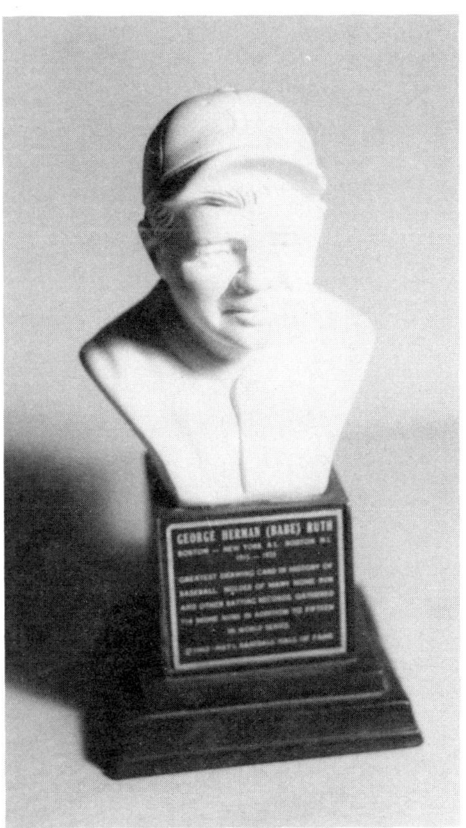

Babe Ruth.

Jackie Robinson.

Joe DiMaggio.

Hank Greenberg.

Bob Feller.

Tris Speaker.

Ty Cobb.

Pie Traynor.

Lou Gehrig.

Christy Mathewson in original unopened box.

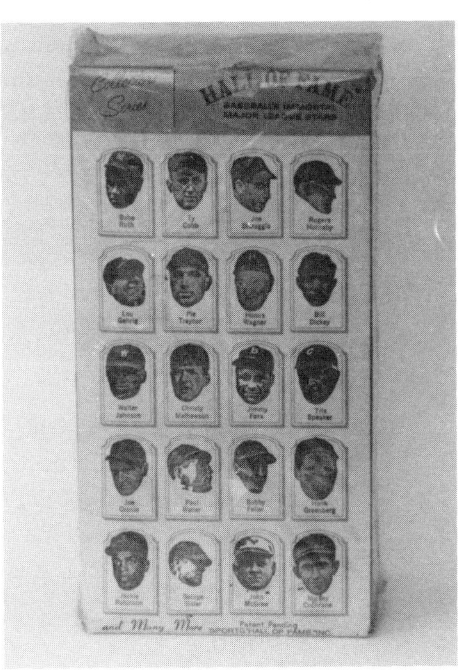

Reverse of unopened box listing players in set of busts.

CHAPTER V
Books and Periodicals

Periodicals

Collectors of sports related periodicals can find copies of *Baseball Magazine* or *The Sporting News* at flea markets, garage sales, or in their uncle's basement in a trunk filled with beer bottles and Christmas tree ornaments.

As is the case with most collectibles, to have value the magazine or newspaper must be in especially good condition and be focused on an indivudual or moment in baseball history that is memorable.

Age is not necessarily the major factor in the evaluation process. A *Sports Illustrated* cover from the 1950's with bridge expert Charles Goren or pitcher Art Mahaffey has minimal interest for collectors regardles of age or condition.

The magazines and periodicals that are priced on the pages that follow all have baseball-related covers. Issues without "baseball" covers are not evaluated. The prices for each publication assume "near mint" condition.

The following criteria should be considered in collecting and evaluating baseball periodicals.

1. Subject matter or personality featured on the cover
2. Articles that detail important or historical events or feats
3. Condition
    a. water stains?
    b. tears?
    c. creases?
    d. missing pages?
    e. covers intact?
    f. mailing label?
4. Age of the publication

Sport Magazine

Sport Magazine has been issued monthly since September 1946. Issues in excellent condition with the cover and all pages intact are fairly uncommon because almost every 12-year-old fan in America cut out the full-page color photographs each month of their heroes and took great delight in taping them to a bedroom wall. The first issue of *Sport* was offered for sale in December 1991 in "excellent" condition for $350.00.

Month	Year	Cover/Feature Article	Value
April	1947	Durocher - Dodgers	25.00
June	1947	Bob Feller	25.00
July	1947	Joe Cronin - Red Sox	18.00
August	1947	Ted Williams	55.00
September	1947	Joe DiMaggio	65.00
April	1948	Ted Williams	45.00
May	1948	Babe Ruth	40.00
July	1948	Ewell Blackwell	18.00
August	1948	Stan Musial	28.00
September	1948	Ted Williams and Joe DiMaggio	55.00
October	1948	Lou Gehrig	40.00
February	1949	Lou Boudreau	22.00
April	1949	Bob Feller	22.00
May	1949	Enos Slaughter	22.00
June	1949	Hal Newhouser	17.00
July	1949	Lou Boudreau and Joe Gordon	22.00
August	1949	Jackie Robinson	40.00
September	1949	Joe DiMaggio	45.00
October	1949	Christy Mathewson	20.00
February	1950	Tommy Henrich	20.00
April	1950	Casey Stengel	25.00
May	1950	Ralph Kiner	25.00
June	1950	Bob Lemon	22.00
July	1950	Stan Musial	38.00
September	1950	Don Newcombe	20.00
October	1950	World Series Issue	18.00
November	1950	Harry Agganis	15.00
May	1951	Ruth, DiMaggio, Cobb	25.00
July	1951	Ewell Blackwell	16.00
August	1951	Yogi Berra	25.00
September	1951	Ted Williams	45.00
October	1951	Jackie Robinson	35.00
March	1952	Gil McDougald	15.00
April	1952	Chico Carrasquel	13.00
May	1952	Alvin Dark	15.00
June	1952	Ralph Kiner	22.00
July	1952	Stan Musial	32.00
August	1952	Yogi Berra and Allie Reynolds	20.00
September	1952	Mike Garcia	15.00
October	1952	Jackie Robinson and Pee Wee Reese	35.00
November	1952	Robinson, Reynolds, Agganis	18.00
February	1953	Bobby Shantz	15.00
May	1953	Bob Lemon	13.00
June	1953	Hank Sauer	15.00
July	1953	Ferris Fain	13.00
August	1953	Warren Spahn	13.00
September	1953	Robin Roberts	18.00
October	1953	Roy Campanella	27.00
November	1953	Phil Rizzuto	18.00
February	1954	Eddie Mathews	14.00
March	1954	Casey Stengel	25.00
April	1954	Don Newcombe	18.00
July	1954	Stan Musial	25.00
August	1954	Minnie Minoso	16.00
September	1954	Duke Snider	20.00
October	1954	Al Rosen	15.00
February	1955	Alvin Dark	15.00
April	1955	Bob Turley	15.00
May	1955	Bobby Thompson	11.00
June	1955	Johnny Antonelli	13.00
August	1955	Paul Richards	11.00
September	1955	Duke Snider	25.00
October	1955	Yogi Berra	25.00
February	1956	Mickey Mantle	15.00
March	1956	Walter Alston	17.00
April	1956	Larry Doby	14.00
May	1956	Bob Lemon	13.00
June	1956	Willie Mays	20.00
July	1956	Williams	30.00
August	1956	Vinegar Bend Mizell	10.00
September	1956	10th Anniversary Issue	20.00
March	1957	Mickey Mantle	25.00
April	1957	Eddie Mathews	16.00
May	1957	Spahn, Roberts, Campanella	16.00
June	1957	Early Wynn	15.00
July	1957	Al Kaline	18.00
August	1957	Joe Adcock	13.00
September	1957	Duke Snider	18.00
Ocotber	1957	Billy Pierce	13.00
January	1958	Mays, Snider, Reese Robinson	20.00
April	1958	Nellie Fox	16.00
May	1959	Yogi Berra	18.00
June	1958	Willie Mays	16.00
July	1958	Herb Score	14.00
August	1958	Billy Martin	12.00
September	1958	Eddie Mathews	15.00
October	1958	Bob Turley	13.00
December	1958	Willie Mays	14.00
February	1959	Lew Burdette	10.00
March	1959	Al Kaline	12.00
April	1959	Rocky Colavito	15.00
May	1959	Gil Hodges	12.00
June	1959	Mantle, Ted Williams	22.00
July	1959	Don Newcombe and Jimmy Piersall	11.00

Month	Year	Cover/Feature Article	Value
August	1959	Mantle, Mays, Colavito, Mathews	22.00
September	1959	Ted Williams, Musial	24.00
October	1959	Warren Spahn	14.00
March	1960	Willie Mays	12.00
April	1960	Duke Snider	13.00
May	1960	Killebrew, Willie McCovey	14.00
June	1960	Don Drysdale	14.00
July	1960	Frank Howard, Aparicio	10.00
August	1960	Mickey Mantle	21.00
October	1960	Ruth, Larry Sherry	15.00
November	1960	Roger Maris	14.00
February	1961	Danny Murtaugh	9.00
April	1961	Frank Howard	9.00
May	1961	Dick Groat	8.00
June	1961	Willie Mays	11.00
July	1961	Colavito, Cepeda	11.00
August	1961	Spahn, Ken Boyer	10.00
September	1961	Mantle, DiMaggio	25.00
October	1961	Wally Moon	9.00
February	1962	Roger Maris	15.00
April	1962	Norm Cash, Vada Pinson	11.00
July	1962	Mantle	18.00
August	1962	Colavito	11.00
September	1962	Musial, Ken Boyer	13.00
October	1962	Willie Mays	13.00
February	1963	Maury Wills	9.00
April	1963	Stan Musial	10.00
May	1963	Mantle, Berra	18.00
June	1963	Maury Wills	9.00
July	1963	Kaline, Colavito	10.00
August	1963	Mays	15.00
September	1963	Sandy Koufax	13.00
October	1963	Mantle	19.00
November	1963	Whitey Ford	13.00
February	1964	Sandy Koufax	13.00
May	1964	Spahn	10.00
June	1964	Dick Stuart	10.00
July	1964	Yastrzemski, Tommy Davis, Tom Tresh	10.00
August	1964	DiMaggio, Mays	18.00
September	1964	Mantle	15.00
October	1964	Mays	13.00
November	1964	Killebrew	11.00
February	1965	Fred Hutchinson	8.00
April	1965	Dean Chance	7.00
May	1965	Sandy Koufax	12.00
June	1965	Mays	13.00
September	1965	Gehrig, DiMaggio, Frank Robinson	15.00

Month	Year	Cover/Feature Article	Value
October	1965	Sandy Koufax, Maury Wills	12.00
February	1966	Koufax	11.00
April	1966	Mays	11.00
May	1966	Maury Wills	8.00
August	1966	Frank Robinson	10.00
September	1966	20th Anniversary Issue, Willie Mays	15.00
October	1966	Sandy Koufax	10.00
June	1967	Willie Mays	11.00
August	1967	Roberto Clemente	12.00
September	1967	Pete Rose	18.00
October	1967	Orlando Cepeda	9.00
February	1968	Yastrzemski	15.00
May	1968	Willie Mays	11.00
June	1968	Yastrzemski	12.00
July	1968	Henry Aaron	10.00
August	1968	Pete Rose	13.00
September	1968	Don Drysdale	10.00
June	1969	Ted Williams	15.00
August	1970	Henry Aaron	10.00
May	1971	Ted Williams, Curt Flood	12.00
July	1971	Carl Yastrzemski	10.00
September	1971	25th Anniversary Issue, Mays	10.00
October	1971	Vida Blue	7.00
June	1972	Brooks Robinson	8.00
August	1972	Tom Seaver	11.00
September	1972	Frank Robinson	8.00
August	1973	Bobby Murcer	7.00
October	1973	Pete Rose, Ferguson Jenkins	7.00
June	1974	Pete Rose	12.00
October	1974	Reggie Jackson	11.00
May	1975	Frank Robinson	7.00
July	1975	Bobby Bonds	6.00
August	1975	Billy Martin	8.00
April	1976	Steve Garvey	6.00
May	1976	Tom Seaver	9.00
August	1976	Joe Morgan/Rose	9.00
July	1977	Mark Fidrych	6.00
October	1977	Rod Carew	7.00
April	1978	Goose Gossage, Sparky Lyle	6.00
May	1978	Nettles	7.00
July	1978	Jim Rice	8.00
October	1978	Yastrzemski	10.00
April	1979	Pete Rose	10.00
May	1979	Ron Guidry	6.00
June	1979	Dave Parker	6.00
July	1979	Graig Nettles	6.00

Month	Year	Cover/Feature Article	Value	Month	Year	Cover/Feature Article	Value
August	1979	Rod Carew	7.00	June	1984	Dale Murphy	5.00
October	1979	Reggie Jackson	8.00	July	1984	Baseball managers	4.00
April	1980	Willie Stargell	6.00	February	1985	Doc Gooden	4.00
May	1980	George Brett	7.00	June	1985	George Brett	5.00
June	1980	Bill Russell	4.00	July	1985	Kirk Gibson	4.00
July	1980	Gorman Thomas	5.00	April	1986	Saberhagen	4.00
September	1980	T. John	6.00	May	1986	George Brett	5.00
May	1981	Billy Martin	6.00	July	1986	Rose, Jackson, Carter	3.00
June	1981	Don Sutton	4.00	March	1987	Schmidt, Clemens, Eric Davis	4.00
July	1981	Goose Gossage, Sutter	5.00				
April	1982	Valenzuela	5.00	April	1987	Strawberry	4.00
May	1982	Reggie Jackson	6.00	April	1988	Will Clark, Keith Hernandez	4.00
June	1982	Tom Seaver	6.00				
July	1982	Billy Martin	5.00	June	1988	McGuire, Stawberry	3.00
April	1983	Steve Garvey	4.00	March	1989	Orel Hershiser	3.00
May	1983	Steve Carlton	6.00	April	1989	Mattingly, Gibson, Eckersley, Hernandez	3.00
June	1983	Yount, Schmidt, Carter, Dawson	6.00	July	1989	Jose Canseco	3.00
July	1983	Reggie Jackson	6.00	October	1989	43rd Anniversary Issue, Doc Gooden	3.00
April	1984	C. Ripken	6.00				

The Sporting News

The *Sporting News* has been published weekly since 1886. Until the early 1960's the paper was devoted strictly to baseball. Today the *Sporting News* covers every aspect of American college and professional sport with an emphasis on major league baseball.

In 1964 "full cover" photographs began to appear. In 1969 the *Sporting News* went to color photographs on the front page.

To have collectible value an issue of the paper must have all its pages intact and be in a minimum of "very good" to "excellent" condition.

A complete year of the *Sporting News* in "very good" to "excellent" condition would be priced as follows for 52 issues.

Year	Value	Year	Value	Year	Value
1946	1,350.00	1956	950.00	1966	400.00
1947	1,350.00	1957	700.00	1967	400.00
1948	1,350.00	1958	600.00	1968	300.00
1949	1,150.00	1959	600.00	1969	300.00
1950	850.00	1960	500.00	1970	300.00
1951	950.00	1961	800.00	1971	225.00
1952	800.00	1962	600.00	1972	225.00
1953	900.00	1963	450.00	1973	225.00
1954	800.00	1964	500.00	1974	250.00
1955	900.00	1965	400.00	1975-1991	each year 200.00

Individual issues during the baseball season (April-October) have more value than "off season" editions (November-March) of the paper. The individual issues priced below are in a minimum of "very good" condition and are complete with no tears or cuttings.

Year	April-Oct.	Nov.-March	Year	April-Oct.	Nov.-March	Year	April-Oct.	Nov.-March
1946-1949	20.00	15.00	1963-1964	8.00	7.00	1971-1985	5.00	4.00
1950-1956	15.00	12.00	1965-1967	7.00	6.00	1985 to date	4.00	3.00
1957-1962	10.00	8.00	1968-1970	6.00	5.00			

Selected issues of the *Sporting News* have significantly more value than "common" issues. An issue that contains a story about an historic baseball event (Don Larsen's perfect game, Nolan Ryan's 300th victory) has more interest for collectors and is more expensive.

Among the most valuable individual issues of the *Sporting News* over the past 45 years are the following.

Date	Event	Value	Date	Event	Value
10-30-1946	The Sporting News 60 Year Anniversary Issue	250.00	4-13-1949	Joe DiMaggio/Ted Williams cover - Opening Day issue	100.00
4-23-1947	Babe Ruth's life story	250.00	4-25-1951	Mickey Mantle cover	150.00
6-23-1948	Babe Ruth on the cover	150.00	10-17-1956	Don Larsen's World Series perfect game	100.00
8-25-1948	Babe Ruth's death	400.00			

The April 22, 1953 issue of the Sporting News is worth about $15.00, a standard price for issues published between April and October of that year. The April 15, 1953 issue is worth $30.00 because it is an Opening Day edition. The April 29, 1953 issue is priced at $20.00 because it carries an article about Mickey Mantle's 565 foot home run in Washington against the Senators.

Collectors should give some thought to putting aside the World Series, All-Star game, and Opening Day issues of the *Sporting News* each year. In addition to containing important information about the event, the papers have more long term investment potential than the standard weekly edition.

Issue Date	Cover or Lead Feature	Value	Issue Date	Cover or Lead Feature	Value
1-31-1946	Ted Williams/Joe DiMaggio	100.00	8-7-1946	Dizzy Dean	25.00
2-7-1947	Mel Ott	20.00	8-28-1946	Feller's 98.6 mph fastball	30.00
2-21-1946	Hank Greenberg	20.00	9-11-1946	Jackie Robinson	30.00
3-7-1946	Bob Feller	25.00	9-18-1946	Ted Williams/Mickey Vernon	40.00
3-14-1946	Ted Williams	25.00	9-25-1946	Ted Williams/Stan Musial	60.00
4-18-1946	Peacetime baseball begins	40.00	10-9-1946	Frank Frisch resigns	75.00
5-9-1946	Joe Cronin/Joe McCarthy	25.00	10-16-1946	MacPhail/Gordon/DiMaggio	50.00
5-23-1946	Ted Williams	25.00	10-23-1946	Harry "The Cat" Brecheen	50.00
6-5-1946	Bill Dickey/Ted Lyons	25.00	10-30-1946	40 Year Anniversary Issue	250.00
6-12-1946	Babe Ruth	30.00	11-6-1946	Bob Feller	25.00
6-19-1946	Red Sox Tear League Apart	25.00	11-13-1946	Ted Williams MVP	20.00
7-10-1946	Bill Veeck	40.00	11-27-1946	Stan Musial MVP	20.00
7-17-1946	Ted Williams	30.00	12-18-1946	Walter Johnson dies	30.00

Issue Date	Cover or Lead Feature	Value
12-25-1946	Billy Evans	20.00
1-1-1947	Stan Musial/Man of the Year Issue	75.00
1-15-1947	Joe DiMaggio	40.00
1-29-1947	Bob Feller	20.00
2-12-1947	Stan Musial/Sam Breadon	20.00
2-26-1947	Spearker/Hornsby	20.00
4-2-1947	Hank Greenberg	25.00
4-9-1947	Yogi Berra/Joe Medwick	25.00
4-16-1947	Leo Durocher suspended for one year	40.00
4-23-1947	Babe Ruth	250.00
5-7-1947	Babe Ruth Day	50.00
5-21-1947	Johnny Mize	25.00
7-9-1947	P.K. Wrigley	40.00
7-16-1947	Larry Doby breaks "color line"	25.00
9-17-1947	Jackie Robinson	30.00
10-1-1947	Burt Shotton/Bucky Harris	75.00
10-8-1947	Joe McCarthy	50.00
10-15-1947	George Weiss	50.00
11-5-1947	Red Ruffing retires	20.00
12-3-1947	Joe DiMaggio MVP	25.00
12-31-1947	Ted Williams/Branch Rickey	75.00
1-7-1948	Roy Campanella	40.00
1-28-1948	Bob Feller/Bill Veeck	25.00
2-11-1948	Herb Pennock dies	20.00
3-24-1948	Babe Ruth	25.00
4-21-1948	1948 predictions	35.00
6-2-1948	Stan Musial	25.00
6-23-1948	Babe Ruth	25.00
7-14-1948	Roy Campanella	40.00
7-21-1948	All-Star Game	25.00
8-25-1948	Babe Ruth dies at 53	400.00
9-1-1948	Carl Erskine/Babe Ruth	30.00
10-6-1948	1914 Miracle Braves	60.00
10-13-1948	Sporting News All-Star Team	50.00
10-20-1948	George Weiss/Casey Stengel	50.00
12-1-1948	Lou Boudreau MVP	20.00
12-8-1948	Stan Musial MVP	20.00
12-29-1948	Boudreau/Veeck	40.00
1-5-1949	Pete Reiser	35.00
2-16-1949	Joe DiMaggio/Bob Feller	20.00
4-13-1949	DiMaggio/Ted Williams	100.00
7-6-1949	Joe DiMaggio returns	25.00
7-13-1949	Ebbets Field	40.00
7-20-1949	All-Star Game	25.00
7-27-1949	Casey Stengel	25.00
8-3-1949	Stan Musial	25.00
10-5-1949	Williams/Slaughter	60.00

Issue Date	Cover or Lead Feature	Value
10-12-1949	Casey Stengel	50.00
10-19-1949	Branch Rickey	50.00
11-23-1949	Jackie Robinson MVP	20.00
11-30-1949	Ted Williams MVP	30.00
12-28-1949	Williams/Stengel	50.00
1--4-1950	Day-by-day baseball highlights of the 1949 season	30.00
2-15-1950	Ty Cobb player of the half century	20.00
4-5-1950	Connie Mack	20.00
4-19-1950	Branch Rickey/Jackie Robinson	30.00
7-26-1950	Ruth vs. Cobb	20.00
9-13-1950	Gil Hodges four home run game	20.00
10-4-1950	Branch Rickey/Dodger stock sell out	40.00
10-11-1950	Whitey Ford	30.00
10-18-1950	Connie Mack retires	30.00
11-15-1950	Grover Cleveland Alexander retires	20.00
1-3-1951	Phil Rizzuto, Weiss, Rolfe Men of the Year (first time award given)	30.00
1-31-1951	Mickey Mantle	25.00
4-4-1951	Mickey Mantle	25.00
4-25-1951	Mickey Mantle	150.00
5-23-1951	Leo Durocher	25.00
7-11-1951	Cobb/Cochrane/Gehringer	30.00
8-15-1951	Willie Mays	25.00
9-5-1951	Casey Stengel	25.00
10-3-1951	Home Run Baker/World Series issue	40.00
10-10-1951	Musial/Feller/Roe/Fain	40.00
10-17-1951	Warren Giles	35.00
11-14-1951	Stan Musial/Ted Williams	20.00
12-26-1951	DiMaggio retires	25.00
1-2-1952	Musial/Durocher Men of the Year #2	50.00
4-16-1952	Opening Day issue	30.00
7-9-1952	All-Star issue	30.00
10-1-1952	World Series issue	40.00
10-8-1952	1952 Yankees and Dodgers	35.00
11-12-1952	Mantle's life story	25.99
12-31-1952	Roberts/Stanky/Weiss Men of the Year	25.00
1-7-1953	Day-by-day 1952 baseball report	30.00
4-15-1953	Play Ball - opening day issue	30.00

Issue Date	Cover or Lead Feature	Value
4-29-1953	Mantle's 565' home run	20.00
6-17-1953	Mickey Mantle	40.00
7-1-1953	Mantle & Mathews	50.00
7-15-1953	Charley Dressen/Casey Stengel	30.00
8-5-1953	Ted Williams	30.00
9-30-1953	1949-1953 Yankees	40.00
10-14-1953	Bill Veeck/World Series coverage	30.00
12-30-1953	Rosen/Stengel Men of the Year	35.00
1-6-1954	Day-by-day 1953 baseball report	25.00
4-14-1954	Baseball's back in Baltimore	30.00
5-12-1954	Stan Musial 5 home run day	30.00
7-14-1954	All-Star Game issue	30.00
9-15-1954	Willie Mays	30.00
9-29-1954	World Series issue	40.00
10-13-1954	Mays/Bobby Avila/World Series	30.00
1-5-1955	Mays/Durocher Men of the Year	40.00
4-13-1955	Opening Day issue	30.00
7-13-1955	All-Star Game issue	30.00
9-28-1955	World Series issue	50.00
10-12-1955	Johnny Podres/World Series	50.00
1-4-1956	Duke Snider/Walter Alston Men of the Year	40.00
3-21-1956	10 greatest players of 1946-1956 decade	30.00
3-28-1956	Stan Musial	30.00
4-18-1956	Opening Day issue	30.00
6-13-1956	Mickey Mantle	50.00
7-4-1956	Williams/Musial/DiMaggio	35.00
7-11-1956	Musial/All-Star Game	50.00
10-3-1956	Casey Stengel/World Series	40.00
10-10-1956	Mantle/Aaron/Newcombe	40.00
10-17-1956	Don Larsen's perfect game	100.00
11-14-1956	Mickey Mantle	25.00
1-2-1957	Mickey Mantle/Birdie Tebbets Men of the Year	50.00
1-23-1957	Mantle/George Weiss	30.00
2-20-1957	Ted Williams	
4-17-1957	Opening Day issue	25.00
5-15-1957	Ted Williams	25.00
7-10-1957	Musial/Williams	25.00
10-2-1957	World Series issue	35.00
10-16-1957	Dodgers to L.A.	30.00
1-1-1958	Williams/Hutchinson Men of the Year	40.00
4-16-1958	Opening Day issue	25.00
5-14-1958	Stan Musial 3000 hits	25.00
7-9-1958	All-time all-stars All-Star Game issue	25.00
8-27-1958	Ted Williams	25.00
10-1-1958	World Series issue	30.00
10-15-1958	Player-manager's success	25.00
12-31-1958	Men of the Year issue and day-by-day diary	35.00
4-8-1959	Opening Day issue	25.00
7-8-1959	All-Star game issue Ted Williams/Carl Hubbell	25.00
8-12-1959	Willie McCovey	20.00
9-30-1959	World Series issue/1919 Black Sox	30.00
10-14-1959	World Series summary	25.00
12-30-1959	Men of the Year issue/day-by-day diary of the season	30.00
4-13-1960	Opening Day issue	20.00
7-13-1960	All-Star Game issue	25.00
8-17-1960	Ted Williams/Player of the Decade	30.00
10-5-1960	1927 Yankees	25.00
1-4-1961	Men of the Year/Mazeroski and Murtaugh	25.00
3-29-1961	Mickey Mantle	25.00
4-12-1961	Opening Day issue	30.00
6-28-1961	Mantle/Maris	50.00
7-5-1961	300 game winners	20.00
7-12-1961	All-Star Game issue	30.00
8-2-1961	Red Sox immortals	25.00
9-6-1961	Mantle/Maris home run race	20.00
9-27-1961	Ruth/Mantle/Maris	25.00
10-4-1961	World Series issue	40.00
10-11-1961	Maris hits 61st home run	75.00
10-18-1961	World Series coverage	30.00
11-22-1961	Roger Maris MVP	25.00
1-3-1962	Maris/Houk Men of the Year issue	50.00
3-7-1962	New York Yankee history	20.00
4-11-1962	Opening Day issue	25.00
7-7-1962	All-Star Game issue	25.00
7-28-1962	Chicago All-Star Game issue	25.00
10-6-1962	World Series issue	25.00
12-29-1962	Don Drysdale/Maury Wills	25.00
4-13-1963	Opening Day issue	15.00
7-13-1963	All-Star Game issue	20.00
10-5-1963	World Series issue	20.00
10-12-1963	Musial's final game	20.00
12-14-1963	Koufax Player of the Year	20.00
7-11-1964	Willie Mays	20.00
10-10-1964	World Series issue	20.00

Issue Date	Cover or Lead Feature	Value
8-21-1965	Pete Rose	30.00
10-9-1965	World Series issue	20.00
4-15-1966	Opening Day issue	15.00
5-21-1966	Willie Mays	15.00
7-16-1966	All-Star Game issue	15.00
10-8-1966	World Series issue	15.00
4-15-1967	Opening Day issue	15.00
4-29-1967	Roger Maris (color)	25.00
7-15-1967	All-Star Game issue	15.00
10-14-1967	Carl Yastrzemski	20.00
10-7-1967	World Series issue	15.00
3-2-1968	Spring training issue	15.00
4-6-1968	Mantle and family	25.00
4-20-1968	Pete Rose (color)	25.00
10-12-1968	Roger Maris and family	20.00
4-5-1969	100 Years of Baseball	15.00
7-26-1969	Reggie Jackson	20.00
10-11-1969	Tom Seaver	15.00
5-23-1970	Hank Aaron	12.00
7-18-1970	Pete Rose	15.00
10-17-1970	World Series issue	15.00
10-24-1970	Johnny Bench	15.00
7-17-1970	All-Star Game issue	12.00
10-30-1970	Roberto Clemente	15.00
10-28-1970	Johnny Bench	15.00
4-14-1970	Steve Carlton	10.00
10-6-1973	Willie Mays	10.00
10-20-1973	World Series issue	10.00
4-6-1974	Opening Day issue	10.00
4-20-1974	Aaron/Ruth	15.00
8-17-1974	Reggie Jackson	10.00
10-19-1974	World Series issue	10.00
4-12-1975	Opening Day issue	10.00
7-19-1975	Mays/Musial/Ruth/Williams	10.00
10-18-1975	Stengel dies	10.00
4-10-1976	Opening Day issue	10.00
7-17-1976	All-Star game preview	10.00
4-9-1977	Opening Day issue	10.00
10-23-1977	World Series issue	10.00
7-15-1978	All-Star issue	10.00
10-21-1978	World Series issue	10.00

The *Sporting News* Baseball Guides

Year	Value
1942	175.00
1943	60.00
1944	45.00
1945	42.00
1946	42.00
1947	42.00
1948	60.00
1949	60.00
1950	60.00
1951	60.00
1952	60.00
1953	55.00
1954	55.00
1955	55.00
1956	55.00
1957	60.00
1958	50.00
1959	45.00
1960	40.00
1961	40.00
1962	40.00
1963	38.00
1964	38.00
1965	35.00
1966	35.00
1967	35.00
1968	35.00
1969	30.00
1970	27.00
1971	25.00
1972	22.00
1973	20.00
1974	20.00
1975	20.00
1976	18.00
1977	15.00
1978	15.00
1979	11.00
1980	11.00
1981	11.00
1982	11.00
1983	11.00
1984	11.00
1985	11.00
1986	10.00
1987	10.00

The *Sporting News* Baseball Registers

Value	Year	Value	Year	Year	Value	Year	Value
1940	100.00	1953	35.00	1965	25.00	1977	18.00
1941	45.00	1954	30.00	1966	25.00	1978	17.00
1942	45.00	1955	30.00	1967	25.00	1979	17.00
1943	40.00	1956	30.00	1968	22.00	1980	17.00
1944	40.00	1957	30.00	1969	22.00	1981	17.00
1945	40.00	1958	30.00	1970	22.00	1982	17.00
1946	40.00	1959	30.00	1971	23.00	1983	16.00
1947	45.00	1960	27.00	1972	20.00	1984	16.00
1948	35.00	1961	27.00	1973	20.00	1985	16.00
1949	40.00	1962	27.00	1974	20.00	1986	14.00
1950	40.00	1963	25.00	1975	18.00	1987	14.00
1951	35.00	1964	25.00	1976	18.00	1988	10.00
1952	35.00						

The *Sporting News* Dope Books

The first issue in 1942 was primarily a record book. It was not issued again until 1948 and continued until 1985.

Year	Value	Year	Value	Year	Value	Year	Value
1942	35.00	1957	28.00	1967	16.00	1977	8.00
1948	30.00	1958	35.00	1968	16.00	1978	7.00
1949	30.00	1959	25.00	1969	16.00	1979	6.00
1950	30.00	1960	25.00	1970	15.00	1980	6.00
1951	30.00	1961	20.00	1971	12.00	1981	6.00
1952	30.00	1962	20.00	1972	11.00	1982	8.00
1953	30.00	1963	18.00	1973	11.00	1983	8.00
1954	28.00	1964	16.00	1974	9.00	1984	7.00
1955	28.00	1965	16.00	1975	8.00	1985	7.00
1956	28.00	1966	16.00	1976	8.00		

Baseball Magazine

Copies of *Baseball Magazine* in a minimum of excellent condition should have the front and back covers intact without creases, discoloration or tears. Inside pages should be complete and free from damage or pencil markings.

It is not unusual to find a copy of the magazine with the back cover removed because the inside back cover often carried a portrait of a contemporary player that was ideal for display on a bedroom wall or in a scrapbook.

Before 1920	45.00-55.00 per issue	1940's	10.00-12.00 per issue
1920's	25.00-35.00 per issue	1950's	10.00-15.00 per issue
1930's	20.00-30.00 per issue	1960's	6.00-10.00 per issue

As is the case with any baseball related periodical, an issue with Cobb, Ruth, DiMaggio, Mantle, or Gehrig on the cover or specifically devoted to an All Star Game or World Series will have a considerably higher value than a "common" issue.

Issue Date	Cover or Article	Condition	Value
September 1915	Federal League stories	very good/excellent	50.00
November 1915	World Series issue	excellent	75.00
November 1919	Reds/Black Sox World Series	excellent	150.00
November 1920	World Series articles	good/very good	55.00
November 1921	World Series articles	excellent	50.00
February 1922	Frank Frisch cover	very good/excellent	50.00
March 1922	Harry Heilmann cover	excellent/mint	55.00
November 1922	World Series issue	excellent	30.00
February 1923	Christy Mathewson article	very good/excellent	25.00
August 1923	Ken Williams cover	excellent/mint	20.00
May 1923	Yankee Stadium cover	excellent	65.00
November 1923	World Series issue	excellent/mint	75.00
January 1924	Edd Roush cover	excellent/mint	25.00
March 1924	Eddie Collins cover	excellent	30.00
April 1924	Polo Grounds cover	very good	100.00
August 1924	Grover Cleveland Alexander cover	near excellent	75.00
October 1924	Max Carey cover	good/very good	50.00
January 1925	Dazzy Vance cover	very good/excellent	20.00
March 1925	Rogers Hornsby cover	excellent	35.00
November 1925	World Series issues	excellent/mint	50.00
January 1927	Ty Cobb retirement story and cover	excellent	175.00
April 1928	Paul Waner cover	excellent	25.00
August 1929	Mickey Cochrane cover	excellent	20.00
July 1930	Grover Cleveland Alexander cover	excellent	25.00
November 1930	World Series issue	excellent	25.00
June 1936	Roger Cramer cover	excellent/mint	25.00
June 1937	Burleigh Grimes cover	excellent/mint	25.00
May 1938	Joe DiMaggio cover	excellent/mint	60.00
October 1938	World Series cover	excellent/mint	20.00
August 1939	Lou Gehrig cover	excellent/mint	85.00
January 1943	Pee Wee Reese cover	excellent/mint	15.00
July 1944	Jimmie Foxx cover	excellent/mint	20.00

Who's Who in Baseball by *Baseball Magazine*

(Red Cover)

Year	Value	Year	Value	Year	Value	Year	Value
1926	75.00	1946	32.00	1960	19.00	1974	12.00
1928	75.00	1947	32.00	1961	19.00	1975	12.00
1932	49.00	1948	32.00	1962	19.00	1976	12.00
1934	49.00	1949	32.00	1963	19.00	1977	12.00
1936	45.00	1950	25.00	1964	19.00	1978	12.00
1937	45.00	1951	25.00	1965	19.00	1979	12.00
1938	45.00	1952	25.00	1966	19.00	1980	8.00
1939	45.00	1953	25.00	1967	19.00	1981	8.00
1940	32.00	1954	25.00	1968	19.00	1982	8.00
1941	32.00	1955	25.00	1969	19.00	1983	8.00
1942	32.00	1956	25.00	1970	12.00	1984	8.00
1943	32.00	1957	25.00	1971	12.00	1985	8.00
1944	32.00	1958	25.00	1972	12.00	1986	8.00
1945	32.00	1959	25.00	1973	12.00		

Sports Illustrated

Ist Cover denotes the initial time a player appeared on the cover of *SI.*

* denotes baseball card insert

Issue date	Cover or Feature	Value
8-16-1954*	Eddie Mathews (first issue)	250.00
1-3-1955	Johnny Podres	20.00
4-11-1955*	Mays, Day, Durocher	125.00
4-18-1955	Al Rosen	50.00
5-30-1955	Herb Score	10.00
6-27-1955	Duke Snider	25.00
7-11-1955	Yogi Berra	25.00
8-1-1955	Ted Williams	45.00
8-22-1955	Don Newcombe	15.00
9-26-1955	Walter Alston	20.00
3-5-1956	St. Louis Cardinals	25.00
4-9-1956	Baseball Preview Issue	25.00
4-23-1956	Billy Martin	20.00
5-14-1956	Kaline, Kuenn	25.00
6-18-1956	Mickey Mantle (Ist Cover)	40.00
7-16-1956	Kluszewski, Post, Bell	25.00
7-30-1956	Joe Adcock	12.00
9-10-1956	Whitey Ford	25.00
10-1-1956	Mantle	35.00
3-4-1957	Mantle	35.00
4-15-1957	Baseball Preview issue	15.00
4-22-1957	Wally Moon	13.00
5-13-1957	Billy Pierce	12.00
5-20-1957	Gussie Busch	6.00
7-8-1957	Musial, Williams All-Star Game preview	35.00
9-2-1957	Roy McMillan	9.00
9-30-1957	World Series report	15.00
12-23-1957	Musial Sportsman of the Year	25.00
3-3-1958	Spring Training	8.00
3-17-1958	Sal Maglie	12.00
3-31-1958	Roy Sievers	12.00
4-14-1958	Special Baseball issue	18.00
4-21-1958	Del Crandall	10.00
5-5-1958	Gil McDougald	12.00
5-19-1958	Richie Ashburn	15.00
6-2-1958	Ed Mathews	15.00
6-23-1958	Jackie Jensen	12.00
7-7-1958	All-Star Game	15.00
7-28-1958	Frank Thomas	10.00
9-29-1958	World Series	15.00
4-13-1959	Willie Mays	25.00

Issue date	Cover or Feature	Value	Issue date	Cover or Feature	Value
5-4-1959	Bob Turley	12.00	8-23-1965	Tony Oliva	9.00
8-10-1959	Fox, Aparicio, White Sox	25.00	10-4-1965	World Series	15.00
9-28-1959	Chicago White Sox	23.00	12-20-1965	Sandy Koufax	15.00
3-7-1960	Spring Training	10.00	4-18-1966	Dick Groat	15.00
4-11-1960	Baseball issue	14.00	6-6-1966	Joe Morgan and Sonny Jackson	9.00
6-6-1960	Red Schoendienst	13.00	7-11-1966	Andy Etchebarren	6.00
8-8-1960	Dick Groat	8.00	9-5-1966	Harry Walker	6.00
10-10-1960	Vernon Law	8.00	9-26-1966	Gaylord Perry	10.00
3-6-1961	Spring Training	10.00	10-10-1966	B. and F. Robinson	15.00
4-11-1961	Baseball issue	10.00	3-13-1967	Jim Nash	6.00
5-15-1961	Cookie Lavagetto	7.00	4-17-1967	Maury Wills	8.00
6-26-1961	Ernie Broglio, Mays	10.00	5-8-1967	Mantle	25.00
7-31-1961	Stop-action Baseball	7.00	5-15-1967	Buzzie Bavasi	10.00
10-2-1961	Roger Maris	25.00	6-5-1967	Al Kaline	15.00
10-9-1961	Joey Jay	7.00	7-3-1967	Roberto Clemente	9.00
3-5-1962	Casey Stengel	18.00	7-31-1967	The Spitball	5.00
4-9-1961	Frank Lary	7.00	8-21-1967	Carl Yastrzemski (1st Cover)	20.00
4-30-1962	Louie Aparicio	11.00	9-4-1967	Tim McCarver	8.00
6-4-1962	Willie Mays	14.00	12-25-1967	Yastrzemski	18.00
7-2-1962	Mickey Mantle	20.00	3-11-1968	Best Rookies	20.00
7-30-1962	Ken Boyer	8.00	4-15-1968	Baseball issue	12.00
8-20-1962	Don Drysdale	10.00	5-6-1968	Ron Swoboda	8.00
10-1-1962	World Series issue	15.00	5-27-1968	Pete Rose (1st Cover)	25.00
3-4-1963	Sandy Koufax (1st Cover)	14.00	7-8-1968	Ted Williams	10.00
4-8-1963	Baseball issue	12.00	7-29-1968	Denny McClain	9.00
4-29-1963	Art Mahaffey	5.00	8-19-1968	Curt Flood	8.00
6-24-1963	Roy Face	7.00	9-23-1968	Denny McClain	15.00
7-22-1963	Dick Groat	8.00	10-7-1968	St. Louis Cardinals	12.00
9-2-1963	Ron Fairly	6.00	3-17-1969	Ted Williams	15.00
9-30-1963	Whitey Ford	15.00	4-14-1969	Bill Freehan	10.00
3-2-1964	Stengel and Berra	12.00	7-7-1969	Reggie Jackson (1st Cover)	20.00
4-13-1964	Sandy Koufax	12.00	10-20-1969	World Series	10.00
5-11-1964	Al Kaline	15.00	12-22-1969	Tom Seaver (1st Cover)	18.00
5-25-1964	Frank Howard	7.00	2-23-1970	Denny McClain	9.00
7-6-1964	Alvin Dark	7.00	5-25-1970	Hank Aaron	8.00
8-10-1964	Johnny Callison	8.00	7-27-1970	Willie Mays	15.00
8-31-1964	Brooks Robinson	11.00	9-28-1970	Murtaugh, Hodges, and Durocher	12.00
3-1-1965	Bunning and Belinsky	9.00	10-19-1970	World Series	15.00
4-19-1965	Baseball Preview	15.00			
5-17-1965	Bill Veeck	10.00			
6-21-1965	Mickey Mantle	20.00			
7-12-1965	Maury Wills	10.00			

The vast majority of copies of *Sports Illustrated* from the 1970's are priced at $4.00-7.00. Covers featuring Nolan Ryan or Pete Rose are usually priced at $10.00-15.00.

Issues from the 1980's typically are priced in the $4.00-5.00 range with few exceptions.

Media Guides

Major league baseball teams issue annual guides for the print and electronic media, season ticket holders, and fans. The guides are typically available only from the teams and are not offered on newstands. The guides are filled with a myriad of statistical data, rosters, minor league player information, and team minutia.

Media guides are tailored for the serious baseball fan. Yearbooks are designed to meet the needs of the casual fan.

A's

1968	60.00
1969	27.00
1970	20.00
1971	20.00
1972	20.00
1973	20.00
1974	20.00
1975	13.00
1976	13.00
1977	13.00
1978	13.00
1979	13.00
1980	6.00
1981	6.00
1982	6.00
1983	6.00
1984	6.00
1986	6.00

Angels

1964	25.00
1965	23.00
1967	20.00
1968	20.00
1969	20.00
1970	13.00
1971	13.00
1972	13.00
1973	13.00
1974	13.00
1975	13.00
1976	13.00
1977	13.00
1978	13.00
1979	13.00
1980	6.00
1981	6.00
1982	6.00
1983	6.00
1984	6.00
1985	6.00

Astros

1962	150.00
1963	40.00
1965	22.00
1967	22.00
1968	23.00
1969	18.00
1970	13.00
1971	13.00
1973	13.00
1974	13.00
1975	13.00
1976	13.00
1977	13.00
1978	13.00
1979	13.00
1980	6.00
1981	6.00
1982	6.00
1983	6.00
1984	6.00
1985	6.00
1986	6.00

Blue Jays

1977	22.00
1978	13.00
1979	10.00
1980	6.00
1981	6.00
1982	6.00
1983	6.00
1984	6.00
1985	6.00
1986	6.00

Braves

1960	24.00
1961	20.00
1963	20.00
1964	27.00
1966	40.00
1967	25.00
1969	20.00
1970	18.00
1971	13.00
1972	13.00
1973	13.00
1975	13.00
1976	13.00
1977	13.00
1978	9.00
1979	8.00
1980	6.00
1981	6.00
1982	6.00
1983	6.00
1984	6.00
1985	6.00
1986	6.00

Brewers

1971 ....25.00	1975 ....8.00	1979 ....6.00	1983 ....6.00
1972 ....13.00	1976 ....7.00	1980 ....6.00	1984 ....6.00
1973 ....13.00	1977 ....7.00	1981 ....6.00	1985 ....6.00
1974 ....13.00	1978 ....6.00	1982 ....8.00	1986 ....6.00

Cardinals

1948 ....45.00	1961 ....27.00	1971 ....13.00	1979 ....7.00
1954 ....35.00	1962 ....30.00	1972 ....13.00	1980 ....6.00
1955 ....30.00	1963 ....22.00	1973 ....12.00	1981 ....6.00
1956 ....30.00	1964 ....25.00	1974 ....10.00	1982 ....6.00
1957 ....30.00	1965 ....20.00	1975 ....10.00	1983 ....6.00
1958 ....30.00	1966 ....25.00	1976 ....8.00	1984 ....6.00
1959 ....40.00	1969 ....27.00	1977 ....8.00	1985 ....6.00
1960 ....27.00	1970 ....13.00	1978 ....8.00	1986 ....6.00

Cubs

1958 ....30.00	1967 ....20.00	1974 ....8.00	1981 ....6.00
1959 ....30.00	1968 ....15.00	1975 ....8.00	1982 ....6.00
1960 ....28.00	1969 ....27.00	1976 ....8.00	1983 ....6.00
1961 ....25.00	1970 ....13.00	1977 ....8.00	1984 ....6.00
1964 ....20.00	1971 ....13.00	1978 ....8.00	1985 ....6.00
1965 ....20.00	1972 ....13.00	1979 ....8.00	1986 ....6.00
1966 ....20.00	1973 ....13.00	1980 ....7.00	1987 ....4.00

Dodgers

1958 ....45.00	1966 ....22.00	1973 ....13.00	1980 ....6.00
1959 ....25.00	1967 ....20.00	1974 ....13.00	1981 ....6.00
1960 ....20.00	1968 ....20.00	1975 ....8.00	1982 ....6.00
1961 ....20.00	1969 ....20.00	1976 ....7.00	1983 ....6.00
1962 ....20.00	1970 ....13.00	1977 ....9.00	1984 ....6.00
1963 ....27.00	1971 ....13.00	1978 ....11.00	1985 ....6.00
1964 ....20.00	1972 ....10.00	1979 ....6.00	1986 ....6.00
1965 ....20.00			

Expos

1969 ....45.00	1974 ....12.00	1978 ....11.00	1982 ....6.00
1970 ....15.00	1975 ....9.00	1979 ....6.00	1983 ....6.00
1971 ....19.00	1976 ....8.00	1980 ....6.00	1984 ....6.00
1972 ....13.00	1977 ....7.00	1981 ....6.00	1985 ....6.00
1973 ....13.00			

Giants

1958 .... 45.00
1959 .... 30.00
1961 .... 22.00
1963 .... 22.00
1964 .... 22.00
1965 .... 22.00
1966 .... 22.00
1967 .... 20.00
1968 .... 20.00
1970 .... 20.00
1971 .... 13.00
1972 .... 13.00
1973 .... 13.00
1974 .... 13.00
1975 .... 13.00
1976 .... 13.00
1977 .... 13.00
1978 .... 13.00
1979 .... 13.00
1980 .... 6.00
1981 .... 6.00
1982 .... 6.00
1983 .... 6.00
1984 .... 6.00
1985 .... 6.00
1986 .... 6.00

Indians

1950 .... 40.00
1952 .... 40.00
1953 .... 40.00
1954 .... 40.00
1955 .... 20.00
1956 .... 20.00
1960 .... 27.00
1961 .... 20.00
1963 .... 20.00
1964 .... 20.00
1965 .... 20.00
1966 .... 20.00
1968 .... 20.00
1969 .... 20.00
1970 .... 13.00
1971 .... 13.00
1972 .... 10.00
1973 .... 10.00
1974 .... 10.00
1975 .... 10.00
1976 .... 10.00
1977 .... 10.00
1978 .... 10.00
1979 .... 10.00
1980 .... 6.00
1981 .... 6.00
1982 .... 6.00
1983 .... 6.00
1984 .... 6.00
1985 .... 6.00

K.C. A's

1956 .... 45.00
1957 .... 45.00
1960 .... 27.00
1962 .... 27.00
1964 .... 27.00
1965 .... 40.00
1966 .... 40.00
1967 .... 35.00

Mariners

1977 .... 20.00
1978 .... 12.00
1979 .... 12.00
1980 .... 6.00
1981 .... 6.00
1982 .... 6.00
1983 .... 6.00
1984 .... 6.00
1985 .... 6.00
1986 .... 6.00

Mets

1964 .... 50.00
1965 .... 45.00
1966 .... 45.00
1972 .... 20.00
1973 .... 13.00
1974 .... 13.00
1975 .... 13.00
1976 .... 13.00
1977 .... 13.00
1978 .... 13.00
1979 .... 13.00
1980 .... 6.00
1981 .... 6.00
1982 .... 6.00
1983 .... 6.00
1984 .... 6.00
1985 .... 6.00
1986 .... 6.00

Orioles

1954 .... 50.00
1955 .... 30.00
1958 .... 30.00
1959 .... 28.00
1960 .... 25.00
1964 .... 20.00
1965 .... 20.00
1966 .... 18.00
1967 .... 25.00
1968 .... 25.00
1969 .... 20.00
1970 .... 13.00
1972 .... 13.00
1973 .... 10.00
1974 .... 8.00
1975 .... 8.00
1976 .... 8.00
1977 .... 8.00
1978 .... 8.00
1979 .... 8.00
1980 .... 6.00
1981 .... 6.00
1982 .... 6.00
1983 .... 6.00
1984 .... 6.00
1985 .... 6.00

Padres

1969 ....40.00
1970 ....20.00
1971 ....9.00
1972 ....9.00
1973 ....8.00
1974 ....8.00
1975 ....7.00
1976 ....6.00
1977 ....6.00
1978 ....6.00
1979 ....6.00
1980 ....6.00
1981 ....6.00
1982 ....6.00
1983 ....6.00
1984 ....6.00
1985 ....6.00
1986 ....6.00

Phillies

1965 ....65.00
1966 ....25.00
1973 ....13.00
1974 ....11.00
1975 ....13.00
1976 ....13.00
1977 ....13.00
1978 ....13.00
1979 ....8.00
1980 ....12.00
1981 ....6.00
1982 ....6.00
1983 ....6.00
1984 ....6.00
1985 ....6.00
1986 ....6.00
1987 ....6.00

Seattle Pilots

1969 ....125.00
1970 ....115.00

Pirates

1964 ....30.00
1965 ....25.00
1966 ....25.00
1967 ....25.00
1968 ....15.00
1969 ....15.00
1970 ....20.00
1971 ....20.00
1972 ....13.00
1973 ....35.00
1974 ....13.00
1975 ....13.00
1976 ....13.00
1977 ....6.00
1978 ....6.00
1979 ....13.00
1980 ....6.00
1981 ....6.00
1982 ....6.00
1983 ....6.00
1984 ....6.00
1985 ....6.00
1986 ....6.00

Rangers

1972 ....25.00
1973 ....15.00
1974 ....15.00
1975 ....8.00
1976 ....8.00
1977 ....8.00
1978 ....7.00
1979 ....7.00
1980 ....6.00
1981 ....6.00
1982 ....6.00
1983 ....6.00
1984 ....6.00
1986 ....6.00
1987 ....3.00
1988 ....3.00

Red Sox

1956 ....35.00
1957 ....35.00
1958 ....35.00
1959 ....30.00
1960 ....25.00
1962 ....20.00
1963 ....20.00
1965 ....20.00
1966 ....20.00
1967 ....33.00
1968 ....20.00
1969 ....20.00
1970 ....13.00
1971 ....13.00
1972 ....13.00
1973 ....9.00
1974 ....9.00
1975 ....16.00
1976 ....8.00
1977 ....7.00
1978 ....7.00
1979 ....7.00
1980 ....6.00
1981 ....6.00
1982 ....6.00
1983 ....6.00
1984 ....6.00
1985 ....6.00
1986 ....8.00

Reds

1968 ....15.00
1969 ....15.00
1970 ....18.00
1971 ....12.00
1972 ....13.00
1973 ....13.00
1974 ....13.00
1975 ....18.00
1976 ....18.00
1977 ....8.00
1978 ....8.00
1979 ....9.00
1980 ....6.00
1981 ....6.00
1982 ....6.00
1983 ....6.00
1984 ....6.00
1985 ....6.00
1986 ....6.00

Royals

1969 ....25.00
1970 ....20.00
1971 ....13.00
1972 ....13.00
1973 ....13.00
1974 ....13.00
1975 ....13.00
1976 ....13.00
1977 ....13.00
1978 ....13.00
1979 ....13.00
1980 ....6.00
1981 ....6.00
1982 ....6.00
1983 ....6.00
1984 ....6.00
1985 ....6.00
1986 ....6.00

Tigers

1960 ....27.00
1961 ....25.00
1962 ....25.00
1963 ....23.00
1965 ....27.00
1966 ....27.00
1967 ....27.00
1968 ....55.00
1969 ....20.00
1970 ....13.00
1972 ....13.00
1973 ....13.00
1974 ....13.00
1975 ....13.00
1976 ....13.00
1977 ....13.00
1978 ....13.00
1979 ....13.00
1980 ....6.00
1981 ....6.00
1982 ....6.00
1983 ....6.00
1984 ....6.00
1986 ....6.00

Twins

1961 ....40.00
1962 ....35.00
1963 ....25.00
1964 ....25.00
1965 ....25.00
1966 ....20.00
1967 ....20.00
1968 ....20.00
1969 ....20.00
1970 ....30.00
1971 ....20.00
1972 ....10.00
1973 ....10.00
1974 ....8.00
1975 ....8.00
1976 ....8.00
1977 ....8.00
1979 ....6.00
1980 ....6.00
1981 ....6.00
1982 ....6.00
1983 ....6.00
1984 ....6.00
1985 ....6.00
1986 ....6.00
1987 ....3.00
1988 ....3.00

White Sox

1957 ....30.00
1958 ....30.00
1959 ....40.00
1960 ....20.00
1961 ....20.00
1962 ....20.00
1963 ....20.00
1965 ....20.00
1966 ....20.00
1967 ....18.00
1968 ....18.00
1969 ....15.00
1970 ....13.00
1971 ....13.00
1972 ....13.00
1973 ....8.00
1974 ....8.00
1975 ....8.00
1976 ....6.00
1977 ....6.00
1978 ....6.00
1979 ....6.00
1980 ....6.00
1981 ....6.00
1982 ....5.00
1983 ....7.00
1984 ....3.00
1985 ....4.00
1986 ....3.00

Yankees

1960 .... 40.00
1961 .... 75.00
1962 .... 40.00
1963 .... 35.00
1964 .... 35.00
1965 .... 30.00
1966 .... 30.00
1967 .... 20.00
1968 .... 20.00
1969 .... 25.00
1970 .... 18.00
1971 .... 13.00
1972 .... 13.00
1973 .... 13.00
1974 .... 10.00
1975 .... 12.00
1976 .... 12.00
1977 .... 13.00
1978 .... 20.00
1979 .... 13.00
1980 .... 10.00
1981 .... 7.00
1982 .... 7.00
1983 .... 7.00
1984 .... 7.00
1985 .... 7.00
1986 .... 7.00
1987 .... 7.00

Baseball Yearbooks

Astros

1965 .... 100.00
1982 .... 15.00

Atlanta Braves

1966 .... 50.00
1967 .... 30.00
1968 .... 20.00
1969 .... 25.00
1970 .... 20.00
1971 .... 18.00
1972 .... 15.00
1974 .... 13.00
1975 .... 15.00
1976 .... 15.00
1979 .... 15.00
1982 .... 18.00
1983 .... 8.00
1987 .... 8.00
1988 .... 8.00

Blue Jays

1977 .... 40.00
1979 .... 15.00
1984 .... 10.00

Boston Braves

1946 .... 350.00
1947 .... 200.00
1950 .... 150.00
1951 .... 150.00
1952 .... 150.00

Brewers

1970 .... 60.00
1979 .... 12.00
1978 .... 12.00
1980 .... 12.00
1981 .... 12.00
1983 .... 12.00
1984 .... 12.00
1985 .... 8.00
1988 .... 7.00

Brooklyn Dodgers

1949 .... 350.00
1950 .... 200.00
1951 .... 200.00
1952 .... 200.00
1953 .... 200.00
1954 .... 135.00
1955 .... 175.00
1956 .... 135.00
1957 .... 135.00

California Angels
Los Angeles Angels (1961-65)

1962 .... 85.00
1963 .... 50.00
1964 .... 30.00
1965 .... 30.00
1966 .... 30.00
1967 .... 35.00
1983 .... 10.00
1984 .... 10.00
1985 .... 10.00

Cardinals

1951 .... 200.00
1953 .... 140.00
1955 .... 85.00
1957 .... 80.00
1958 .... 70.00
1959 .... 100.00
1960 .... 60.00
1961 .... 50.00
1962 .... 55.00
1963 .... 50.00
1964 .... 40.00
1965 .... 45.00
1966 .... 55.00
1968 .... 30.00
1969 .... 35.00
1970 .... 20.00
1971 .... 25.00
1972 .... 20.00
1973 .... 18.00
1974 .... 20.00
1975 .... 18.00
1977 .... 18.00

(Houston) Colt 45's

1962 .... 175.00
1964 .... 125.00

Cubs

1948 .... 125.00
1949 .... 100.00
1950 .... 85.00
1952 .... 80.00
1954 .... 70.00
1955 .... 70.00
1956 .... 65.00
1957 .... 75.00

Expos

1969 .... 40.00
1970 .... 25.00
1971 .... 20.00
1972 .... 25.00

Indians

1949 .... 130.00
1950 .... 115.00
1951 .... 100.00
1952 .... 90.00
1953 .... 90.00
1954 .... 120.00
1955 .... 75.00
1956 .... 75.00
1958 .... 125.00
1959 .... 75.00
1960 .... 75.00
1962 .... 55.00
1963 .... 75.00
1964 .... 75.00
1965 .... 65.00
1966 .... 65.00
1968 .... 30.00
1969 .... 30.00
1970 .... 25.00
1971 .... 25.00
1972 .... 25.00
1978 .... 10.00
1984 .... 6.00

KC Athletics

1955 .... 195.00
1956 .... 125.00
1957 .... 100.00
1958 .... 95.00
1959 .... 125.00
1962 .... 175.00
1963 .... 75.00
1964 .... 40.00
1965 .... 40.00
1966 .... 65.00
1967 .... 40.00

L.A. Dodgers

1958 .... 150.00
1959 .... 100.00
1960 .... 50.00
1961 .... 35.00
1962 .... 35.00
1963 .... 55.00
1964 .... 30.00
1965 .... 50.00
1966 .... 35.00
1967 .... 25.00
1968 .... 25.00
1969 .... 25.00
1970 .... 20.00
1971 .... 15.00
1972 .... 15.00
1973 .... 35.00
1974 .... 25.00
1975 .... 12.00
1976 .... 12.00
1977 .... 20.00
1978 .... 18.00
1979 .... 12.00
1980 .... 10.00
1981 .... 15.00
1982 .... 10.00
1983 .... 12.00
1984 .... 10.00
1985 .... 10.00
1988 .... 8.00

Mariners

1985 .... 12.00

Mets

1962 .... 325.00
1963 .... 125.00
1964 .... 70.00
1965 .... 60.00
1966 .... 60.00
1967 .... 60.00
1968 .... 50.00
1969 .... 135.00
1970 .... 45.00
1971 .... 40.00
1972 .... 25.00
1973 .... 30.00
1974 .... 25.00
1975 .... 20.00
1976 .... 15.00
1977 .... 15.00
1978 .... 15.00
1979 .... 20.00
1980 .... 35.00
1981 .... 15.00
1982 .... 13.00
1983 .... 11.00
1984 .... 9.00
1985 .... 10.00
1986 .... 12.00
1987 .... 8.00

Milwaukee Braves

1953 .... 175.00
1954 .... 100.00
1955 .... 75.00
1956 .... 55.00
1957 .... 100.00
1958 .... 85.00
1959 .... 55.00
1960 .... 60.00
1961 .... 45.00
1962 .... 35.00
1963 .... 30.00
1964 .... 30.00
1965 .... 65.00

N.Y. Giants

1947 .... 200.00
1951 .... 100.00
1952 .... 100.00
1953 .... 75.00
1954 .... 125.00
1955 .... 65.00
1956 .... 70.00
1957 .... 85.00

Oakland A's

1968 .... 100.00
1969 .... 60.00
1970 .... 40.00
1971 .... 35.00
1972 .... 25.00
1973 .... 25.00
1974 .... 20.00
1975 .... 20.00
1976 .... 15.00
1977 .... 15.00
1978 .... 18.00
1979 .... 18.00
1980 .... 15.00
1982 .... 15.00
1983 .... 15.00

Orioles

1954 .... 250.00
1955 .... 150.00
1956 .... 125.00
1957 .... 100.00
1958 .... 80.00
1959 .... 70.00
1960 .... 100.00
1961 .... 75.00
1962 .... 75.00
1963 .... 50.00
1964 .... 75.00
1966 .... 50.00
1968 .... 40.00
1969 .... 30.00
1970 .... 50.00
1971 .... 25.00
1972 .... 20.00
1973 .... 20.00
1974 .... 18.00
1980 .... 12.00
1981 .... 10.00
1983 .... 8.00
1984 .... 8.00
1985 .... 8.00
1986 .... 8.00

Padres

1969 .... 75.00
1979 .... 15.00
1980 .... 10.00
1982 .... 8.00
1983 .... 8.00
1984 .... 15.00
1985 .... 8.00
1986 .... 8.00

Philadelphia A's

1949 .... 135.00
1950 .... 135.00
1951 .... 100.00
1952 .... 85.00
1953 .... 55.00
1954 .... 100.00

Phillies

1949 .... 200.00
1950 .... 150.00
1951 .... 575.00
1952 .... 125.00
1953 .... 65.00
1955 .... 100.00
1956 .... 125.00
1957 .... 100.00
1958 .... 100.00
1959 .... 95.00
1960 .... 85.00
1962 .... 75.00
1963 .... 75.00
1965 .... 75.00
1966 .... 45.00
1967 .... 45.00
1968 .... 45.00
1969 .... 35.00
1970 .... 40.00
1971 .... 35.00
1972 .... 25.00
1974 .... 15.00
1976 .... 15.00
1977 .... 15.00
1978 .... 15.00
1979 .... 11.00
1980 .... 35.00
1982 .... 9.00
1984 .... 8.00
1987 .... 8.00

Pilots

1969 .... 225.00

Pirates

1951 .... 200.00
1952 .... 100.00
1953 .... 100.00
1954 .... 100.00
1955 .... 85.00
1956 .... 60.00
1957 .... 60.00
1958 .... 50.00
1959 .... 60.00
1960 .... 85.00
1961 .... 40.00
1962 .... 35.00
1963 .... 35.00
1964 .... 35.00
1965 .... 35.00
1966 .... 30.00
1967 .... 30.00
1968 .... 30.00
1969 .... 30.00
1970 .... 25.00
1972 .... 30.00
1973 .... 30.00
1974 .... 25.00
1975 .... 20.00
1976 .... 12.00
1977 .... 12.00
1978 .... 12.00
1979 .... 20.00
1980 .... 9.00
1981 .... 8.00
1983 .... 8.00
1985 .... 8.00
1986 .... 8.00

Rangers

1976 .... 25.00
1977 .... 12.00
1979 .... 9.00
1981 .... 8.00
1984 .... 7.00
1985 .... 6.00

Red Sox

1951 .... 200.00
1952 .... 125.00
1955 .... 125.00
1956 .... 75.00
1957 .... 75.00
1958 .... 65.00
1959 .... 65.00
1960 .... 50.00
1963 .... 40.00
1964 .... 40.00
1969 .... 40.00
1970 .... 22.00
1971 .... 20.00
1972 .... 18.00
1975 .... 25.00
1976 .... 15.00
1977 .... 18.00
1978 .... 12.00
1979 .... 12.00
1980 .... 10.00
1981 .... 8.00
1983 .... 8.00
1984 .... 8.00
1986 .... 8.00

Reds

1948 .... 275.00
1949 .... 125.00
1951 .... 150.00
1952 .... 125.00
1953 .... 100.00
1954 .... 100.00
1955 .... 75.00
1956 .... 70.00
1957 .... 90.00
1958 .... 85.00
1959 .... 55.00
1960 .... 50.00
1961 .... 50.00
1962 .... 50.00
1963 .... 50.00
1964 .... 30.00
1965 .... 30.00
1966 .... 30.00
1967 .... 30.00
1968 .... 30.00
1969 .... 30.00
1970 .... 20.00
1971 .... 25.00
1972 .... 25.00
1973 .... 25.00
1974 .... 25.00
1975 .... 20.00
1976 .... 15.00
1977 .... 15.00
1978 .... 12.00
1979 .... 12.00
1980 .... 8.00
1981 .... 8.00
1982 .... 8.00
1983 .... 8.00
1984 .... 8.00

Royals

1969 .... 50.00
1970 .... 25.00
1971 .... 20.00
1972 .... 18.00
1973 .... 18.00
1975 .... 15.00
1984 .... 10.00
1986 .... 8.00
1987 .... 8.00
1988 .... 8.00

S.F. Giants

1958 .... 250.00
1959 .... 75.00
1960 .... 40.00
1961 .... 45.00
1962 .... 60.00
1963 .... 40.00
1964 .... 40.00
1965 .... 35.00
1966 .... 30.00
1967 .... 30.00
1968 .... 35.00
1969 .... 30.00
1970 .... 25.00
1971 .... 75.00
1972 .... 25.00
1973 .... 20.00
1974 .... 15.00
1975 .... 15.00
1976 .... 15.00
1980 .... 10.00
1981 .... 10.00
1982 .... 12.00
1983 .... 12.00
1984 .... 10.00
1985 .... 7.00
1986 .... 7.00

Senators

1957 .... 100.00
1958 .... 90.00
1959 .... 75.00
1963 .... 50.00
1964 .... 40.00
1965 .... 35.00
1966 .... 30.00
1967 .... 35.00
1968 .... 35.00

St. Louis Browns

1944 ..... 350.00
1945 ..... 300.00
1946 ..... 250.00
1947 ..... 225.00
1951 ..... 200.00
1952 ..... 250.00

Tigers

1957 ..... 150.00
1958 ..... 135.00
1966 ..... 45.00
1967 ..... 45.00
1969 ..... 30.00
1970 ..... 24.00
1971 ..... 20.00
1972 ..... 20.00
1973 ..... 20.00
1974 ..... 15.00
1975 ..... 12.00
1976 ..... 12.00
1977 ..... 12.00
1978 ..... 12.00
1979 ..... 12.00
1980 ..... 8.00
1981 ..... 8.00
1982 ..... 8.00
1983 ..... 8.00
1984 ..... 8.00
1987 ..... 8.00

Twins

1961 ..... 200.00
1962 ..... 55.00
1964 ..... 35.00
1967 ..... 30.00
1968 ..... 25.00
1969 ..... 30.00
1970 ..... 30.00
1971 ..... 25.00
1972 ..... 25.00
1973 ..... 20.00
1974 ..... 20.00
1975 ..... 20.00
1977 ..... 15.00
1978 ..... 12.00
1979 ..... 12.00
1980 ..... 8.00
1981 ..... 8.00
1985 ..... 8.00
1988 ..... 8.00

White Sox

1952 ..... 100.00
1953 ..... 75.00
1955 ..... 60.00
1956 ..... 55.00
1957 ..... 60.00
1958 ..... 55.00
1962 ..... 40.00
1965 ..... 24.00
1967 ..... 15.00
1968 ..... 20.00
1969 ..... 25.00
1982 ..... 10.00
1983 ..... 17.00

Yankees

1950 ..... 350.00
1951 ..... 250.00
1952 ..... 225.00
1953 ..... 225.00
1954 ..... 200.00
1955 ..... 175.00
1956 ..... 150.00
1957 ..... 200.00
1958 ..... 150.00
1959 ..... 100.00
1960 ..... 100.00
1961 ..... 125.00
1962 ..... 75.00
1963 ..... 65.00
1964 ..... 65.00
1965 ..... 65.00
1966 ..... 50.00
1967 ..... 50.00
1968 ..... 40.00
1969 ..... 40.00
1970 ..... 35.00
1971 ..... 25.00
1972 ..... 25.00
1973 ..... 25.00
1974 ..... 15.00
1975 ..... 15.00
1976 ..... 25.00
1977 ..... 20.00
1978 ..... 20.00
1979 ..... 15.00
1980 ..... 10.00
1981 ..... 8.00
1982 ..... 8.00
1983 ..... 8.00
1984 ..... 8.00
1985 ..... 8.00
1986 ..... 8.00
1987 ..... 8.00
1988 ..... 6.00
1989 ..... 6.00

World Series Programs

The most collectible World Series programs are those made prior to the 1974 fall classic. After that date a single program has been made with the contributions of the teams in the playoffs and major league baseball.

Prior to the joint effort adoption in 1974 each team produced a program for the games played in its park.

A World Series program with **maximum** value should be 1) unscored; 2) complete wth any game day inserts; and 3) contain no stains, tears, creases, folds, discolorations, or water marks.

The values that follow assume the programs are unscored and in at least excellent condition with very minor problems (no creases, tears, stains, etc.)

Year	Teams	Value
1940	Cincinnati/	250.00-275.00
	Detroit	200.00-250.00
1941	New York Yankees/	200.00-225.00
	Brooklyn	225.00-240.00
1942	St. Louis Cards/	150.00-175.00
	New York Yankees	150.00-175.00
1943	New York Yankees/	150.00-175.00
	S. Louis Cards	150.00-175.00
1944	St. Louis Cards/	150.00-175.00
	St. Louis Browns	150.00-175.00
1945	Detroit/	250.00-275.00
	Chicago Cubs	175.00-200.00
1946	St. Louis Cards/	125.00-150.00
	Boston Red Sox	125.00-150.00
1947	New York Yankees/	150.00-175.00
	Brooklyn	175.00-200.00
1948	Cleveland/	100.00-115.00
	Boston Braves	135.00-145.00
1949	New York Yankees/	175.00-185.00
	Brookyn	150.00-165.00
1950	New York Yankees/	150.00-175.00
	Philadelphia Phillies	100.00-125.00
1951	New York Yankees/	150.00-175.00
	New York Giants	100.00-125.00
1952	New York Yankees/	140.00-150.00
	Brooklyn	150.00-175.00
1953	New York Yankees/	125.00-135.00
	Brooklyn	125.00-135.00
1954	New York Giants/	140.00-150.00
	Cleveland	125.00-135.00
1955	Brooklyn/	175.00-200.00
	New York Yankees	150.00-175.00
1956	New York Yankees/	135.00-150.00
	Brooklyn	135.00-150.00
1957	Milwaukee Braves/	65.00-75.00
	New York Yankees	75.00-85.00
1958	New York Yankees/	100.00-115.00
	Milwaukee Braves	65.00-75.00
1959	Los Angeles/	95.00-110.00
	Chicago White Sox	75.00-85.00
1960	Pittsburgh/	100.00-110.00
	New York Yankees	100.00-110.00
1961	New York Yankees/	100.00-110.00
	Cincinnati	100.00-110.00
1962	New York Yankees/	65.00-75.00
	San Francisco	100.00-115.00
1963	Los Angeles Dodgers/	30.00-35.00
	New York Yankees	35.00-40.00
1964	St. Louis/	100.00-115.00
	New York Yankees	60.00-70.00
1965	Los Angeles Dodgers/	30.00-35.00
	Minnesota	45.00-65.00
1966	Baltimore/	75.00-85.00
	Los Angeles Dodgers	40.00-50.00
1967	St. Louis Cards/	75.00-85.00
	Boston	75.00-85.00
1968	Detroit/	110.00-130.00
	St. Louis Cards	75.00-85.00
1969	New York Mets/	100.00-125.00
	Baltimore	60.00-70.00
1970	Baltimore/	20.00-25.00
	Cincinnati	20.00-25.00
1971	Pittsburgh/	20.00-25.00
	Baltimore	20.00-25.00
1972	Oakland/	35.00-40.00
	Cincinnati	25.00-30.00
1973	New York Mets/	16.00-19.00
	Oakland	45.00-50.00

Year	Teams	Value	Year	Teams	Value
1974	Oakland/Los Angeles	13.00-15.00	1983	Baltimore/Philadelphia	7.00-9.00
1975	Cincinnati/Boston	20.00-30.00	1984	Detroit/San Diego	5.00-6.00
1976	Cincinnnati/Yankees	13.00-15.00	1985	Kansas City/St. Louis	4.00-5.00
1977	Yankees/Los Angeles	10.00-12.00	1986	New York Mets/Boston	7.00-8.00
1978	Yankees/Los Angeles	10.00-12.00	1987	Minnesota/St. Louis	4.00-5.00
1979	Pittsburgh/Baltimore	12.00-14.00	1988	Los Angeles/Oakland	4.00-5.00
1980	Philadelphia/Kansas City	7.00-9.00	1989	Oakland/San Francisco	4.00-5.00
1981	Los Angeles/Yankees	8.00-10.00	1990	Cincinnati/Oakland	4.00-5.00
1982	St. Louis/Milwaukee	7.00-9.00	1991	Atlanta/Minnesota	4.00-5.00

Books

The Library of Congress lists more than 3,500 baseball books that have been published since 1900 in the United States. In the decade of the 1980's there were more baseball related titles published than at any other period.

Collectors can find baseball books from a variety of sources. Among the most commonly used are flea markets, tag or house sales, antiques shops, book sales at local libraries, used book stores, antiques malls, auctions (local or mail), and book sellers who specialize in old, rare, and out-of-print sports books.

Purchasing baseball books from specialized book sellers will probably cost the collector several more dollars for each purchase but will provide security about the condition and degree of rarity of the book.

A dealer who understands the marketplace usually prices his goods at their "fair market" retail value. Antiques or flea market dealers often don't have much knowledge about the price structure of baseball books and price their items dramatically high or at bargain prices.

The professional book seller is also selective in regards to the condition of the books he purchases for resale. Usually, the hard cover books have dust jackets and all their pages. Occasionally, autographed copies or special editions are offered.

Several sports book sellers have detailed catalogs that list hundreds of baseball related titles for sale. These catalogs can provide collectors with a wealth of information about the availability, scarcity, and value of baseball books. They were as an invaluable resource to the libraries of most collectors.

The 263 titles that follow are priced at their **retail** values. They are in a minimum of "very good" condition and are evaluated with dust jackets and contents complete. Most are first editions.

A collector wishing to sell books to a dealer can typically expect **no** more than 50% to 60% of the retail value for the items he wishes to sell.

It is interesting to note that age is not necessarily a major factor in the value of a baseball book. The "Baseball Joe" series written between 1910 and the 1920's seldom are worth more than $15.00-25.00 each and a paperbound history of the Peoria franchise in the Three Eye League may be well worth $75.00 even though it was completed in 1972. The "Baseball Joe" series was printed in huge quantities and individual books are not difficult to locate. The Peoria baseball history had a limited printing because it holds minimal interest for anyone not interested in the Three Eye League and is extremely difficult to find.

Aaron, Henry and Furman Bisher. *Aaron,* 1974. $20.00.
Aaron, Hank and Joel Cohen. *Hitting the Aaron Way.* 1974. $20.00.
Aaseng, Nathan. *Baseball's Hottest Hitters.* 1983. $18.00.
Adelman, Bob and Susan Hall. *Out of the Left Field: Willie Stargell and the Pittsburgh Pirates.* 1976. $25.00.
Alexander, Charles. *Ty Cobb.* 1984. $25.00.
Allen, Archie. *Handbook of Baseball Drills.* 1959. $25.00.
Allen, Ethan. *Baseball Techniques Illustrated.* 1951. $18.00.
Allen, Ethan. *Major League Baseball: Technique and Tactics.* 1938. $28.00.
Allen, Lee and Tom Meany. *Kings of the Diamond.* 1965. $28.00.
Allen, Lee. *The National League Story.* 1961. $10.00.
Allen, Lee. *The World Series.* 1969. $30.00.
Allen, Maury. *Bo: Pitching and Wooing.* 1973. $18.00.
Allen, Maury. *Damn Yankee: The Billy Martin Story.* 1980. $18.00.
Allen, Maury. *Roger Maris: A Man for All Seasons.* 1986. $25.00.
Allen, Maury. *Where Have You Gone, Joe DiMaggio?* 1975. $18.00.
Allen, Mel. *It Takes Heart.* 1959. $18.00.
Allen, Mel. *You Can't Beat the Hours.* 1974. $20.00.
Alou, Felipe. *My Life and Baseball.* 1967. $45.00 (autographed).
Alston, Walter. *A Year At a Time.* 1976. $20.00.
Anderson, Clary. *Make the Team in Baseball.* 1966. $25.00.
Anderson, Dave. *The Yankees.* 1979. $20.00.
Anderson, Sparky. *Bless You Boys: The Diary of the Detroit Tigers 1984 Season.* 1984. $20.00.
Anderson, Sparky and Si Burick. *The Main Spark: Sparky Anderson & the Cincinnnati Reds.* 1978. $20.00
Andreano, Ralph. *No Joy In Mudville.* 1965. $25.00.
Angell, Roger. *Five Seasons.* 1977. $35.00 (autographed).
Angell, Roger. *The Summer Game.* 1972. $30.00.
Antonacci, Robert. *Baseball for Young Champions.* 1956. $13.00.
Appel, Martin and Burt Goldblatt. *Baseball's Best.* 1977. $35.00.
Arnow, Jan. *Louisville Slugger: The Making of a Baseball Bat.* 1984. $22.00.
Asinof, Eliot. *Eight Men Out.* 1963. $45.00.
Axelson, G.W. *Commy.* 1919. $285.00 (autographed by Eliot Asinof and James T. Farrell).
Balter, Sam and Cy. *One of the Book of Sports.* 1955. $18.00.
Banks, Ernie. *Mr. Cub.* 1971. $20.00.
Barber, Red and Robert Creamer. *Rhubard in the Catbird Seat.* 1968. $35.00.
Barber, Red and Robert Creamer. *Rhubard in the Catbird Seat.* 1968. $70.00 (autographed by Creamer).
Barbour, Ralph. *Double Play.* 1910. $45.00.
Barbour, Ralph. *The New Boy at Hilltop and Other Stories.* 1910. $65.00.
Barbour, Ralph. *Weatherby's Inning.* 1903. $65.00.
Barrow, Edwared. *My Fifty Years in Baseball.* 1951. $35.00.
Bartell, Dick. *Rowdy Richard.* 1987. $25.00.
Bartlett, Arthur. *Baseball and Mr. Spalding.* 1951. $32.50.
Batson, Larry. *Frank Robinson.* 1974. $13.00.
Bauer, Hank. *Championship Baseball.* 1968. $25.00.
Bavasi, Buzzie. *Off the Record.* 1968. $25.00.
Baylor, Don. *Don Baylor: Northing But the Truth: A Baseball Life.* 1989. $17.00.
Beard, Gordon. *Birds on the Wings: The Story of the Baltimore Orioles.* 1967. $25.00.
Bell, Joseph. *World Series Thrills.* 1966. $20.00.
Bench, Johnny. *Catch You Later.* 1979. $25.00.
Bench, Johnny. *From Behind the Plate.* 1972. $20.00.
Berke, Art. *Unsung Heroes of the Major Leagues.* 1976. $23.00.
Berkow, Ira. *Pitchers Do Get Lonely.* 1988. $20.00.
Berra, Yogi and Ed Fitzgerald. *Yogi.* 1961. $20.00.
Berra, Yogi and Tom Horton. *Yogi: It Ain't Over.* 1989. $35.00 (signed by Berra).
Berry, Henry. *Boston Red Sox.* 1975. $23.00.
Bethel, Dell. *Inside Baseball.* 1969. $25.00.
Binette, Wilfred. *Knuckler: The Phil Niekro Story.* 1970. $25.00.
Bridsall, Ralph. *The Story of Cooperstown.* 1954. $25.00.
Bisher, Furman. *Miracle in Atlanta.* 1966. $25.00.
Blackwell, Ewell. *Secrets of Pitching.* 1949. $35.00.
Blue, Vida and Bill Libby. *Vida: His Own Story.* 1972. $20.00.
Bonner, M.G. *The Big Baseball Book for Boys.* 1931. $45.00.
Boone, Robert and Gerald Grunska. *Hack.* 1978. $30.00.
Borst, Bill. *Baseball Through a Knothole: A St. Louis History.* 1980. $35.00.
Boswell, Thomas. *The Heart of the Order.* 1989. $17.00.
Boswell, Thomas. *How Life Imitates the World Series.*

1982. $28.00.

Boswell, Thomas. *Why Time Begins on Opening Day.* 1984. $23.00.

Boudreau, Lou. *Player-Manager.* 1949. $25.00.

Bouton, Jim. *Ball Four.* 1970. $28.00.

Bove, Vincent. *And On the Eighth Day God Created the Yankees.* $23.00.

Bowman, John and Joel Zoss. *The Pictorial History of Baseball.* 1986. $45.00.

Boyd, Brendan. *The Great American Baseball Card Flipping, Trading and Bubble Gum Book.* 1973. $23.00.

Boy's Life. *The Boys' Life Book of Baseball Stories.* 1964. $23.00.

Brashler, William. *The Bingo Long Traveling All Stars & Motor Kings.* 1973. $45.00 (autographed).

Brashler, William. *Josh Gibson: A Life in the Negro Leagues.* 1978. $45.00.

Breslin, Jimmy. *Can't Anybody Here Play This Game?* 1963. $18.00.

Brewster, Benjamin. *The First Book of Baseball.* 1950. $23.00.

Broadus, Catherine and Loren. *Laughing and Crying with Little League.* 1972. $20.00.

Brock, Lou and Franz Schulze. *Stealing Is My Game.* 1976. $25.00.

Broeg, Bob. *The Pilot Light and the Gashouse Gang.* 1980. $45.00 (autographed).

Brosnan, Jim. *The Long Season.* 1960. $35.00.

Brosnan, Jim. *Pennant Race.* 1962. $30.00.

Brosnan, Jim. *The Ted Simmons Story.* 1977. $27.00.

Brown, Heywood. *Tumultous Merriment.* 1979. $25.00.

Brown, Warren. *The Chicago Cubs.* 1946. $45.00.

Brown, Warren. *The Chicago White Sox.* 1952. $35.00.

Buchanan, Lamont. *The World Series.* 1951. $35.00.

Burchard, Marshall. *Sports Hero: Brooks Robinson.* 1972. $20.00.

Burchard, Marshall. *Mark "The Bird" Fidrych.* 1977. $20.00.

Burchard, S.H. *Sports Star: George Brett.* 1982. $20.00.

Burnett, W.R. *The Roar of the Crowd.* 1964. $20.00.

Bütler, Hal. *Baseball All Star Game Thrills.* 1968. $20.00.

Butler, Hal. *Al Kaline and the Detroit Tigers.* 1973. $25.00.

Butler, Hal. *The Bob Allison Story.* 1967. $20.00.

Berg, Ethel. *My Brother Morris Berg: The Real Moe.* 1975. $75.00.

Camp, Walter. *The Book of Sports and Games.* 1923. $45.00.

Campanella, Roy. *It's Good to be Alive.* 1959. $25.00.

Campanis, Al. *Play Ball with Roger the Dodger.* 1980. $13.00.

Caray, Harry. *Holy Cow!* 1989. $16.00.

Carew, Rod, *Carew.* 1979. $20.00.

Carmichael, John. *My Great Day in Baseball.* 1946. $25.00.

Carrieri, Joe. *Yankee Batboy.* 1955. $20.00.

Caus, Louis. *Baseball's Back in Town.* 1977. $125.00 (autographed by the author).

Cepeda, Orlando. *My Ups and Downs in Baseball.* 1968. $20.00.

Chadwick, Lester. *Baseball Joe at Yale.* 1925. $20.00.

———. *Baseball Joe, Captain of the Team.* 1924. $22.00.

———. *Baseball Joe, Champion of the League.* 1925. $18.00.

———. *Baseball Joe, Club Owner.* 1926. $23.00.

———. *Baseball Joe, Homerun King.* 1922. $18.00.

———. *Baseball Joe in the Central League.* 1914. $23.00.

———. *Baseball Joe on the School Nine.* 1912. $23.00.

———. *Baseball Joe Saving the League.* 1923. $23.00.

———. *Batting to Win.* 1911. $35.00.

Charboneau, Joe. *Super Joe: The Life and Legend of Joe Charboneau.* $15.00.

Child, Malcolm. *How to Play Big League Baseball.* 1951. $23.00.

Chrisman, David. *The History of the International League.* 1981. $45.00 (autographed by the author).

Christopher, Matt. *Baseball Flyhawk.* 1963. $20.00.

———. *Catcher with a Glass Arm.* 1964. $20.00.

———. *Challenge at Second Base.* 1962. $18.00.

———. *Little Lefty.* 1959. $20.00.

Christine, Bill. *Roberto!* 1973. $20.00.

Clark, Steve. *The Complete Book of Baseball Cards.* 1976. $20.00.

Clemens, Roger. *Rocket Man.* 1987. $18.00.

Cleveland, Charles. *The Greatest Baseball Managers.* 1950. $23.00.

Cobb, Mickey. *Baseball Injuries and Training Tips.* 1974. $28.00 (autographed by the author).

Coffin, Tristram. *The Illustrated Book of Baseball Folklore.* 1975. $30.00.

———. *The Old Ball Game.* 1971. $23.00.

Cohen, Barbara. *Thank You, Jackie Robinson.* 1974. $18.00.

Cohen, Joel. *Jim Palmer.* 1977. $18.00.

———. *Steve Garvey: Storybook Star.* 1977. $20.00.

Cohen, Richard and Roland Johnson. *The World Series.* 1976. $20.00.

Collett, Ritter. *The Cinnati Reds.* 1976. $45.00.

Colletti, Nick. *You Gotta Have Heart.* 1985. $23.00.

Colton, Matthew. Frank Armstrong, *Captain of the Nine*. 1913. $65.00.

———. *Frank Armstrong's Second Team*. 1911. $65.00.

Conigliaro, Tony. *Seeing It Through*. 1970. $25.00.

Conlan, Jocko and Robert Creamer. *Jocko*. 1967. $25.00.

Connor, Anthony. *Baseball For the Love of It*. 1982. $23.00.

Cooke, Edmund. *Baseballogy*. 1912. $150.00.

Coombs, Jack. *Baseball*. 1937. $25.00.

Cosell, Howard. *I Never Played the Game*. 1985. $20.00.

Creamer, Robert. *Babe: The Legend Comes to Life*. 1974. $45.00 (autographed by Robert Creamer and Lawrence Ritter).

———. *Stengel: His Life and Times*. 1984. $18.00.

Crepeau, Richard. *Baseball: America's Diamond Mind, 1919-1941*. 1980. $35.00.

Crissey, Harrington. *Teenagers, Gray Beards and 4-F's*. 1981. $25.00.

Curran, William. *Mitts*. 1985. $23.00.

Daley, Arthur. *Kings of the Homerun*. 1962. $28.00.

———. *Times At Bat*. 1950. $18.00.

Dark, Alvin. *When in Doubt, Fire the Manager*. 1980. $23.00.

Davids, Robert. *Insider's Baseball*. 1983. $20.00.

Davidson, Donald. *Caught Short*. 1972. $75.00 (autographed by the author, Eddie Mathews, Hank Aaron).

Davis, Mac. *The Lore and Legends of Baseball*. 1953. $20.00.

Day, Laraine. *Day with the Giants*. 1952. $65.00 (autographed by the author and Leo Durocher).

———. *Day with the Giants*. 1952. $25.00.

Deford, Frank. *Casey on the Loose*. 1989. $18.00.

DeGregorio, George. *Joe DiMaggio*. 1981. $20.00.

Dellinger, H.L. *The 1884 Kansas City Unions*. 1977. $45.00.

Deliquanti, Don. *Baseball: The New Champions*. 1973. $20.00.

Deitsch, Jordan and Richard Cohen. *The Scrapbook History of Baseball*. 1975. $20.00.

Devaney, John. *Baseball's Youngest Big Leaguers*. 1971. $18.00.

Devaney, John and Burt Goldblatt. *The World Series: A Complete Pictorial History*. 1972. $45.00.

Dews, Robert. *The Georgia-Florida League 1935-1958*. 1979. $45.00.

Dickey, Glenn. *The Great No-Hitters*. 1976. $23.00.

———. *The History of American League Baseball*. 1980. $28.00.

———. *The History of National League Baseball*. 1979. $28.00.

Dolan, Edward and Richard Lyttle. *Fred Lynn: The Hero From Boston*. 1978. $18.00.

Dorer, Skip. *In the "O" Zone*. 1980. $23.00.

Doyle, Ed. *The Forgotten Ones*. 1972. $23.00.

———. *The Only One: The Babe*. 1974. $20.00.

Drucker, Malka and Tom Seaver. *Tom Seaver: Portrait of a Pitcher*. 1978. $20.00.

Dunne, Bert. *Play Ball!* 1945. $27.00.

Durant, John. *The Story of Baseball*. 1947. $25.00.

———. *The Yankees*. 1950. $25.00.

Duren, Ryne. *The Comeback*. 1978. $18.00.

Durocher, Leo. *Nice Guys Finish Last*. 1975. $23.00.

Durso, Joseph. *Baseball and the American Dream*. 1986. $23.00.

———. *Casey: The Life and Legend of C.D. Stengel*. 1967. $23.00.

———. *The Days of Mr. McGraw*. 1969. $25.00.

———. *Whitey and Mickey*. 1977. $20.00.

———. *Yankee Stadium: 50 Years of Drama*. 1972. $65.00.

Dykes, Jimmie and Charles Dexter. *You Can't Steal First Base*. 1967. $28.00.

Enstein, Charles. *The Fireside Book of Baseball*. 1956. $30.00.

———. *The Second Fireside Book of Baseball*. 1958. $35.00.

———. *The Third Fireside Book of Baseball*. 1968. $65.00.

———. *Willie Mays, Coast to Coast Giant*. 1963. $25.00.

———. *Willie's Time*. 1979. $23.00.

Ellis, William. *Billy Sunday: The Man and the Message*. 1914. $28.00.

Enright, Jim. *The Chicago Cubs*. 1975. $30.00.

———. *Trade Him!* 1977. $35.00.

Epstein, Ben. *Yogi Berra, The Muscle Man*. 1951. $18.00.

Eskenazi, Gerald. *Bill Veeck: A Baseball Legend*. 1988. $25.00.

Etkins, Jack. *Innings Ago*. 1987. $25.00.

Evers, John. *How to Play Second Base*. 1917. $45.00.

Fabbri, Helen. *Dear Pete: The Life of Pete Rose*. 1985. $18.00.

Falkner, David. *The Short Season*. 1986. $18.00.

Falls, Joe. *The Detroit Tigers*. 1975. $30.00.

Farrell, James T. *My Baseball Diary*. 1957. $25.00.

Felker, Clay. *Casey Stengel's Secret*. 1961. $20.00.

Feller, Bob. *Strikeout Story*. 1947. $30.00 (autogrpahed by Feller).

———. *Pitching to Win*. 1952. $28.00 (autographed by Feller).

Fidrych, Mark. *No Big Deal*. 1977. $23.00.

Fiffer, Steve. *How to Watch Baseball*. 1987. $13.00.

Figueroa, Ed and Dorothy Harshaman. *Yankee Stranger*. 1982. $35.00.
Fine, Gary. *With the Boys*. 1987. $25.00.
Finlayson, Ann. *Champions at Bat: Three Power Hitters*. 1970. $23.00.
Fitzgerald, Ed. *The American League*. 1952. $20.00.
———. *The Ballplayer*. 1957. $23.00.
———. *The National League*. 1952. $20.00.
Fleming, G.H. *The Dizziest Season*. 1984. $20.00.
———. *Murderer's Row*. 1985. $28.00.
———. *The Unforgettable Season*. 1981. $18.00.
Flood, Curt. *The Way It Is*. 1971. $20.00.
Foley, Red. *Red Foley's Best Baseball Book Ever*. 1987. $23.00.
Fonseca, Lew. *How To Pitch Baseball*. 1942. $25.00.
Ford, Whitey and Phil Pepe. *Slick*. 1987. $35.00 (autographed by Ford).
Forker, Dom. *The Men of Autumn*. 1989. $17.00.
Foster, John. *How to Bat*. 1921. $23.00.
———. *How to Catch & How to Run the Bases*. 1922. $18.00.
Fox, Larry. *Last to First: The Story of the Mets*. 1970. $18.00.
Freehan, Bill. *Behind the Mask*. 1970. $25.00.
Frick, Ford. *Games, Asterisks, and People*. 1973. $23.00.
Frisch, Frank. *Frank Frisch: The Fordham Flash*. 1962. $23.00.
Garagiola, Joe. *Baseball Is A Funny Game*. 1960. $25.00 (autographed by Garagiola).
Garreau, Garth. *Bat Boy of the Giants*. 1948. $23.00.
Gehrig, Eleanor. *My Luke and I*. 1976. $35.00.
Gerlach, Larry. *The Men in Blue*. 1980. $35.00.
Getz, Mike. *Baseball's 3000 Hit Club*. 1982. $25.00.
Gibson, Bob. *From Ghetto to Glory*. 1968. $40.00 (autographed by Gibson).
Gibson, Jerry. *Big League Batboy*. 1970. $23.00.
Godden, Dwight. *Rookie*. 1985. $20.00.
Goodman, Irv. *Stan the Man Musial*. 1961. $25.00.
Gorman, Tom. *Three and Two*. 1979. $25.00.
Green, Paul. *Forgotten Fields*, 1984. $25.00.
Harris Stanley. *Playing the Game*. 1925. $65.00.
Henderson, Robert. *Ball, Bat, and Bishop*. 1947. $95.00.
Henrich, Tommy. *The Way to Better Baseball*. 1951. $45.00 (autographed by Henrich).
Heward, Bill. *Some Are Called Clowns*. 1974. $28.00.
Hirschberg, Al. *The Braves, The Pick and the Shovel*. 1948. $45.00 (autographed by the author).
———. *The Red Sox, The Bean and the Cod*. 1947. $35.00.
Holway, John. *Smokey Joe and the Cannonball*. 1983. $45.00.
———. *Voices From the Great Black Baseball Leagues*. 1975. $45.00.
Honig, Donald. *Baseball When the Grass Was Real*. 1975. $47.00 (autographed by the author).
Hornsby, Rogers. *My Kind of Baseball*. 1953. $35.00.
Jackson, Reggie. *Reggie: The Autobiography*. 1984. $20.00.
Kahn, Roger. *The Boys of Summer*. 1971. $45.00 (autographed by the author and Lawrence Ritter).
Lowry, Phillip. *Green Cathedrals*. 1986. $95.00.
Murmane, Tim. *How to Play Baseball*. 1909. $95.00.
Murphy, James. *The Gabby Hartnett Story*. 1983. $20.00.
Obojski, Robert. *Bush League*. 1975. $35.00.
Oliver, Ted. *Kings of the Mound*. 1944. $45.00.
Overfield, Joseph. *The 100 Seasons of Buffalo Baseball*. 1985. $45.00.
Pinelli, Babe. *Mr. Ump*. 1953. $30.00.
Poiner, Murray. *Branch Rickey: A Biography*. 1982. $32.00.
Quigley, Martin. *The Crooked Pitch: The Curveball in American Baseball History*. 1984. $20.00.
Roseboro, John. *Glory Days with the Dodgers and Other Days with Others*. 1978. $28.00.
Rust, Art Jr. *Recollections of a Baseball Junkie*. 1985. $53.00.
Schacht, Al. *Clowning Through Baseball*. 1945. $25.00.
Tunis, John. *World Series*. 1950. $65.00. (Japanese edition signed by the author).
Veeck, Bill. *Veeck As in Wreck*. 1962. $125.00 (autographed by the author).
Williams, Billy. *Billy: The Classic Hitter*. 1974. $35.00 (autographed by the author).
Williams, Ted. *My Turn At Bat*. 1969. $25.00.
Young, Dick. *Roy Campanella*. 1952. $22.00.
Zimmerman, Paul. *The Los Angeles Dodgers*. 1960. $25.00.

Time Magazine With Baseball Covers

Year	Subject	Value
1929	Bill Wrigley	90.00-100.00
1930	Wilbert Robinson	90.00-100.00
1932	Col. Jacob Ruppert	75.00-85.00
1934	Lefty Gomez	50.00-60.00
1935	Mickey Cochrane	35.00-45.00
1936	Lou Gehrig/Carl Hubbell	65.00-75.00
1937	Bob Feller	65.00-75.00
1938	Happy Chandler	55.00-65.00
1947	Leo Durocher	35.00-45.00
1948	Joe DiMaggio	75.00-85.00
1950	Ted Williams	65.00-75.00
1952	Eddie Stanky	30.00-40.00
1954	Willie Mays	35.00-45.00
1955	Broadway play "Damn Yankees"	20.00-30.00
1955	Augie Busch	15.00-25.00
1955	Casey Stengel	20.00-30.00
1956	Robin Roberts	15.00-25.00
1957	Birdie Tebbetts	15.00-20.00
1958	Walter O'Malley	20.00-25.00
1959	Rocky Colavito	35.00-45.00
1968	Denny McLain	15.00-20.00
1969	N.Y. Mets	30.00-40.00
1971	Vida Blue	10.00-15.00
1972	Johnny Bench	20.00-25.00
1974	Reggie Jackson	15.00-20.00
1975	Charley Finley	10.00-15.00
1976	Babe Ruth	15.00-20.00
1977	Rod Carew	15.00-20.00
1979	Earl Weaver	10.00-15.00
1981	Billy Martin	10.00-15.00
1982	Carl Yastrzemski/Pete Rose	10.00-15.00
1985	Peter Ueberroth	10.00-15.00
1985	Pete Rose	15.00-20.00
1986	Dwight Gooden	15.00-20.00
1989	Pete Rose	5.00-10.00

Newsweek Magazine with Baseball Covers

* - indicates more than one picture and several subjects on the cover

Issue	Cover	Value
April 15, 1933	Catcher tagging sliding runner	15.00-20.00
April 29, 1933*	Carl Hubbell	18.00-22.00
July 29, 1933*	House of David signs girl pitcher	15.00-20.00
September 9, 1933*	Connie Mack	18.00-22.00
September 30, 1933*	Clark Giffith	18.00-22.00
December 23, 1933*	Judge Landis	18.00-22.00
February 17, 1934*	Babe Ruth contest	20.00-30.00
March 17, 1934*	Mel Ott in spring training	18.00-22.00
October 6, 1934	Mickey Cochrane	20.00-25.00
April 20, 1935	Judge Kenesaw Mountain Landis	20.00-25.00
October 3, 1936	Carl Hubbell	20.00-25.00
Ocotber 11, 1937*	Carl Hubbell	18.00-22.00
Spril 18, 1938	Rudy York	15.00-18.00
October 10, 1938	Yankee-Cub World Series	25.00-30.00
June 19, 1939	Abner Doubleday and Cooperstown	35.00-40.00
September 16, 1946	Ted Williams	24.00-30.00
June 2, 1947	Bob Feller	15.00-20.00
October 6, 1947	Bruce Edwards and the Dodger Farm system	10.00-12.00

Issue	Cover	Value
April 26, 1948	Billy Southworth and Joe McCarthy	15.00-18.00
August 8, 1949	Branch Rickey	15.00-18.00
April 17, 1950	Mel Parnell	8.00-10.00
March 24, 1952	Dodgers' spring training	8.00-10.00
October 4, 1954	Bob Feller and Bob Lemon	10.00-12.00
October 3, 1955	Basebal and color television	8.00-10.00
June 25, 1956	Mickey Mantle	15.00-20.00
July 1, 1957	Stan Musial	10.00-12.00
August 3, 1959	Casey Stengel	15.00-18.00
August 14, 1961	Year of the Home Run	8.00-10.00
April 26, 1965	The Astro Dome	7.00-9.00
October 11, 1965	Sandy Koufax	8.00-10.00
October 2, 1967	Carl Yastrzemski	8.00-10.00
August 13, 1975	Aaron and Ruth	12.00-15.00
June 16, 1975	Nolan Ryan	8.00-10.00
Jule 28, 1976	Vida Blue and Big Salaries	5.00-7.00
August 6, 1990	George Steinbrenner	3.00-4.00

Newspapers

Collectors of historic sports newspapers are faced with a difficult task in a "throw away" society. Most libraries today use microfilm rather than keeping the original newspapers. The quality of newsprint continues to decline which makes the long term storage of contemporary papers almost impossible.

Libraries that closed or had periodic sales to reduce their overcrowded holdings have been exceptional sources for collectors in the past.

The newspapers described below are complete editions that feature significant moments in baseball history. In addition to the specific event that is described, most of the articles have photographs and box scores.

The entire edition is infinitely more collectible and desireable than a portion of the page or a clipping and much more of a challenge to locate.

Date	Newspaper	Headline	Condition	Value
6-4-1905	L.A. Times	"Christy Mathewson Perfect Game"	Excellent	150.00
10-10-1906	L.A. Times	"Chicago White Sox Win From Cubs" (World Series)	Excellent	225.00
10-11-1906	L.A. Times	"Chicago White Sox World Champions"	Very Good	250.00
10-9-1909	L.A. Times	"Captain Clark's Home Run Breaks the Tigers' Back"	Very Good	150.00
10-12-1909	L.A. Times	"Wagner & Team-mates Storm Tiger Strong-hold 8-6"	Very Good	150.00
10 12-1913	L.A. Times	"Plank Outpitches Mathewson, Athletics Win Championship"	Very Good	150.00

Date	Newspaper	Headline	Condition	Value
10-10-1914	L.A. Times	"Boston's Young Hitters Drive Chief Bender Out" (1914 World Series)	Excellent	85.00
10-12-1914	L.A. Times	"Mack Up Against It for Slab Artist to Oppose the Braves"	Excellent	65.00
10-19-1915	L.A. Times	"Opening World Series Game Full of Thrills" (Grover Cleveland Alexander wins for Philadelphia)	Excellent	100.00
10-8-1917	L.A. Times	"American League Champs Grab Second World Series Game"	Excellent	75.00
10-11-1917	L.A. Times	"Giants Turn on White Sox in 3rd World Series Game and Win"	Excellent	75.00
9-25-1918	L.A. Times	"Babe Ruth Breaks all Records for One Season's Home Runs"	Excellent	150.00
9-25-1919	L.A. Times	"White Sox Grab Pennant"	Excellent	150.00
9-23-1920	L.A. Times	"Comiskey Has Little To Say - Can't Explain What Happened in World Series"	Excellent	125.00
9-25-1920	L.A. Times	"Did Gamblers Fix Games?"	Excellent	150.00
9-28-1920	LA. Times	"Eddie Cicotte Accused"	Excellent	200.00
9-30-1920	L.A. Times	"Williams & Felsch Admit to Taking Bribes"	Very Good	250.00
10-6-1920	L.A. Times	"Investigation of Fixed 1919 World Series Goes On While Cleveland Beats Brooklyn"	Excellent	100.00
10-7-1920	L.A. Times	"Cincinnati Says Reds Are Okay"	Excellent	75.00
10-7-1920	L.A. Times	"Dodgers Come Back Strong on 2nd Game & Even Up Series"	Excellent	75.00
8-2-1921	L.A. Times	"Can't Hang It on 'Black Sox' ... Claims Attorneys in Ball Scandal Defense"	Very Good	85.00
7-2-1920	L.A. Times	"Walter Johnson No-Hitter"	Excellent	100.00
10-9-1922	L.A. Times	"N.Y. Giants Win World's Championship in Decisive Fashion"	Excellent	100.00
10-7-1924	L.A. Times	"Ty Cobb Retires From Active Baseball – Georgia Peach Admits He's Through For Good"	Excellent	125.00
10-8-1925	L.A. Times	"Christy Mathewson Dies"	Excellent	100.00
10-19-1925	L.A. Times	"Lazzeri Shatters World Home Run Record"	Excellent	10.00
4-19-1929	N.Y. Times	"Ruth & Gehrig Hit Homers as Yanks Win in Opener, 7-3"	Near Mint	40.00
8-12-1929	N.Y. Times	"Ruth Hits His 500th Major League Homer"	Near Mint	150.00
8-22-1931	N.Y. Herald Tribune	"Ruth Hits 600th Homer of Career and Buys Ball from Boy Finder"	Excellent	125.00
8-22-1931	L.A. Times	"Bambino Pikes Six Hundredth"	Excellent	150.00
10-2-1932	L.A. Times	"Ruth & Gehrig Bat Out Home Run Barrage to Crush Cubs"	Very Good	125.00
10-9-1934	N.Y. Times	"Ruth to Return Unless He Gets a Manager's Job Next Season"	Excellent	100.00
5-26-1935	N.Y. Times	"Ruth Hits Three Homers But Braves Lose 11-7" (These were Ruth's final home runs.)	Excellent	100.00
6-3-1935	N.Y. Herald Tribune	"Babe Ruth Quits Braves As He and Fuchs Split"	Excellent	100.00
10-17-1936	N.Y. Times	"Second MVP Award Bolsters Gehrig's All-Time Star Rating"	Near Mint	125.00

Date	Newspaper	Headline	Condition	Value
5-3-1939	N.Y. Times	"Gehrig Voluntarily Ends Streak at 2130 Straight Games"	Excellent	750.00
6-13-1939	N.Y. Times	"Baseball Pageant Thrills 10,000 at Games 100 Birthday Party"	Excellent	250.00
10-25-1939	N.Y. Times	"DiMaggio Voted MVP in American League"	Excellent	150.00
4-17-1940	N.Y. Times	"Feller Opens Season with No-Hit Shutout"	Excellent	100.00
7-3-1941	N.Y. Times	"DiMaggio Sets All-Time Hitting Record as Yanks Win" (The Yankee Clipper broke Willie Keeler's record of 45 games.)	Excellent	200.00
7-3-1941	L.A. Times	"DiMaggio Hangs Up New Major League Hitting Record"	Excellent	175.00
9-29-1941	L.A. Times	"Ted Williams Ends at .405"	Excellent	125.00
9-29-1941	N.Y. Times	"Batting Mark of .4057 for Williams"	Near Mint	100.00
10-2-1941	N.Y. Times	"Yankees Beat Dodgers 3-2, Before 68,540"	Very Good	50.00
11-12-1941	N.Y. Times	"Di Maggio Most Valuable American Leaguer for 2nd Time in 3 Years"	Near Mint	100.00
5-1-1946	N.Y. Times	"Feller Tops Yanks with No-Hitter, 1-0"	Near Mint	85.00
12-13-1951	N.Y. Herald Tribune	"Yanks Retire DiMaggio's '5' "	Excellent	100.00
7-26-1955	N.Y. Times	"DiMaggio, Vance Among Six Honored at Baseball HOF"	Excellent	175.00
10-3-1961	N.Y. Herald Tribune	"I Love Maris" (This is a column by Jim Murray.)	Excellent	50.00
7-24-1962	N.Y. Herald Tribune	"Hall of Fame Links Baseball's Golden Past to Future" (Jackie Robinson, Feller, Roush go into the Hall of Fame.)	Excellent	75.00
6-5-1964	N.Y. Herald Tribune	"Koufax Pitches No-Hitter Against Phils"	Excellent	75.00
10-13-1967	L.A. Times	"Gibson Ends It - Midnight Comes Early for Cinderella Sox"	Excellent	50.00
10-11-1968	L.A. Times	"Tigers Win It"	Excellent	50.00

Street and Smith's Baseball Yearbooks

Street and Smith's Baseball Yearbook has been published annually since 1941. The Baseball Yearbook followed the debut of the College Football Yearbook in 1940.

Street and Smith went to regional covers in 1963 to boost sales. The 1963 editions featured Tom Tresh (New York and the East Coast), Stan Musial (middle America and the South), and Don Drysdale (California and the West Coast).

Issues from the 1941-1945 period are especially desireable because many potential customers were in the military and could not purchase the magazine. World War II paper drives also took away many copies from contemporary collectors.

Year	Cover	Ex./Mint Condition	Good Condition
1941	Bob Feller	175.00-200.00	75.00-95.00
1942	Howie Pollett	150.00-175.00	65.00-75.00
1943	Charlie Keller	95.00-125.00	45.00-60.00
1944	Joe McCarthy	85.00-100.00	45.00-60.00
1945	New York Giants	85.00-100.00	45.00-60.00
1946	Dick Fowler	60.00-80.00	25.00-35.00
1947	Leo Durocher	60.00-80.00	25.00-35.00
1948	Joe DiMaggio	75.00-100.00	45.00-60.00
1949	Lou Boudreau	65.00-80.00	25.00-35.00
1950	Joe DiMaggio, Ted Williams	75.00-100.00	45.00-60.00
1951	Joe DiMaggio, Ralph Kiner	65.00-75.00	30.00-45.00
1952	Stan Musial	60.00-70.00	20.00-35.00
1953	Mickey Mantle	60.00-75.00	25.00-40.00
1954	Eddie Mathews	55.00-65.00	20.00-40.00
1955	Yogi Berra	55.00-65.00	15.00-20.00
1956	Mickey Mantle, Duke Snider	55.00-65.00	15.00-20.00
1957	Mickey Mantle, Don Larsen, Yogi Berra	50.00-60.00	20.00-25.00
1958	Bob Buhl, Lew Burdette	45.00-55.00	10.00-15.00
1959	Mickey Mantle, Warren Spahn, Lew Burdette	50.00-60.00	10.00-15.00
1960	Nellie Fox, Luis Aparicio	45.00-50.00	10.00-15.00
1961	Dick Groat	45.00-50.00	10.00-15.00
1962	Roger Maris	45.00-50.00	10.00-15.00
1963	Tom Tresh	20.00-25.00	8.00-12.00
1963	Stan Musial	35.00-40.00	15.00-20.00
1963	Don Drysdale	20.00-25.00	5.00-6.00
1964	Mickey Mantle	30.00-35.00	10.00-12.00
1964	Warren Spahn	18.00-22.00	6.00-10.00
1964	Sandy Koufax	25.00-35.00	10.00-15.00
1965	Dean Chance	18.00-22.00	6.00-10.00
1965	Ken Boyer	20.00-25.00	5.00-8.00
1965	Brooks Robinson	20.00-25.00	8.00-12.00
1966	Sandy Koufax	35.00-40.00	12.00-15.00
1966	Ron Swodoba	25.00-30.00	10.00-15.00
1966	Rocky Colavito	35.00-40.00	12.00-18.00
1967	Juan Marichal	20.00-25.00	8.00-12.00
1967	Harmon Killebrew	20.00-25.00	8.00-12.00
1967	Andy Etchebarren	15.00-18.00	5.00-10.00
1968	Jim Lonborg	15.00-18.00	5.00-10.00
1968	Orlando Cepeda	15.00-18.00	5.00-10.00
1968	Jim McGlothlin	15.00-18.00	5.00-10.00
1969	Bob Gibson, Denny McLain	20.00-25.00	8.00-12.00
1970	Tom Seaver	20.00-25.00	8.00-12.00
1970	Bill Singer	15.00-18.00	5.00-10.00
1970	Harmon Killebrew	20.00-25.00	8.00-12.00
1971	Johnny Bench	20.00-25.00	8.00-12.00
1971	Boog Powell	15.00-18.00	5.00-10.00
1971	Gaylord Perry	18.00-22.00	6.00-12.00
1972	Vida Blue	15.00-18.00	5.00-10.00

Year	Cover	Ex./Mint Condition	Good Condition
1972	Joe Torre	15.00-18.00	5.00-10.00
1972	Roberto Clemente	18.00-20.00	5.00-10.00
1973	Steve Carlton	15.00-18.00	5.00-10.00
1973	Reggie Jackson	15.00-18.00	5.00-10.00
1973	Johnny Bench	15.00-18.00	5.00-10.00
1974	Nolan Ryan	20.00-25.00	8.00-12.00
1974	Pete Rose	20.00-25.00	8.00-12.00
1974	Hank Aaron	20.00-25.00	8.00-12.00
1975	Catfish Hunter	15.00-18.00	5.00-10.00
1975	Mike Marshall	15.00-18.00	5.00-10.00
1975	Lou Brock	15.00-18.00	5.00-10.00
1976	Joe Morgan	12.00-15.00	5.00-7.00
1976	Fred Lynn	12.00-15.00	5.00-7.00
1976	Dave Lopes	12.00-15.00	5.00-7.00
1977	Thurman Munson	15.00-20.00	6.00-12.00
1977	Mark Fidrych	15.00-20.00	6.00-12.00
1977	Randy Jones	15.00-20.00	6.00-12.00
1978	Steve Garvey	15.00-18.00	7.00-10.00
1978	Rod Carew	15.00-18.00	7.00-10.00
1978	Reggie Jackson	15.00-18.00	7.00-10.00
1979	Ron Guidry	12.00-15.00	4.00-6.00
1979	J.R. Richard	12.00-15.00	4.00-6.00
1979	Burt Hooten	12.00-15.00	4.00-6.00
1980	Brian Downing	8.00-12.00	3.00-5.00
1980	Joe Niekro	8.00-12.00	3.00-5.00
1980	Mike Flanagan	8.00-12.00	3.00-5.00
1981	Mike Schmidt	10.00-13.00	4.00-6.00
1981	George Brett	8.00-10.00	3.00-4.00
1981	Rickey Henderson	8.00-10.00	3.00-4.00
1982	Nolan Ryan	10.00-12.00	4.00-6.00
1982	Rollie Fingers, Tom Seaver	10.00-12.00	4.00-6.00
1982	Fernando Valenzuela, Billy Martin	10.00-12.00	4.00-6.00
1982	Rich Gossage, Pete Rose	10.00-12.00	4.00-6.00
1983	Steve Carlton	8.00-10.00	3.00-4.00
1983	Phil Niekro	8.00-10.00	3.00-4.00
1983	Doug De Cinces	8.00-10.00	3.00-4.00
1983	Robin Yount	8.00-10.00	3.00-4.00
1984	Dale Murphy	6.00-8.00	2.00-4.00
1984	Carlton Fisk	3.00-4.00	1.00-2.00
1984	Pedro Guerrero	3.00-4.00	1.00-2.00
1984	Scott McGregor, Rick Dempsey	3.00-4.00	1.00-2.00
1985	Dwight Gooden	3.00-4.00	1.00-2.00
1985	Detroit Tigers	3.00-4.00	1.00-2.00
1985	Steve Garvey	3.00-4.00	1.00-2.00
1986	Nolan Ryan	5.00-7.00	2.00-3.00
1986	Orel Hershiser	5.00-7.00	2.00-3.00
1986	Dwight Gooden, Don Mattingly	5.00-7.00	2.00-3.00
1986	Kansas City Royals	5.00-7.00	2.00-3.00
1987	Gary Carter, Jesse Orosco	4.00-5.00	2.00-3.00
1987	Joe Carter	3.00-4.00	1.00-2.00

Year	Cover	Ex./Mint Condition	Good Condition
1987	Jesse Barfield	4.00-7.00	1.00-2.00
1987	Mike Scott	4.00-7.00	1.00-2.00
1987	Roger Clemens	4.00-7.00	1.00-2.00
1987	Wally Joyner	4.00-7.00	1.00-2.00
1988	Ozzie Smith	4.00-7.00	1.00
1988	George Bell	4.00-7.00	1.00
1988	Jeff Reardon	4.00-7.00	1.00
1988	Don Mattingly	4.00-7.00	1.00
1988	Dale Murphy	4.00-7.00	1.00
1988	Mark McGwire, Benito Santiago	4.00-7.00	1.00
1989	Orel Hershiser	3.00-6.00	1.00
1989	Jose Canseco	3.00-6.00	1.00
1989	Mike Greenwell	3.00-6.00	1.00
1989	Andres Galarraga, Fred McGriff	3.00-6.00	1.00
1989	Kevin McReynolds	3.00-6.00	1.00
1989	Chris Sabo, Mark Grace	3.00-6.00	1.00
1990	Anniversary issue, 50 years of covers	6.00-8.00	2.00-3.00

Baseball Digest

1943

July	Play at 2nd Base	20.00
October	S. Chandler	20.00

1944

February	Bill Johnson	16.00
March	Sewell and Nicholson	16.00
April	D. Walker	16.00
May	L. Boudreau	18.00
July	V. Stephens	16.00
August	B. Walters	16.00
September	C. Grimm and G. Barr	16.00
October	Walker Cooper	16.00
November	M. Marion	14.00

1945

March	G. Hartley	12.00
May	B. Voiselle	12.00
July	H. Borowy	15.00
August	T. Holmes	15.00
September	S. Hack	15.00
October	H. Greenberg	30.00
November	A. Lopez	22.00

1946

February	C. Keller	16.00
March	B. Considine	16.00
April	B. Doerr	22.00
May	B. Feller	22.00
July	T. Williams, J. DiMaggio	40.00
August	J. Cronin	22.00
September	H. Wyse	14.00
October	Dave Ferriss	16.00
November	J. Pesky, R. Schoendienst	25.00

1947

February	B. Harris	18.00
March	J. Rigney, P. Knudsen	14.00
April	J. Van Cuyk	14.00
May	B. Herman, H. Greenberg	25.00
July	Boudreau, Gordon	22.00
August	B. Kerr	14.00
September	E. Blackwell	14.00
October	J. DiMaggio	28.00
November	Dodgers and Phillies	14.00

1948

January	J. Page	14.00
February	L. Durocher, B. Rickey	23.00
March	Meyer, Ennis, Hubbard	13.00
April	J. McCarthy	18.00
May	A. Houtteman	13.00
June	W. Marshall	13.00
July	R. Kiner	18.00
August	L. Boudreau	18.00
September	S. Musial	25.00
October	H. Sauer	13.00
November	G. Bearden	13.00

1949

January	J. Hegan	13.00
February	R. Rolfe	13.00
March	T. Williams	25.00
April	J. DiMaggio	25.00
May	Play at Plate	15.00
June	R. Roberts	22.00
July	J. Groth	13.00
August	F. Frisch	20.00
September	V. Raschi	13.00
October	Parnell, Tebbetts	13.00
November	J. Jorgensen	10.00
December	Henrich, Reynolds	15.00

1950

January	R. Smalley, R. Ashburn	14.00
February	Dave Koslo	12.00
March	1950 Baseball Rules	12.00
April	Feller	18.00
June	J. DiMaggio	24.00
July	P. Rizzuto	13.00
August	D. Sisler	12.00
September	Jansen, Houtteman	12.00
October	Evers	12.00
November	Konstanty	12.00

1951

January	Berra, Ford	18.00
February	Hodges	16.00
March	Yost	11.00
April	J. DiMaggio	25.00
May	Earnshaw	11.00
June	T. Williams	32.00
July	I. Noren	11.00
August	N. Fox and P. Richards	18.00
September	S. Musial	20.00
October	Gil McDougald	11.00
November	Charlie Dressen	11.00

1952

January	Lopat, Rizzuto	12.00
February	Stanky	10.00
March	S. Gordan	10.00
April	M. Garcia	12.00
May	G. Staley	10.00
June	Pee Wee Reese	16.00
July	T. Kluszewski	11.00
August	B. Shantz	11.00
September	S. Maglie, Campanella	15.00
October	C. Erskine	10.00
November	D. Snider	16.00

1953

January	R. Roberts	13.00
February	E. Matthews	13.00
March	Billy Martin	10.00
April	Musial, Mantle	24.00
May	C. Furillo	10.00
June	B. Lemon	12.00
July	Logan, Kellner, Dorish	7.00
August	R. Roberts	12.00
September	O'Connell, Strickland, Trucks	7.00
October	Stengel	13.00

1954

January	Billy Martin	10.00
March	J. Piersall	8.00
April	W. Ford	14.00
May	H. Kuenn	8.00
June	Morgan, Mathews	9.00
July	B. Turley	7.00
August	Keegan	7.00
September	W. Mays	14.00
October	World Series Issue	7.00
Nov./Dec.	D. Rhodes	7.00

1955

Jan./Feb.	Kiner, Sarni	9.00
March	Rookies of 1955	10.00
April	A. Dark	7.00
May	Mueller and Lemon	7.00
June	Bobby Avila	6.00
July	B. Skowron	6.00
August	McMillian, Al Smith	6.00
September	D. Newcombe	6.00
October	W. Alston, T. Byrne	8.00
November	J. Podres	6.00

1956

February	A. Kaline	10.00
March	Rookie report	8.00
April	L. Aparicio	11.00

May	P. Higgins	6.00
June	Labine	6.00
July	Mickey Mantle	17.00
August	Dale Long	6.00
September	Berra	9.00
October	World Series	9.00
Nov./Dec.	D. Larsen	7.00

1957

Jan./Feb.	R. Roberts	10.00
March	Scouting Reports	8.00
April	K. Farrell, J. Tighe, B. Scheffing	8.00
May	D. Blasingame	6.00
June	B. Martin	7.00
July	D. Hoak	5.00
August	S. Musial	11.00
September	B. Shantz	5.00
Oct./Nov.	B. Ruth - World Series	13.00

1958

January	L. Burdette	5.00
February	V. McDaniel	5.00
March	Scouting Reports	9.00
April	Snider, Mays	14.00
May	T. Williams	15.00
June	S. Musial	15.00
July	W. Spahn	10.00
August	B. Turley	6.00
September	P. Runnels	5.00
Oct./Nov.	Martin, Mays	9.00

1959

Dec./Jan.	B. Turley, J. Jensen, R. Roberts	8.00
February	Baseball's Darling Daughters	7.00
March	Scouting Reports	9.00
April	E. Banks	11.00
May	J. Pizarro	6.00
June	Antonelli, Pascual, Landis	6.00
July	Pinson	6.00
August	Wilhelm	8.00
September	Face and Colavito	6.00
Oct,/Nov.	World Series/H. Wilson	9.00

1960

January	L. Sherry, J. Roseboro	6.00
February	H. Kuenn	8.00
March	Scouting Reports	8.00
April	McCovey	8.00
May	E. Wynn	8.00
June	Bunning, McDaniel, Francona	6.00
July	V. Law	6.00
August	D. Stuart	5.00
September	R. Hansen	5.00
Oct./Nov.	D. Groat	6.00
December	Clemente	7.00

1961

February	R. Houk	6.00
March	Scouting reports	8.00
April	Tony Kubek	7.00
May	G. Hobbie	4.00
June	E. Battey	4.00
July	Moon	4.00
August	Cash	4.00
September	Ford	8.00
Oct./Nov.	Mantle, Maris	20.00
Dec./Jan.	E. Howard	6.00

1962

February	Joe Jay	4.00
March	Scouting Reports	9.00
April	Cepeda	7.00
May	Jim Landis	5.00
June	Mantle	15.00
July	Donovan	4.00
August	20 Dramatic Home Runs	10.00
September	R. Rollins	4.00
Oct./Nov.	T. Tresh, F. Howard	4.00
Dec./Jan.	R. Terry	4.00

1963

February	Cobb, Wills	8.00
March	Scouting Reports	8.00
April	Rosters	6.00
May	Drysdale, Dean, Grove	8.00
June	Al Kaline	8.00
July	O'Toole	4.00
August	J. Bouton	4.00
September	Lemaster	4.00
Oct./Nov.	Downing	4.00
Dec./Jan.	Koufax, Drysdale	9.00

1964

February	R. Maris	11.00
March	Scouting Reports	9.00
April	S. Koufax	10.00
May	Killebrew	8.00
June	T. Davis and Yaz	8.00
July	Maloney	4.00
August	D. Nicholson	4.00
September	D. Bennett, W. Smith	3.00
Oct./Nov.	1914 Miracle Braves	6.00
Dec./Jan.	Groat	4.00

1965

February	Rose	9.00
March	Scouting Reports	9.00
April	B. Williams	6.00
May	Freehan	4.00
June	Tony Conigiliaro	4.00
July	W. Bond	3.00
August	Drysdale	6.00
September	Ward, Morgan	6.00
Oct./Nov.	1955 Series	4.00
Dec./Jan.	Koufax	8.00

1966

February	Mays	9.00
March	Scouting Reports	6.00
April	Rosters	6.00
May	McDowell	4.00
June	C. Bazzani	3.00
July	Marichal	6.00
August	Alley, Mazeroski	5.00
September	G. Scott	4.00
Oct./Nov.	World Series Special	4.00
Dec./Jan	J. Palmer	6.00

1967

February	Allison, Drysdale, Mathews	5.00
March	Scouting Reports	5.00
April	Rosters	6.00
May	Roger Maris	10.00
June	G. Perry, Marichal	7.00
July	J. Wynn	4.00
August	J. Horlen	3.00
September	McCarver	4.00
Oct./Nov.	Burdette, R. Faber	4.00
Dec./Jan.	B. Gibson	5.00

1968

February	B.Williams	5.00
March	J. Bench	13.00
April	Rosters	6.00
May	Carew, Johnstone, Nye	5.00
June	Rojas, Briles	3.00
July	Koosman	4.00
August	A. Kosco	3.00
mber	M. Alou, K. Harrelson	4.00
Oct./Nov.	Gibson, McClain	5.00
Dec./Jan.	Lou Brock	5.00

1969

February	Mantle	18.00
March	Scouting Reports	6.00
April	Rosters	6.00
May	Lopez	5.00
June	E. Banks	8.00
July	Tony C.	3.00
August	F. Robinson	6.00
September	K. Holtzman	3.00
October	World Series	3.00
November	Seaver	8.00
December	Tom Seaver	6.00

1970

January	Killebrew	6.00
February	Pepitone	3.00
March	G. Alley	3.00
April	T. Perez	5.00
May	Clemente	7.00
June	Stottlemyre	3.00
July	Holtzman	3.00
August	Bando	3.00
September	J. Hickman, T. Perez	3.00
October	Jim Palmer	5.00
November	Bench	5.00
December	B. Williams	4.00

1971

January	B. Robinson	4.00
February	Marichal, Bando	4.00
March	Carl Yastrzemski	5.00
April	Gibson	5.00
May	Mays	5.00
June	T. Oliva	3.00
July	Aaron	5.00
August	Blue	3.00
September	Pepitone	3.00
October	World Series	3.00
November	B. Murcer	3.00
December	Torre	3.00

1972

January	S. Blass	3.00
February	E. Williams	3.00
March	F. Robinson	5.00
April	Melton	3.00
May	Yaz, Bench	5.00
June	R. Jackson, Mays, Rose	7.00
July	R. Allen	3.00
August	Bud Harrelson	3.00
September	Clemente	6.00
October	Gary Nolan	3.00
November	Fisk, Carlton	5.00
December	R. Allen	3.00

1973

January	P. Rose	5.00
February	Cedeno	3.00

March	Killebrew	4.00
April	Kessinger	3.00
May	Ryan	6.00
June	Seaver	6.00
July	Rose	6.00
August	C. May, R. Allen, Melton	3.00
September	Ken Holtzman	3.00
October	Bill Russell	3.00
November	Jose Cardenal	3.00
December	W. Stargell	5.00

1974

January	World Series, Y. Berra	5.00
February	B. Bonds	3.00
March	B. Grich	3.00
April	H. Aaron	6.00
May	T. Sizemore	3.00
June	F. Millan	3.00
July	B. Robinson	4.00
August	T. Perez, G. Perry	5.00
September	T. John	3.00
October	D. Allen	3.00
November	Jackson, Campaneris, Bando	6.00
December	L. Brock	5.00

1975

January	R. Fingers	3.00
February	Garvey	3.00
March	J. Burroughs	2.00
April	Hunter	4.00
May	Schmidt	5.00
June	R. Carew	4.00
July	N. Ryan	5.00
August	R. Monday	2.00
September	J. Bench	4.00
October	Blue	3.00
November	Lynn	2.00
December	Morgan	4.00

1976

January	P. Rose	5.00
February	J. Palmer	4.00
March	Brett	4.00
April	Fisk	3.00
May	Tanana	2.00
June	R. Manning	2.00
July	B. Madlock	3.00
August	Randy Jones	3.00
September	Bowa	2.00
October	M. Rivers	2.00
November	M. Fidrych	3.00
December	J. Morgan	4.00

1977

January	World Series Highlights	3.00
February	T. Munson	4.00
March	Otis	3.00
April	M. Fidrych	3.00
May	J. Montefusco	2.00
June	S. Carlton	4.00
July	D. Parker	3.00
August	Trillo, DeJesus	2.00
September	Carl Yastrzemski	5.00
October	Steve Garvey	4.00
November	Bump Wills	2.00
December	George Foster	2.00

1978

January	Reggie Jackson	5.00
February	McCovey	4.00
March	Carew	4.00
April	Seaver	4.00
May	Cedeno	2.00
June	Templeton	2.00
July	Kingman	3.00
August	J. Rice	3.00
September	Ron Guidry	3.00
October	Hurdle, Gale	2.00
November	Reggie Smith	2.00
December	D. Parker	3.00

1979

January	World Series Highlights	4.00
February	D. Winfield	3.00
Mach	Greg Luzinski	2.00
April	Rich Gossage	2.00
May	Jack Clark	3.00
June	Steve Garvey	3.00
July	Al Oliver	2.00
August	Bill Buckner	2.00
September	Tommy John	3.00
October	Mike Schmidt	4.00
November	O. Moreno	2.00
December	George Brett	4.00

1980

January	Al Oliver, M. Flanagan	2.00
February	Molitor	3.00
March	Carter	3.00
April	Stargell	4.00
May	Don Baylor	2.00
June	J.R. Richard and N. Ryan	4.00
July	Burns, Baumgarten, Trout	2.00
August	Landreaux	2.00
September	Carlton	4.00
October	Reggie Jackson	4.00

November	Charboneau	2.00
December	Brett	4.00

1981

January	McGraw	3.00
February	Murray	3.00
March	Henderson	5.00
April	Schmidt	5.00
May	Carter	3.00
June	C. Cooper	3.00
July	Fisk	4.00
August	Valenzuela	3.00
September	Darwin	2.00
October	Ron Davis	2.00
November	Pete Rose	4.00
December	T. Raines	3.00

1982

January	Garvey	3.00
February	Lansford	2.00
March	Fingers	3.00
April	Winfield	4.00
May	Ryan	5.00
June	Reuss	2.00
July	S. Barojas	2.00
August	D. Murphy	4.00
September	R. Henderson	3.00
October	Yount	4.00
November	Hrbek	3.00
December	O. Smith and L. Smith	3.00

1983

January	D. Porter	2.00
February	Soto	2.00
March	Decinces	2.00
April	McGee	3.00
May	Vuckovich	2.00
June	Ripken	4.00
July	T. Pena	3.00
August	Stieb	3.00
September	Chambliss	2.00
October	Kittle	2.00
November	Carlton	4.00
December	Fisk	4.00

1984

January	Dempsey	2.00
February	Boggs	4.00
March	Dale Murphy	4.00
April	Boddicker	2.00
May	Dawson	3.00
June	Parrish	3.00
July	Madlock	3.00
August	Durham	2.00
September	Martinez, Gwynn, McReynolds	3.00
October	Sandberg	5.00
November	K. Hernandez	2.00
December	M. Langston	3.00

1985

January	A. Trammell	3.00
February	Mattingly	5.00
March	Viola	3.00
April	J. Morris	3.00
May	Gwynn	3.00
June	Gooden	5.00
July	B. Sutter	3.00
August	Rose	4.00
September	L. Smith	2.00
October	Guidry	2.00
November	Guerrero	2.00
December	Gooden	3.00

1986

January	McGee	2.00
February	Saberhagen	2.00
March	Browning	2.00
April	H. Baines	3.00
May	Strawberry	4.00
June	E. Murray	3.00
July	Blyleven	2.00
August	Clemons	4.00
September	G. Carter	3.00
October	Joyner and Canseco	5.00
November	B. Doran	3.00
December	Clemons and Higuera	3.00

1987

January	Mattingly and Boggs	4.00
February	S. Fernandez	3.00
March	M. Scott	2.00
April	C. Brown	1.00
May	P. O'Brien	2.00
June	E. Davis and J. Davis	3.00
July	M. Witt	2.00
August	R. Henderson	3.00
September	J. Clark and O. Smith	2.00
October	M. McGwire	3.00
November	G. Bell	2.00
December	K. Seitzer	1.00

1988

January	Dawson	3.00
February	Viola	2.00
March	J. Key	1.00
April	McReynolds and Pagliarulo	2.00

May	E. Davis	3.00	February	Hershiser	2.00
June	Royals pitchers	2.00	March	Jefferies	2.00
July	Van Slyke	2.00	April	K. Gibson	2.00
August	Winfield	3.00	May	C. Snyder	2.00
September	G. Maddux	2.00	June	McGriff	2.00
October	Puckett	3.00	July	W. Clark	2.00
November	Canseco	3.00	August	N. Ryan	3.00
December	D. Jackson	2.00	September	B. Jackson	3.00
			October	P. Stewart	2.00
	1989		November	H. Johnson	2.00
January	Canseco	3.00	December	Walton/D. Smith	2.00

Famous Slugger Yearbooks

Hillerich and Bradsby's Famous Slugger Yearbooks were promotional booklets given away in sporting goods stores. Each Yearbook summarized the previous season's leading hitters from the major and minor leagues. The booklets were also filled with hitting statistics and records.

Most of the Yearbooks contained stories about the evolution of baseball and the Louisville Slugger. The 1959 Famous Slugger Yearbook is typical of many with a "how to hit" article written by Stan Musial and a recap of the 1958 baseball season.

Year	Value	Year	Value	Year	Value
1931	60.00	1949	28.00	1964	14.00
1933	39.00	1950	23.00	1965	14.00
1934	39.00	1951	23.00	1966	14.00
1935	39.00	1952	23.00	1967	11.00
1937	39.00	1953	23.00	1968	11.00
1939	29.00	1954	23.00	1969	11.00
1940	32.00	1955	18.00	1970	11.00
1941	32.00	1956	18.00	1971	11.00
1942	32.00	1957	18.00	1972	11.00
1943	32.00	1958	18.00	1973	7.00
1944	32.00	1959	18.00	1974	7.00
1945	28.00	1960	14.00	1975	7.00
1946	28.00	1961	14.00	1976	7.00
1947	28.00	1962	14.00	1977	7.00
1948	28.00	1963	14.00	1978	7.00

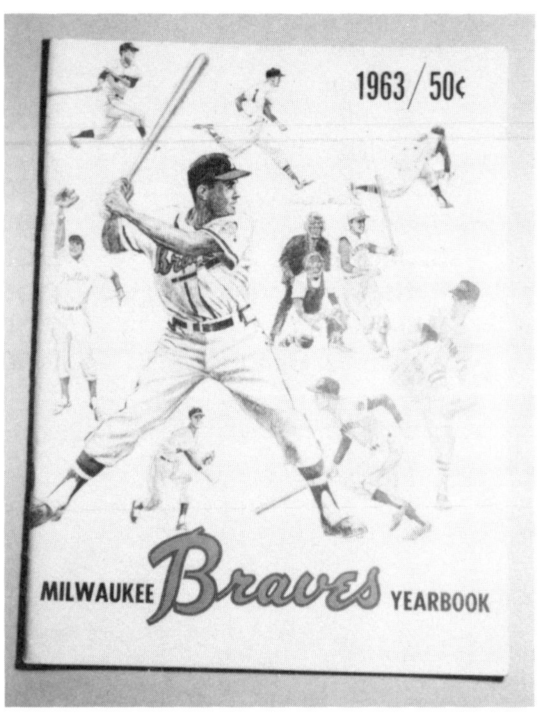

1963 Milwaukee Braves yearbook. $25.00-30.00.

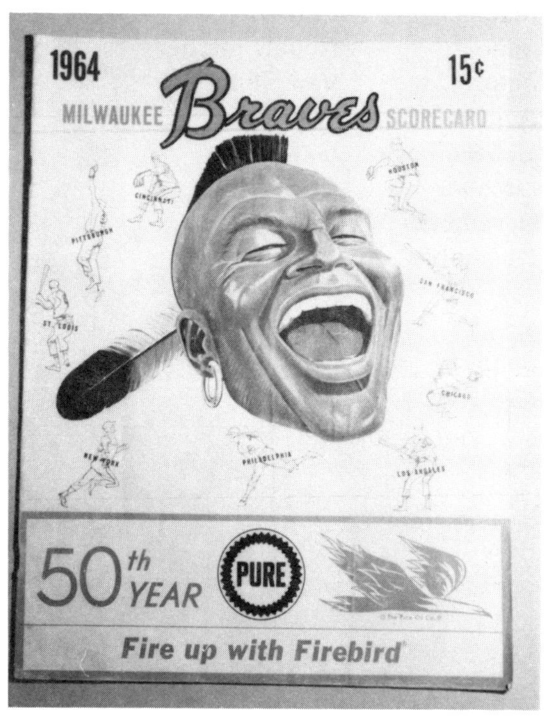

1964 Braves scorecard (unscored). $8.00-10.00.

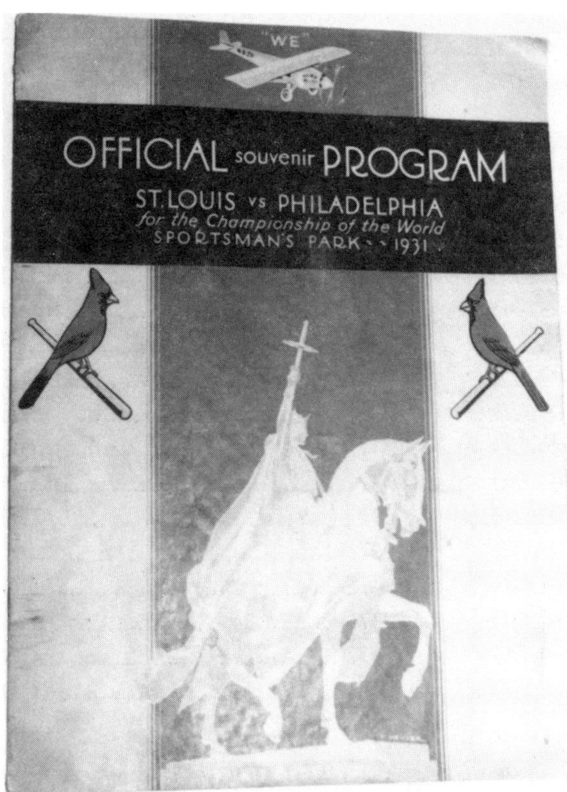

1931 World Series Program, St. Louis Cardinals vs. Philadelphia. $135.00-150.00.

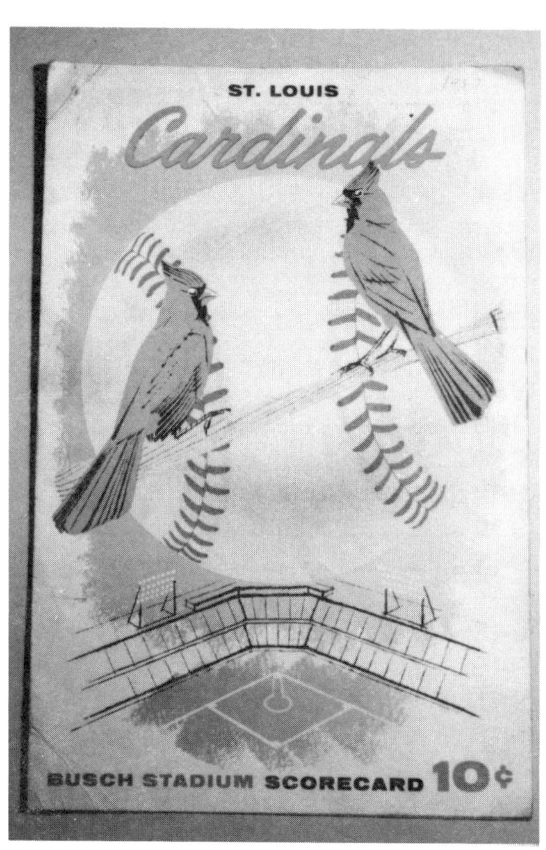

1957 Cardinal scorecard (unscored). $12.00-14.00.

1958 Cardinal scorecard (unscored). $12.00-14.00.

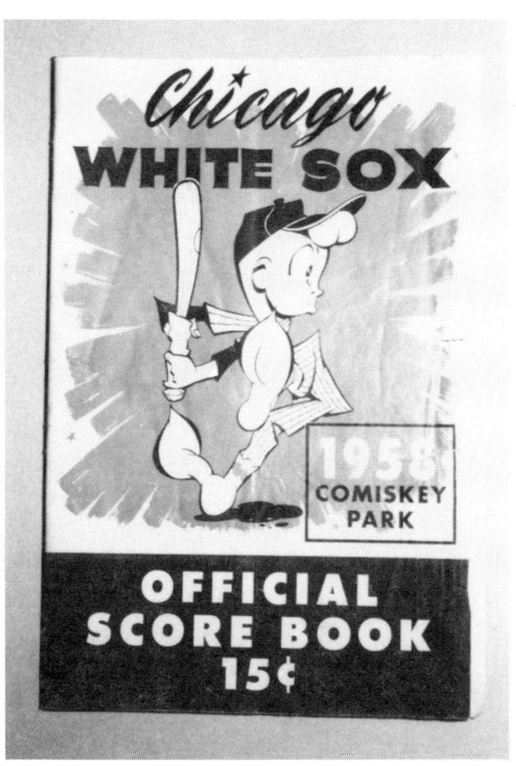

1958 White Sox scorecard (unscored). $14.00-16.00.

Late 1950's Dizzy Dean Baseball Guide premium. $15.00-20.00.

CHAPTER VI
Bats

"Game-Used" Major League Bats

"Game-used" major league equipment is eagerly collected by baseball fans across America.

Cracked and uncracked "game-used" bats from major leagure players are usually secured directly from the team, bat boys, equipment managers, clubhouse employees, and, on occasion, the individual players.

The bats that follow all have been recently offered for sale.

Model - manufacturer of the bat
C - Cooper
LS - Louisville Slugger
A - Adirondak
HB - Hillerich and Bradsby
W - Worth
Cond. - Condition
UC - uncracked
C - cracked

Name	Model	Model#	Cond.	Value
Aaron, Hank	HB		UC	1,495.00
Agosto, Juan	LS	R161	C	20.00
Aldrete, Mike	LS	C234	C	15.00
Allenson, Andy	LS		UC	12.00
Allison, Bob	LS		C	350.00
Alomar, Sandy	C		UC	175.00
Alou, Jose	LS	S2	C	20.00
Anderson, Dave	LS	P72	UC	10.00
Anderson, Russell	A		C	6.00
Aparicio, Luis	HB		UC	675.00
Aquino, Luis	LS	R161	UC	40.00
Ashby, Allen	A		UC	14.00
Ayala, Benny	LS	K55	C	25.00
Baines, Harold	LS	B345	C	65.00
Baker, Dusty	LS	M110	UC	55.00
Balboni, Steve	LS	P89	UC	45.00
Balboni, Steve	LS	P89	C	35.00
Baldwin, Bill	LS	P72	C	25.00
Barfield, Jessee	A		C	75.00
Barnes, Skeeter	LS	P72	C	10.00
Bass, Kevin	LS	S226	C	15.00
Baylor, Don	LS	R161	UC	40.00
Belcher, Tim	LS	W248	UC	50.00
Bell, Buddy	LS	S2	C	45.00
Bell, George	LS	S44	C	85.00
Belliard, Rafael	LS	B267	UC	30.00
Benedict, Bruce	LS	K455	C	25.00
Beniquez, Juan	W	WC178	C	20.00
Bergman, Dave	LS	S188	C	15.00
Bernazard, Tony	LS	B343	C	15.00
Berra, Dale	LS	P72	C	45.00
Berra, Dale	A	225B	C	12.00
Berta, Nick	LS	M110	C	20.00
Billardello, Dan	LS	R205	C	12.00
Blanks, Scooter	H&B		C	20.00
Bochte, Bruce	A	413B	UC	35.00
Boggs, Wade	LS	M253	UC	250.00
Boggs, Wade	LS	M253	UC	225.00
Boggs, Wade	LS	M110	UC	225.00
Boroughs, Jeff	H&B	B310	C	25.00

Name	Model	Model#	Cond.	Value
Bosley, Thad	LS	D174	UC	35.00
Boston, Daryl	LS	B345	C	15.00
Bradley, Phil	C		C	30.00
Brenley, Bob	W	W227	C	20.00
Brett, George	LS	K55	UC	295.00
Brookins, Tom	LS	M110	C	20.00
Brooks, Hubie	LS	P89	UC	85.00
Brooks, Hubie	W	WC119	UC	85.00
Buckner, Bill	LS	M110	C	65.00
Buckner, Bill	LS	K55	C	65.00
Buhner, Jay	LS	P80	C	25.00
Burks, Ellis	LS	C271	C	125.00
Burroughs, Jeff	LS	B310	C	75.00
Butera, Sal	LS	K55	C	25.00
Butera, Sal	LS	M110	C	25.00
Cabell, Enos	LS	P89	C	25.00
Calderon, Ivan	LS	P72	UC	70.00
Calderon, Ivan	LS	P72	UC	75.00
Campaneris, Bert	LS	R43	UC	80.00
Canseco, Jose	C	C234R	UC	495.00
Cardenas, Leo	LS		C	100.00
Carew, Rod	LS	C243	UC	595.00
Carter, Joe	LS	W248	C	90.00
Carter, Gary	A	113A	UC	100.00
Cedeno, Caesar	LS	M110	C	35.00
Cedeno, Caesar	LS	M110	C	40.00
Chappas, Harry	LS	K55	C	5.00
Clark, Jack	LS	M253	UC	135.00
Clark, Jack	LS	S44	UC	110.00
Clark, Will	C		UC	375.00
Cobb, Ty	HB		C	9,500.00
Colavito, Rocky	HB	K55	UC	450.00
Coleman, Ray	LS	S2	C	60.00
Coleman, Vince	A	P302	C	75.00
Collins, Dave	LS	M259	UC	30.00
Cooper, Cecil	LS	H176	UC	65.00
Correll, Vic	H&B	S2	UC	40.00
Cronin, Joe	LS		C	795.00
Crowley, Terry	HB	M159	UC	40.00
Cruz, Todd	LS		C	25.00
Cruz, Julio	LS	B267	C	20.00
Cunningham, Joe	A	413B	C	20.00
Daulton, Darren	LS	P72	C	30.00
Daur, Rich	LS	W248	C	15.00
Davidson, Mark	LS	P72	C	10.00
Davis, Mike	LS	M110	C	25.00
Davis, Mike	LS	M110	C	25.00
Davis, Eric	LS	K75	UC	195.00
Dawley, Dave	LS	M253	C	20.00
Dayley, Ken	LS	B267	C	15.00
Decinces, Doug	LS	D113	C	45.00
Dernier, Bob	LS	B267	C	25.00
Diaz, Bo	LS	C235	C	25.00
Diaz, Bo	LS	P216	C	30.00
Doran, Bill	LS	C271	C	50.00
Doyle, Brian	LS	G105	C	25.00
Dressen, Chuck	HB		C	295.00
Ducey, Rob	LS	C271	C	25.00
Ducey, Rob	C	S44	C	25.00
Duncan, Mariano	LS	B267	C	25.00
Dunston, Shawon	LS	M253	C	70.00
Dwyer, Jim	W	WX136	UC	25.00
Dwyer, Jim	A	DD26	C	20.00
Easler, Mike	LS	P72	C	75.00
Eisenreich, Jim	LS	M159	C	50.00
Engle, Dave	LS	U1	C	12.00
Ennis, Del	HB		C	295.00
Esasky, Nick	LS	K55	C	50.00
Evans, Dwight	LS	S2	C	110.00
Falcone, Pete	LS	P72	C	25.00
Farr, Steve	LS	R161	UC	50.00
Fernandez, Tony	A	459B	C	65.00
Figueroa, Ed	LS	R161	C	15.00
Fisk, Carlton	LS	T141	UC	295.00
Fitzgerald, Mike	LS	C271	C	10.00
Fletcher, Scott	LS	M110	C	45.00
Fletcher, Scott	LS		C	35.00
Foley, Tom	LS	R161	C	15.00
Foli, Tim	LS	F148	C	25.00
Ford, Curt	LS	P72	C	20.00
Forrester, Terry	LS	P72	C	10.00
Foster, Leo	LS	S2	C	15.00
Francona, Terry	LS	R219	C	12.00
Gaetti, Gary	LS	S2	C	65.00
Galarraga, Andres	C	C243	UC	100.00
Gant, Ron	LS	M110	C	20.00
Gantner, Jim	LS	T141	C	15.00
Garcia, Damaso	LS	C243	C	25.00
Garner, Phil	LS	K48	C	35.00
Garner, Phil	H&B	K44	C	35.00
Garr, Ralph	LS	U1	C	50.00
Garvey, Steve	LS	C263	C	85.00
Gentile, Jim	LS	M110	C	75.00
Ghert, Scot	LS	M110	UC	8.00
Gibson, Kirk	LS	S216	UC	75.00
Gilbreath, Rod	HB	G105	C	18.00
Girardi, Joe	LS	P89	C	20.00
Glavine, Tom	LS	C243	C	35.00
Grant, U.S.	HB	L1864	C	15.00
Greenwell, Mike	LS	C235	C	150.00
Griffey, Ken	LS	S216	C	50.00
Griffin, Alfredo	LS	C300	UC	25.00

Name	Model	Model#	Cond.	Value
Griffin, Alfredo	LS	R161	UC	55.00
Gross, Kevin	LS	G168	C	18.00
Gross, Greg	A	154B	C	25.00
Gross, Greg	C	S318	C	20.00
Gjroth, Hennie			C	995.00
Grubb, John	LS	S188	C	15.00
Gubicza, Mark	LS	S318	UC	50.00
Guerrero, Pedro	LS	M110	UC	50.00
Guillen, Ozzie	LS	G164	C	65.00
Guillen, Ozzie	AS	279S	UC	70.00
Gwynn, Chris	LS	W248	UC	25.00
Gwynn, Tony	LS	K55	UC	250.00
Hairston, Jerry	LS	M110	UC	50.00
Hairston, Jerry	LS	M110	C	15.00
Hamilton, Jeff	W	WC137	C	10.00
Hamiltin, Daryl	C	H176C	C	20.00
Hargrove, Mike	LS	M110	C	45.00
Harper, Terry	LS	B242	UC	25.00
Harrah, Toby	LS	M110	C	45.00
Hatcher, Mickey	LS	S44	C	25.00
Hearn, Ed	LS	C271	C	25.00
Hearndon, Larry	W	WC135	C	25.00
Hearron, Jeff	LS	M110	C	10.00
Heath, Mike	LS	P72	UC	35.00
Heath, Mike	LS	H260	C	18.00
Heep, Danny	LS	S2	C	10.00
Henderson, Dave	LS	K75	C	75.00
Henderson, Rickey	LS	T141	UC	225.00
Herndon, Larry	W	WC135	UC	45.00
Hill, Donnie	LS	M110	UC	15.00
Hill, Marc	LS	R161	C	15.00
Hobson, Butch	LS	S188	C	30.00
Hodges, Gil	HB		C	1,250.00
Horner, Bob	LS		C	35.00
Horton, Willie	LS	K75	C	90.00
Horwood, Willie	LS	R133	C	5.00
Howe, Art	LS	M253	C	35.00
Howe, Art	LS	K55	UC	35.00
Hrbek, Kent	LS	H258S	UC	150.00
Hubbard, Glenn	LS	P72	C	25.00
Huggins, Miller	SP		C	1,100.00
Hulett, Tim	LS	S44	C	20.00
Iorg, Dane	LS		C	20.00
Jackson, Bo	LS	B310	UC	325.00
Jackson, Ransom	HB		UC	325.00
Jackson, Reggie	A	288RJ	C	650.00
James, Chris	LS	P72	C	40.00
Javier, Julian	LS	F4	C	75.00
Jeltz, Steve	LS	C243	C	15.00
Jeltz, Steve	LS	C243	C	20.00
Johnson, Lance	LS	P72	UC	40.00
Johnson, Lance	LS	P72	UC	25.00
Johnstone, Jay	A		C	75.00
Jorgensen, Mike	LS	B310	C	25.00
Joyner, Wally	LS	C243	UC	75.00
Kaline, Al	HB		C	745.00
Karkovice, Ron	LS	M110	C	18.00
Kellogg, Mathew	LS	P72	UC	12.00
Kelly, Pat	LS	K75	C	30.00
Kelly, George	HB		UC	575.00
Kessinger, Don	LS	K55	UC	225.00
Khalifa, Sammy	LS	S318	UC	25.00
Killebrew, Harmon	HB		C	1,695.00
Kingman, Dave	LS	52	UC	125.00
Knicely, Alan	LS	M110	UC	40.00
Knight, Ray	LS	C271	C	30.00
Krenchicki, Wayne	LS	K75	UC	35.00
Kutcher, Randy	LS	C243	C	25.00
Landreaux, Kenny	A	381B	C	10.00
Larkin, Gene	LS		C	50.00
Larkin, Barry	A	155S	C	65.00
Laudener, Tim	LS	L156	C	28.00
Lavallier, Mike	LS	H176	C	25.00
Lawless, Tom	LS	C311	C	18.00
Lemon, Chet	LS	K48	C	28.00
Leonard, Jeff	LS	G153	C	35.00
Lindeman, Jim	LS	P72	UC	25.00
Little, Bryan	A	369B	C	15.00
Luzinski, Greg	W		UC	85.00
Lynn, Fred	LS	M110	UC	125.00
Lyons, Steve	LS	P72	C	25.00
Madlock, Bill	LS	C235	UC	60.00
Magadan, Dave	LS	C217	UC	65.00
Maldonado, Candy	LS	B267	C	25.00
Manguel, Pepe	LS	D143	C	215.00
Manrique, Fred	LS	S226	C	20.00
Marshall, Mike	LS	D113	C	60.00
Martinez, Ramon	LS	W248	UC	75.00
Martiez, Carmelo	A	CM81	C	30.00
Mattingly, Don	LS	T141	UC	450.00
May, Lee	LS	R161	C	100.00
McGee, Willie	LS	C271	C	85.00
McGee, Willie	LS	C271	UC	75.00
McLemore, Mark	LS	C243	C	24.00
McRae, Hal	LS	R161	C	75.00
McReynolds, Kevin	LS	M110	UC	135.00
McWilliams, Larry	LS	M110	C	25.00
Melendez, Luis	LS	S2	C	25.00
Menke, Dennis	H&B	K55	UC	35.00
Meyeres, Greg	C	S318	C	30.00
Mileey, Dave	LS	M110	C	10.00
Miller, Ed	LS	U1	C	25.00

Name	Model	Model#	Cond.	Value
Milner, John	LS	R43	C	50.00
Milner, Ed	LS	C271	C	15.00
Mitchell, Ron	LS	B267	UC	25.00
Molitor, Paul	C	H176	C	75.00
Montgomery, Jeff	LS	P72	UC	30.00
Moore, Alvin	LS	M110	C	25.00
Morris, John	LS	M110	C	15.00
Morrison, Jim	LS	S44	C	20.00
Moseby, Lloyd	W	WC42	C	45.00
Mota, Manny	LS	150	UC	95.00
Mulinіks, Rance	LS	P72	C	25.00
Murcer, Bobby	HB		C	195.00
Murphy, Dale	LS	S44	UC	110.00
Murray, Eddie	LS	W248	C	150.00
Murray, Rick	LS	J93	C	15.00
Neal, Charlie	A		UC	325.00
Nicosia, Steve	LS	K75	C	35.00
Nokes, Matt	W		UC	60.00
O'Doul, Lefty	LS		UC	395.00
Oberkfell, Ken	LS	K55	C	45.00
Oester, Ron	LS	R161	C	30.00
Ogilvie, Ben	A	377A	C	35.00
Olander, John	LS	S2	C	25.00
Oliva, Tony	LS	K75	C	450.00
Oliver, Al	LS	E43	UC	45.00
Oquendo, Jose	LS		C	30.00
Orta, Jorge	A	240B	C	25.00
Orta, Jorge	A	240B	UC	48.00
Palacios, Rey	LS	S318	C	20.00
Pankovits, Jim	LS	M159	C	25.00
Parker, Dave	LS	M110	UC	80.00
Parrish, Larry	LS	K55	UC	45.00
Parrish, Larry	LS	K55	UC	35.00
Pasqua, Dan	LS	T141	UC	60.00
Pasqua, Dan	LS	T141	C	25.00
Patek, Fred	LS	F3	C	40.00
Pecota, Bill	LS	S44	UC	30.00
Pedrique, Al	LS	S226	C	15.00
Pena, Alejandro	A	184D	UC	15.00
Pena, Hipolito	LS	R161	C	15.00
Pendleton, Terry	LS	T142	UC	65.00
Percotta, Bill	LS	S44	UC	30.00
Perry, Gerald	A	225B	UC	35.00
Pettis, Gary	LS	M110	UC	50.00
Pettis, Gary	LS	K75	C	30.00
Phelps, Ken	LS	M110	C	30.00
Plantier, Phil	LS	C243	UC	11.00
Polidor, Gus	LS	C243	C	15.00
Porter, Darrell	LS	B267	UC	45.00
Porter, Darrell	LS	M235	UC	55.00
Power, Vic	LS	K55	C	125.00
Pruitt, Ron	LS	S2	C	25.00
Puckett, Kirby	LS	S44	UC	175.00
Quinones, Rey	C	S318L	C	35.00
Quirk, Jamie	LS	B310	UC	45.00
Quirk, Jamie	LS	B310	UC	45.00
Randolph, Willie	LS	R43	UC	75.00
Randolph, Willie	W	WC136	C	40.00
Ray, Johnnie	LS	S318	C	45.00
Ready, Randy	LS	M272	C	25.00
Redus, Gary	LS	R205	C	18.00
Revering, Dave	HB	M110	C	20.00
Reynolds, Craig	LS	K55	C	25.00
Reynolds, RJ	A	382A	C	30.00
Rhoden, Rick	LS	K55	C	30.00
Richards, J.R.	LS	P72	UC	95.00
Roberts, Bip	LS	C243	C	25.00
Robinson, Brooks	A		C	745.00
Roenicke, Gary	LS	K75	C	25.00
Romero, Ed	LS	C271	C	20.00
Romine, Kevin	LS	C235	C	18.00
Roseboro, Johnny	HB	G144	UC	185.00
Royster, Jerry	LS	C243	C	25.00
Ruiz, Manuel	LS	U1	C	20.00
Runger, Paul	LS	113	UC	30.00
Ryal, Mark	LS	C235	C	25.00
Sain, Johnny	LS	S2	C	25.00
Salas, Mark	LS	M143	C	20.00
Salazar, Luis	LS	T142	C	30.00
Samuel, Juan	LS	C243	UC	55.00
Santana, Rafael	LS	M110	C	25.00
Santo, Ron	A		UC	100.00
Santovenia, Nelson	C		C	45.00
Sax, Steve	LS	S2	UC	95.00
Schmidt, Mike	A	MS20	C	385.00
Schu, Rick	LS	S318	C	20.00
Sconiers, Daryll	LS	C234	C	15.00
Scott, George	A		C	50.00
Seaver, Tom	LS		UC	895.00
Seitzer, Kevin	LS	C271	C	70.00
Shaperson, Mike	LS	C243	C	10.00
Shelby, John	A	DD26	UC	10.00
Sheridan, Pat	LS	072	UC	35.00
Sheridan, Pat	W	W5K	UC	55.00
Singleton, Kenny	LS	D113	C	35.00
Skinner, Joel	LS	M253	UC	35.00
Skinner, Joel	A	225B	C	25.00
Smalley, Roy	LS	D2	C	15.00
Smalley, Roy	LS	M110	C	20.00
Stargell, Willie	LS	K44	UC	350.00
Stewart, Sammy	LS	C243	C	50.00
Stewart, Luke	LS	R161	C	20.00

Name	Model	Model#	Cond.	Value
Stewart, Jake	LS	K55	C	20.00
Straino, Al	H7B	S2	UC	35.00
Striegel, Eric	LS	K55	UC	25.00
Striegel, Jon	A	368B	C	20.00
Stubbs, Franklin	LS	S318	UC	35.00
Sutton, Don	LS		UC	325.00
Tabler, Pat	LS	S2	UC	50.00
Tabler, Pat	LS	S2	UC	70.00
Thon, Dicky	LS	M110	C	35.00
Tolan, Bobby	LS		C	28.00
Tolleson, Wayne	LS	K55	C	28.00
Trammel, Alan	W	WC127	C	59.00
Treadway, Jeff	LS	H176	C	45.00
Treadway, Jeff	LS	H178	UC	40.00
Trevino, Alex	LS	M110	C	15.00
Trevino, Alex	LS	C300	C	15.00
Upshaw, Willie	C		UC	55.00
Valenzuela, F.	LS	R161	UC	75.00
Valle, Dave	LS	M110	C	25.00
VanSlyke, Andy	LS	M110	UC	95.00
Velarde, Randy	LS	M110	UC	30.00
Vrentas, Steve	C	C2	C	3.00
Walker, Greg	LS	C271	UC	50.00
Wallach, Tim	C		C	75.00
Walling, Denny	LS	M159	UC	50.00
Walling, Denny	LS	M159	UC	50.00
Ward, Gary	A		C	35.00
Watson, Bob	LS	W262	UC	65.00
Welch, Bob	LS	B310	UC	55.00
Wellman, Brad	LS	S44	UC	35.00
Whitaker, Lou	A	326B	UC	115.00
Whitaker, Lou	LS	K48	UC	115.00
Whitfield, Terry	LS	M253	UC	20.00
Wilson, Willie	A	170B	UC	50.00
Wilson, Mookie	LS	R161	UC	70.00
Winfield, Dave	RA	DW20	C	150.00
Winfield, Dave	C	C2	UC	200.00
Woods, Al	LS	R161	C	25.00
Woodward, Woody	H7B	S2	UC	40.00
Wyneger, Butch	A		UC	20.00
Yastrzemski, Carl	LS	K48	UC	500.00
Yount, Robin	LS	P72	UC	225.00
Zisk, Richie	LS	Z19	UC	75.00

World Series Black Bats

These commemorative "World Series Black Bats" date from 1962-1989 and are in their original Hillerich and Bradsby factory shipping boxes and have not been displayed. They are priced as mint bats.

The bats each have the impressed autographs of the team members in gold on each bat. The commemorative bats are provided after each World Series to the participationg teams, team and baseball officials, and "friends" of Hillerich and Bradsby. They are not offered for sale to the general public and are produced in limited numbers.

The prices that follow are for both bats. For example, the 1969 Mets bat and the 1969 Baltimore bat are priced at $905.00 for the pair.

Year	Teams	Value
1962	New York/San Francisco	1,425.00
1963	Los Angeles/New York Yankees	1,380.00
1964	St. Louis/New York	1,330.00
1965	Los Angeles/Minnesota	1,285.00
1966	Baltimore/Los Angeles	1,235.00
1967	St. Louis/Boston	1,210.00
1968	Detroit/St. Louis	935.00
1969	New York Mets/Baltimore	905.00
1970	Baltimore/Cincinnati	830.00
1971	Pittsburgh/Baltimore	780.00
1972	Oakland/Cincinnati	760.00
1973	Oakland/New York	1,140.00
1974	Oakland/Los Angeles	950.00
1975	Cincinnati/Boston	930.00
1976	Cincinnati/New York	1,235.00
1977	New York/Los Angeles	800.00
1978	New York/Los Angeles	1,140.00
1979	Pittsburgh/Baltimore	695.00
1980	Philadelphia/Kansas City	645.00
1981	Los Angeles/New York	740.00
1982	St. Louis/Milwaukee	620.00
1983	Baltimore/Philadelphia	600.00

1984	Detroit/San Diego	950.00	1987	Minnesota/St. Louis	500.00
1985	Kansas City/St. Louis	550.00	1988	Los Angeles/Oakland	465.00
1986	New York/Boston	620.00	1989	Oakland/San Francisco	500.00

Hall of Fame Limited Edition Inductee Bats

Since 1983 the Hall of Fame has issued on a numbered and limited basis a series of brown bats with gold lettering made by Louisville Slugger honoring Cooperstown inductees.

The bats have been numbered 1-500 on all years from 1936 through 1987. Beginning with the 1988 bat, 1,000 of each year were made. The bats numbered 1-500 are sold only by subscription and bats 501-1000 are sold at the gift shop in the Hall of Fame on Saturday morning of Induction Weekend each summer.

Each induction bat carries the signature or printed name of the player, umpire, or executive being honored that particular year impressed into the bat's barrel.

In an effort to put the inductee bats into a logical sequence, a program was devised to release the bats forward from 1936 and backwards or in reverse chronological order from 1983. Eventually there will be only one bat issued a year for each group of Hall of Fame inductees.

1936	Wagner, Ruth, Mathewson, Cobb, W. Johnson	425.00-450.00
1937	B. Johnson, McGraw, G. Wright, Speaker, Lajoie, Mack, Young, Bulkeley	350.00-375.00
1938	Alexander, Cartwright, Chadwick	225.00-250.00
1939	Anson, Ewing, Cummings, Comiskey, E. Collins, Sisler, Gehrig, Keeler, Radbourne, Spalding	350.00-375.00
1942	Hornsby	225.00-250.00
1944	Landis	150.00-175.00
1945	Bresnahan, Brouthers, Clarke, J. Collins, Delahanty, Duffy, Jennings, Kelly, O'Rourke W. Robinson	150.00-175.00
1971	Weiss, Paige, Hooper, Hafey, Bancroft, Marquard	225.00-250.00
1972	Koufax, Berra, Leonard, Wynn Youngs, Gibson, Gomez, Harridge	225.00-250.00
1973	Clemente, Spahn, Irvin, Evans, Kelly, Welch	225.00-250.00
1974	Mantle, Thompson, Bottomley, Conlan, Ford, Bell	500.00-550.00
1975	Kiner, J. Johnson, Averill, Herman, Harris	175.00-200.00
1976	Roberts, Hubbard, Lindstrom, Lemon, Connor, Charleston	200.00-225.00
1977	Banks, Lloyd, Dihigo, Lopez, Ruse, Sewell	175.00-200.00
1978	Joss, Mathews, MacPhail	175.00-200.00
1979	Giles, Wilson, Mays	250.00-275.00
1980	Snider, Klein, Kaline, Yawkey	250.00-275.00
1981	B. Gibson, Foster, Mize	175.00-200.00
1982	Aaron, F. Robinson, T. Jackson, Chandler	250.00-275.00
1983	Alston, Kell, Marichal, B. Robinson	450.00-525.00
1984	Reese, Drysdale, Ferrell, Aparicio, Killebrew	250.00-275.00
1985	Brock, Slaughter, Wilhelm, Vaughan	175.00-200.00
1986	Doerr, McCovey, Lombardi	175.00-200.00
1987	B. Williams, Dandridge, Hunter	200.00-225.00
1988	Stargell	150.00-175.00
1989	Bench, Yastrzemski, Schoendienst, Barlick	300.00-350.00
1990	Palmer, Morgan	200.00-225.00
1991	Carew, Perry, Jenkins, Lazzeri, Veeck	250.00-275.00

CHAPTER VII
Miscellaneous Baseball Collectibles

Press Pins

Notes on Collecting Press Pins

1. The first "press" pins were issued for the 1911 World Series between the Giants and Athletics.
2. World Series press pins have been made available to the press, team guests, and officials since 1911 with the single exception of 1918 when the Chicago Cubs failed to provide pins.
3. Each year there are more World Series pins issued than pins for the All-Star Game and even fewer pins for the Hall of Fame Induction Weekend in Cooperstown, New York.
4. It is estimated that approximately 3,700 pins were handed out for the 1990 World Series and less than 1,000 for the 1990 Induction Ceremony at the Hall of Fame. At the 1982 Induction when pins were initially used only about 600 were made available.
5. The Hall of Fame pins have been made each year since 1982 by L.B. Balfour of Attleboro, Mass. and sequentially numbered on the back of each pin since 1987.
6. The first All-Star Game in 1933 was played without press pins. All-Star Game pins were first issued in 1938. They have been provided at each game since 1946.
7. A "phantom" press pin is a pin produced by a major league team in anticipation of playing in the World Series. When their dreams are destroyed on the last day of the season or in the League Championship Series, the "phantom" press pins are put away. Each year many of the "phantoms" make their way into the hands of collectors.

World Series Press Pins

1913 Phil. A's 9,000.00
1915 Red Sox 4,000.00
1917 New York Giants ... 6,500.00
1920 Brooklyn 4,000.00
1923 New York Yankees . 4,000.00
1924 Washington 2,200.00
1925 Pittsburgh 2,100.00
1925 Washington 2,100.00
1926 New York Yankees . 3,000.00
1927 New York Yankees . 4,000.00
1928 New York Yankees . 2,400.00
1929 Chicago Cubs 2,200.00
1932 Chicago Cubs 2,200.00
1937 New York Yankees .. 1,000.00
1938 New York Yankees .. 1,000.00
1938 Chicago Cubs 2,200.00
1939 New York Yankees 900.00
1939 Cincinnati 550.00
1940 Detroit 825.00
1941 New York Yankees 550.00
1945 Detroit 600.00
1945 Chicago Cubs 475.00
1946 Boston Red Sox 600.00
1947 Brooklyn 800.00
1948 Cleveland 450.00
1949 New York Yankees 650.00
1949 Brooklyn 600.00
1950 New York Yankees 475.00
1951 New York Yankees 325.00
1951 New York Giants 250.00
1952 New York Yankees 350.00
1952 Brooklyn 650.00
1953 New York Yankees 400.00
1953 Brooklyn 400.00
1954 New York Giants 175.00
1955 Brooklyn 500.00
1955 New York Yankees 325.00
1956 Brooklyn 1,600.00
1956 New York Yankees 300.00
1957 New York Yankees 200.00
1958 New York Yankees 200.00
1959 Los Angeles Dodgers 300.00

1960 New York Yankees 250.00
1961 Cincinnati 175.00
1961 New York Yankees 275.00
1962 San Francisco 375.00
1962 New York Yankees 225.00
1963 Los Angeles 200.00
1963 New York Yankees 225.00
1964 St. Louis 150.00
1964 New York Yankees 200.00
1965 Los Angeles 125.00
1965 Minnesota 75.00
1966 Los Angeles 100.00
1968 St. Louis 60.00
1968 Detroit 160.00
1969 New York Mets 400.00
1969 Baltimore 115.00
1970 Cincinnati 95.00
1970 Baltimore 95.00
1971 Pittsburgh 95.00
1972 Cincinnati 75.00
1972 Oakland 275.00
1973 New York Mets 200.00
1973 Oakland 325.00
1974 Oakland 400.00
1975 Cincinnati.....................115.00
1975 Boston 250.00
1976 Cincinnati 125.00
1977 Los Angeles 75.00
1978 Los Angeles 75.00
1978 New York Yankees......100.00
1979 Pittsburgh 45.00
1979 Baltimore 45.00
1980 Philadelphia 35.00
1981 Los Angeles 45.00
1981 New York Yankees.......55.00
1982 St. Louis 20.00
1982 Milwaukee 50.00
1983 Philadelphia 30.00
1983 Baltimore 25.00
1984 Detroit 65.00
1984 San Diego 50.00
1985 St. Louis 75.00
1985 Kansas City 65.00
1986 New York Mets 90.00
1986 Boston 75.00
1987 St. Louis 60.00
1987 Minnesota 50.00
1988 Los Angeles 50.00
1988 Oakland 50.00
1989 San Francisco 95.00
1989 Oakland 100.00
1990 Cincinnati 150.00
1990 Oakland 100.00

"Phantom" World Series Press Pins

1946 Brooklyn 125.00
1949 Boston 1,600.00
1955 Cleveland 750.00
1956 Milwaukee 75.00
1964 Cincinnnati 150.00
1964 Philadelphia 15.00
1965 San Francisco 125.00
1966 Pittsburgh 450.00
1967 Chicago White Sox 75.00
1969 Minnestoa 25.00
1969 San Francisco 150.00
1970 California 500.00
1970 Chicago Cubs 500.00
1971 San Francisco 150.00
1972 Chicago (White Sox) .900.00
1972 Pittsburgh 900.00
1976 Philadelphia 50.00
1977 Boston 75.00
1978 Cincinnati 75.00
1979 Montreal 50.00
1979 California 350.00
1980 Houston 125.00
1981 Oakland 125.00
1983 Pittsburgh 250.00
1983 Chicago White Sox ...35.00
1984 Chicago Cubs 250.00
1986 Houston 150.00

All-Star Game Press Pins

1938 Cincinnati 8,000.00
1941 Detroit 2,500.00
1948 St. Louis Browns 2,500.00
1949 Brooklyn 650.00
1950 Chicago 325.00
1951 Detroit 325.00
1952 Philadelphia 400.00
1953 Cincinnati 350.00
1954 Cleveland 300.00
1955 Milwaukee 250.00
1959 Pittsburgh 275.00
1959 Los Angeles 225.00
1960 Kansas City 350.00
1960 New York 500.00
1961 San Francisco 400.00
1961 Boston 450.00
1962 Chicago 475.00
1963 Cleveland 110.00
1965 Minnesota 110.00
1966 St. Louis 40.00
1967 California 75.00
1968 Houston 100.00
1969 Washington 95.00
1970 Cincinnati 50.00
1972 Atlanta 45.00
1974 Pittsburgh 75.00
1975 Milwaukee 75.00
1976 Philadelphia 80.00
1977 New York Yanks 135.00
1978 San Diego 50.00
1979 Seattle........................45.00
1980 Los Angeles 45.00
1981 Cleveland 30.00

1982 Montreal....................25.00
1983 Chicago......................25.00
1984 San Francisco..........25.00
1985 Minnesota................25.00
1986 Houston......................55.00
1987 Oakland......................55.00
1988 Cincinnati.................100.00
1990 Chicago...................200.00
1991 Toronto.......................150.00

Hall of Fame Press Pins

1982 Hall of Fame...........700.00
1983 Hall of Fame...........675.00
1984 Hall of Fame..........425.00
1985 Hall of Fame..........425.00
1986 Hall of Fame..........425.00
1987 Hall of Fame..........650.00
1988 Hall of Fame..........650.00
1989 Hall of Fame..........650.00
1990 Hall of Fame..........650.00
1991 Hall of Fame............550.00

Hall of Fame Pewter Plates

The pewter plates prices below were issued annually to commemorate the year's inductees into the Hall of Fame. There were 1,000 pewter plates made available each year and sold through the gift shop and catalog in the Hall of Fame.

Year	Inductees	Price
1974	Bell, Bottomley, Conlon, Ford Mantle, Thompson	200.00
1975	Averill, Harris, Herman, J. Johnson, Kiner	60.00
1976	Charleston, Connor, Lemon, Lindstrom, Hubbard, Roberts	60.00
1977	Banks, Lloyd, Dihigo, Lopez, Rusie, Sewell	100.00
1978	Joss, Mathews, MacPhail	60.00
1979	Giles, Wilson, Mays	100.00
1980	Duke Snider, Klein, Kaline, Yawkey	100.00
1981	R. Gibson, R. Foster, Mize	60.00
1982	Aaron, F. Robinson, T. Jackson, Chandler	60.00
1983	Alston, Kell, Marichal, B. Robinson	60.00
1984	Reese, Ferrell, Drysdale, Aparicio, Killebrew	110.00
1985	Brock, Slaughter, Wilhelm, Vaughn	100.00
1986	Doerr, Lombardi, McCovey	100.00
1987	Dandridge, Hunter, Billy Williams	60.00

World Series Ticket Stubs

All the World Series ticket stubs listed below are in a minimum of "excellent" condition unless specifically noted. "VG" indicates the stub is in "very good" condition.

1929 at Shibe, Game 5, VG 95.00
1941 at Ebbets Field, Game 3 ....75.00
1942 at NY, Game 3...75.00
1946 at Fenway, Game 4, VG.........................50.00
1946 at Fenway, Game 4 ....50.00
1946 at Fenway, Game 5, VG..........................50.00
1948 at Cleveland, Game 4, VG 40.00
1948 at Fenway, Game 2 ....50.00
1949 at Ebbets Field, Game 4..........................75.00
1949 at NY, Game 2..40.00

1950at NY, Game 3 ....40.00
1951 at NY, Game 1 ....40.00
1951 at Yanks, Game 1, Fair 10.00
1951 at Yanks, Game 2, VG to EX 30.00
1951 at Giants, Game 3, VG to EX 30.00
1951 at Yanks, Game 6, VG to EX 30.00
1952 at NY, Game 3, VG to EX 30.00
1952 at NY, Game 4, EX 35.00
1952 at NY, Game 5, VG 25.00
1952 at NY, Game 5 ....40.00
1952 at Ebbets Field, Game 7 ....75.00
1953 at Ebbets Field, Game 3 ....75.00
1953 at Ebbets Field, Game 5 ....75.00
1953 at NY, Game 1 ....35.00
1953 at NY, Game 6 ....35.00
1955 at NY, Game 1 ....35.00
1955 at NY, Game 6 ....35.00
1956 at Ebbets Field, Game 2 ....75.00
1956 at NY, Game 3 ....35.00
1956 at Ebbets Field, Game 2 ....75.00
1956 at Ebbets Field, Game 7, VG to EX 65.00
1957 at NY, Game 1 ....35.00
1957 at NY, Game 2 ....35.00
1957 at Milwaukee, Game 4, VG 25.00
1957 at NY, Game 6 ....35.00
1958 at NY, Game 3 ....35.00
1958 at NY, Game 4 ....35.00
1958 at NY, GAme 5 ....35.00
1958 at Milwaukee, Game 6 ....35.00
1959 at Comiskey, Game 1, VG 25.00
1959 at Comiskey, Game 2, VG 25.00
1959 at LA, Game 3, VG 25.00
1959 at LA, Game 4, VG 25.00
1959 at LA, Game 5, VG 25.00
1959 at Comiskey, Game 6, VG 25.00
1960 at Pittsburgh, Game 1 ....35.00
1960 at NY, Game 3 ....35.00
1960 at NY, Game 3, VG 25.00
1960 at NY, Game 4 ....35.00
1960 at NY, Game 5 ....35.00
1961 at NY, Game 1 ....40.00
1961 at NY, Game 2 ....40.00
1962 at NY, Game 4 ....35.00
1962 at NY, Game 5 ....35.00
1963 at NY, Game 1 ....35.00
1964 at St. Louis, Game 2 ....35.00
1964 at NY, Game 4 ....35.00
1967 at Fenway, Game 2 ....35.00
1972 at Cincinnati, Game 1 ....20.00
1972 at Cincinnati, Game 2 ....20.00
1973 at Shea, Game 3 ....35.00
1973 at Shea, Game 5 ....50.00

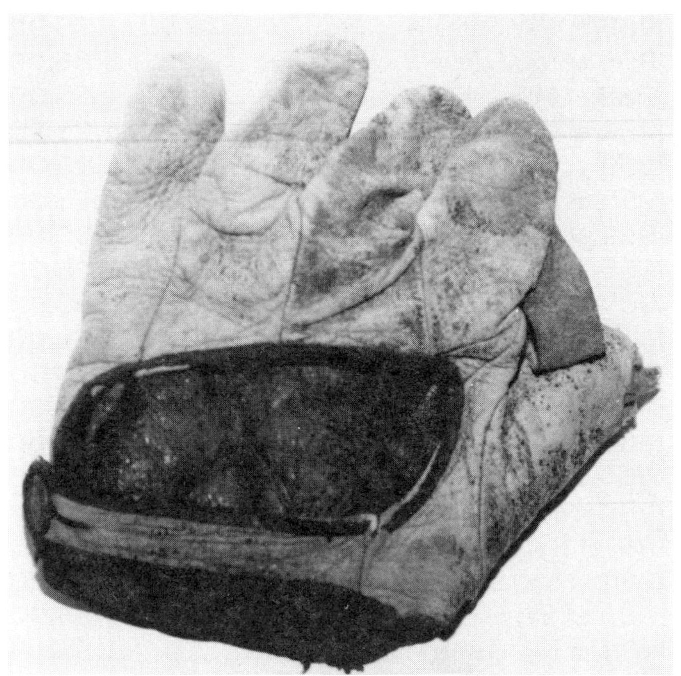

Left: Child's baseball glove, c. 1920's. $45.00-55.00.

Below left: Pair of Vince Coleman's game-worn spikes. $125.00-150.00.

Below right: "Phantom" World Series ticket from 1977 Chicago White Sox. $8.00-10.00.

Bottom: Pair of game-worn and autographed Mike Schmidt's spikes. $300.00-400.00.

Babe Ruth Underwear box, c. 1920's. $500.00-600.00.

Poster from the side of Edd Roush's car in ceremonial parade, 1969. $20.00-25.00.

Adhesive-backed advertising sticker for Ted's Root Beer (Ted Williams), c. 1950's. $15.00-20.00.

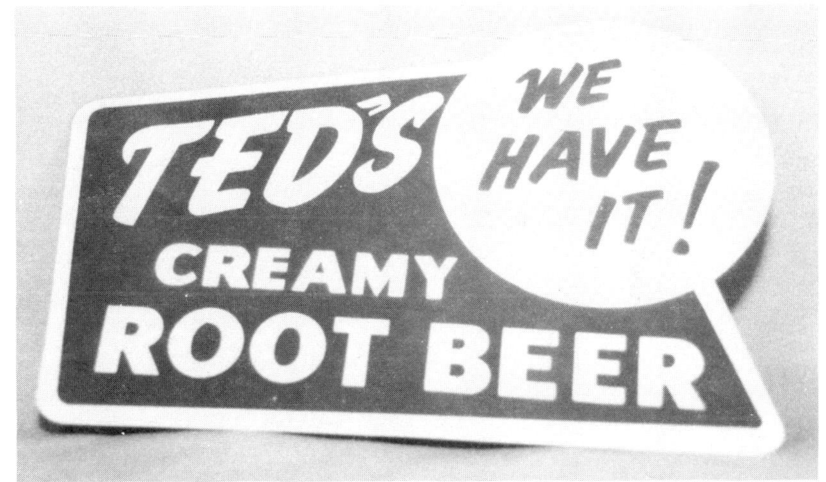

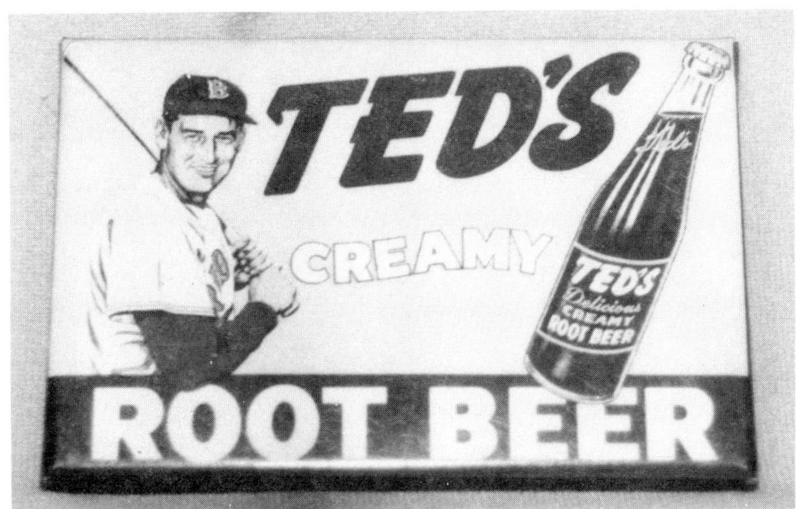

Metal Ted's Root Beer sign (reproduction), c. 1988. $8.00-10.00. The originals of this sign were made of heavy paper and are rare.

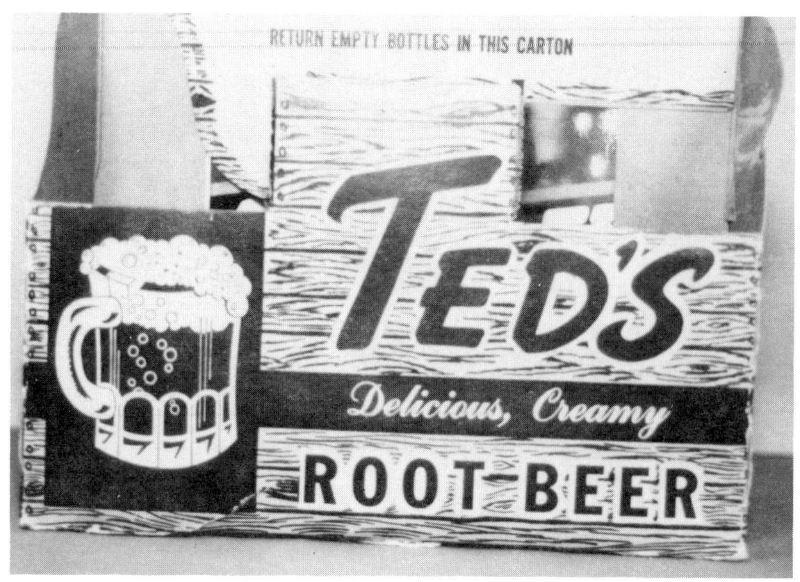

Six pack carton for Ted's Root Beer bottles, C. 1950's. $40.00-50.00.

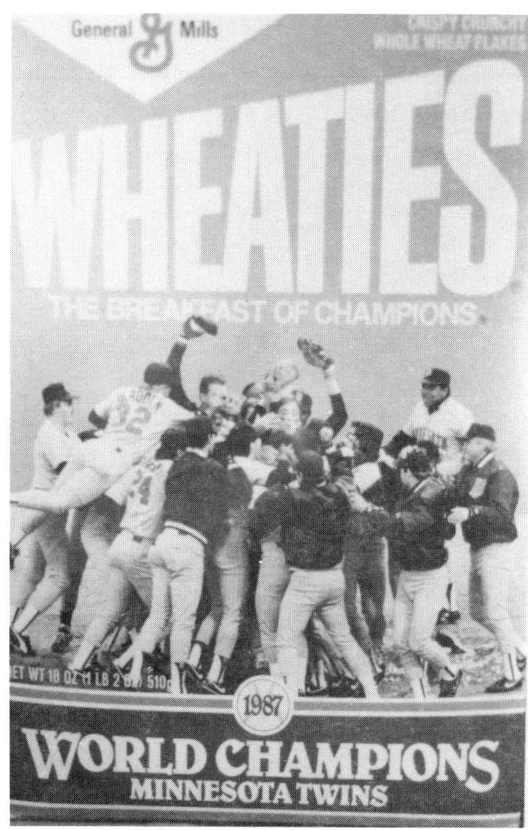

Wheaties box, 1987 World Champion Minnesota Twins. $4.00-5.00.

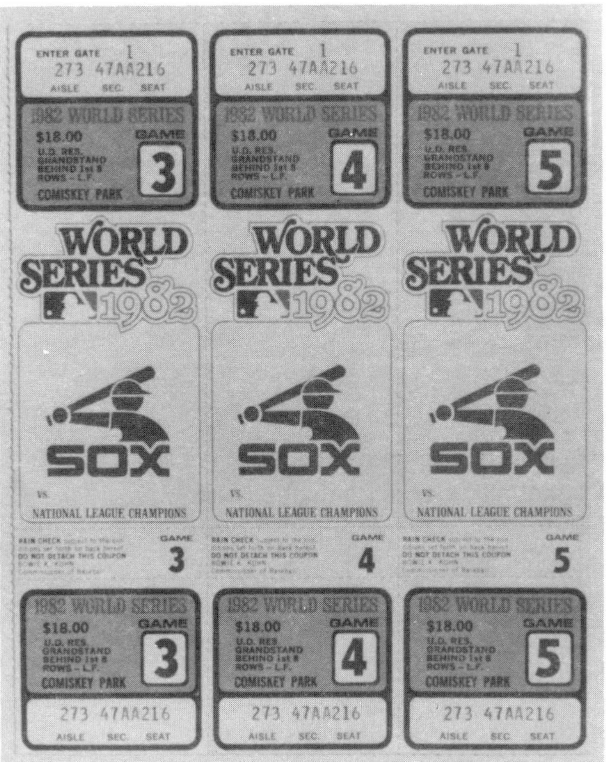

"Phantom" World Series tickets from 1982 Chicago White Sox. $15.00-20.00.

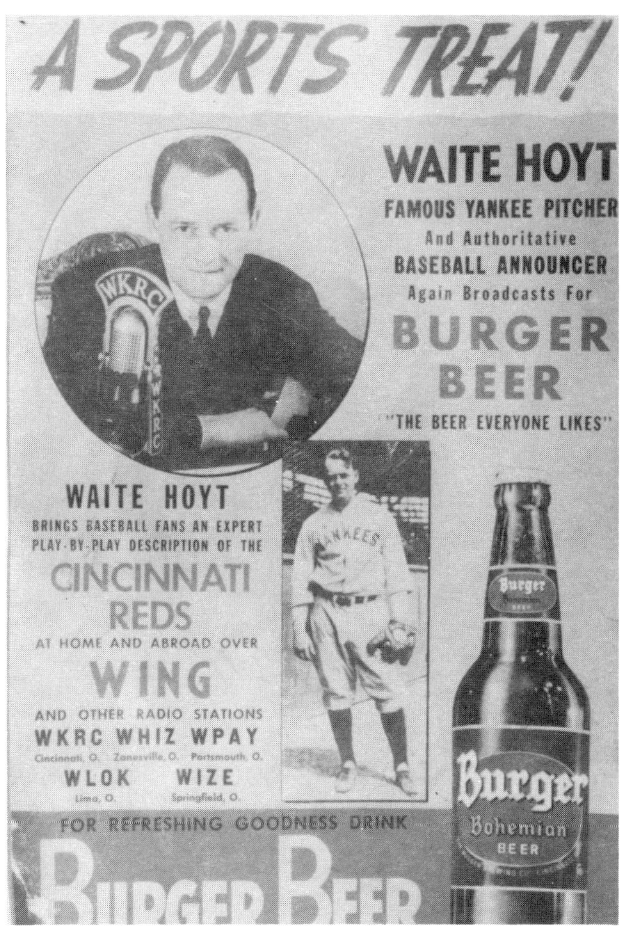

Burger Beer cardboard poster from 1945 season featuring Waite Hoyt, Fall of Fame pitcher, as broadcaster. $50.00-65.00.

Sources

The dealers listed below are specialists in various aspects of baseball collectibles and memorabilia. Most offer extensive catalogs of baseball-related items they have for sale.

Autographs

Greg Tucker
P.O. Box 909
Broken Arrow, OK 74013-0909

John Raybin
527 Third Ave. #294
New York, NY 10016

Mark Jordan
First National Bank Building
Suite 506
Bedford, TX 76022

Mountaineer Sports Cards
Rt. 1 Box 1023
Gerrardstown, WV 25420
(Perez-Steele cards)

Michael Taylor
3910 Hillsborough
Cameron Park, CA 95682-8502
(baseball cards)

Game-Used Equipment and Uniforms

Dick Dobbins
Box 193
Alamo, CA 94507

Murf Denny
Box 125
Brule, WI 54820

Hartel Sports
1004 Glenview Drive
P.O. Box 3
Steelville, IL 62288

Robb Wochnick
29625 S. Jackson Way
P.O. Box 597
Wilsonville, OR 97070

Statues and Figurines

Brian Morris
102 Watchrung Ave.
Montclair, NJ 06042
(Hartland statues)

Jeff Clow
10411 Grand Oak Lane
Cincinnati, OH 45242
(Kenner "Starting Lineup")

Patrick Flynn
Minne Memories
108 Warren
Mankato, MN 56001
(bobbing head dolls)

Tim Hunter
2637 Sunray
Reno, NV 89503
(bobbing head dolls)

Publications

B. and E. Collectibles, Inc.
12 Marble Ave.
Thornwood, NY 10594
(magazines, programs, yearbooks, media guides)

Robert Crestahl
4732 Circle Rd.
Montreal, Quebec,
Canada H3W 1Z1
(*Sporting News* specialist)

Bernard Titowsky
Austin Book Shop
Box 36
Kew Gardens, NY 11415
(baseball books)

Box Seat Collectibles
P.O. Box 2601
Van Nuys, CA
91404-2601
(newspapers)

Hobby Publications

Baseball Card News
700 E. State St.
Iola, WI 54990

Baseball Hobby News
4540 Kearny Villa Rd.
Suite 215
San Diego, CA 92125-1573

Sports Collectors Digest
700 E. State St.
Iola, WI 54990

Tuff Stuff
P.O. Box 1637
Glen Allen, VA
23060-0637

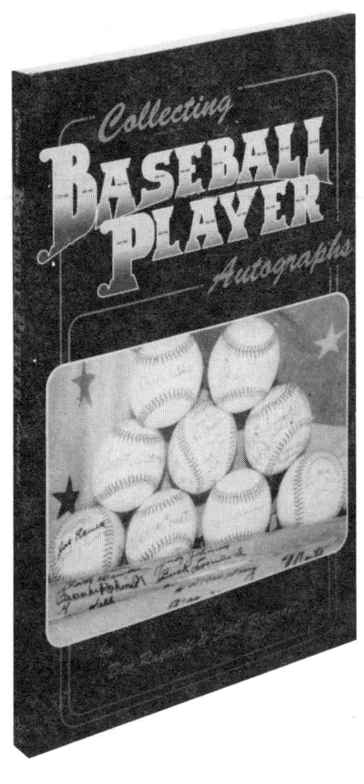

Collecting Baseball Player Autographs

By Don Raycraft and Scott Raycraft

In the 1940's and 1950's baseball player autographs could be received by standing outside the 16 major league parks, hotel lobbies, etc. But today the scene has greatly changed to long lines at card shows, and a fee is now charged between $2.00 and $35.00 to receive these highly sought after autographs. With the increased interest of these people paying top dollar for autographs, the Raycrafts decided to author a book dealing exclusively with these baseball player autographs. This new book has hundreds of illustrations and current values. Also included are chapters on Baseball Card Shows, Autograph Sessions at Shows, Paying for Autographs, Autographs by Mail, Value Guide to Hall of Fame Autographs, Questions and Answers, plus much more.

#2183, 5 ½ x 8 ½, 128 pages, PB $9.95

Schroeder's Antiques Price Guide

Schroeder's Antiques Price Guide has become THE household name in the antiques and collectibles field. Our team of editors works year-round with more than 200 contributors to bring you our #1 best-selling book on antiques and collectibles.

With more than 50,000 items identified and priced, *Schroeder's* is a must for the collector and dealer alike. If it merits the interest of today's collector, you'll find it in *Schroeder's*. Each subject is represented with histories and background information. In addition, hundreds of sharp original photos are used each year to illustrate not only the rare and unusual, but the everyday "fun-type" collectibles as well – not postage stamp pictures, but large close-up shots that show important details clearly.

Our editors compile a new book each year. Never do we merely change prices. Accuracy is our primary aim. Prices are gathered over the entire year previous to publication, from ads and personal contact. Then each category is thoroughly checked to spot inconsistencies, listings that may not be entirely reflective of actual market dealings, and lines too vague to be of merit. Only the best of the lot remains for publication. You'll find *Schroeder's Antiques Price Guide* the one to buy for factual information and quality.

No dealer, collector or investor can afford not to own this book. It is available from your favorite bookseller or antiques dealer at the low price of $12.95. If you are unable to find this price guide in your area, it's available from Collector Books, P.O. Box 3009, Paducah, KY 42002–3009 at $12.95 plus $2.00 for postage and handling.

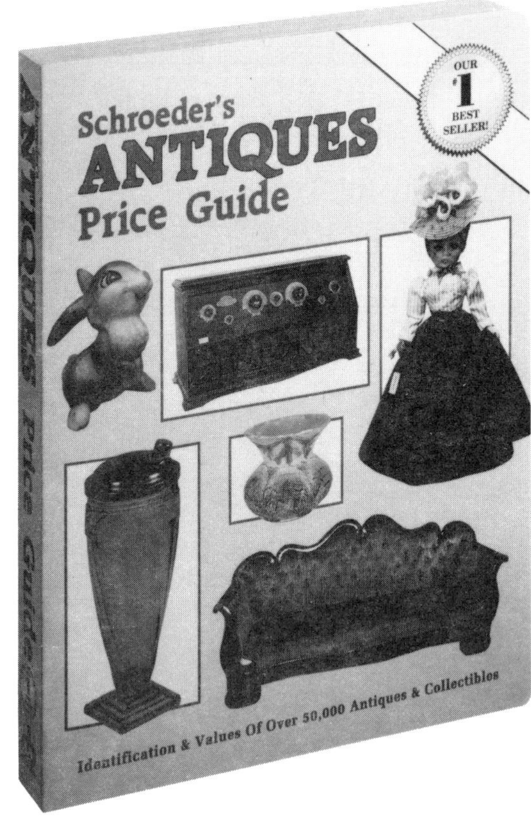

#2281, 8 ½ x 11, 608 pages, PB $12.95